Young People Making a Life

Young People Making a Life

Ani Wierenga
The University of Melbourne, Australia

Foreword by Rob White
University of Tasmania, Australia

First published 2009 by
PALGRAVE MACMILLAN
Houndmills, Basingstoke, Hampshire RG21 6XS and
175 Fifth Avenue, New York, N.Y. 10010
Companies and representatives throughout the world

PALGRAVE MACMILLAN is the global academic imprint of the Palgrave
Macmillan division of St. Martin's Press, LLC and of Palgrave Macmillan Ltd.
Macmillan® is a registered trademark in the United States, United Kingdom
and other countries. Palgrave is a registered trademark in the European
Union and other countries.

ISBN-13: 978-0-230-54928-9   hardback
ISBN-10: 0-230-54928-4   hardback

This book is printed on paper suitable for recycling and made from fully
managed and sustained forest sources. Logging, pulping and manufacturing
processes are expected to conform to the environmental regulations of the
country of origin.

A catalogue record for this book is available from the British Library.

Library of Congress Cataloging-in-Publication Data

Wierenga, Ani, 1968–
    Young people making a life / Ani Wierenga ; foreword by Rob White.
        p. cm.
    Includes bibliographical references and index.
    ISBN-978-0-230-54928-9 (alk. paper)
    1. Youth–Australia–Tasmania–Social conditions. I. Title.

    HQ799.A82T37 2008
    305.23509946'4–dc22   2008030656

10   9   8   7   6   5   4   3   2   1
18   17   16   15   14   13   12   11   10   09

Printed and bound in Great Britain by
CPI Antony Rowe, Chippenham and Eastbourne

Contents

List of Figures and Table

Foreword

Social analysis is at its most powerful when driven by passionate concern, when it is informed by theoretical insight, and when it is documented in clear, simple prose. The combining of the rational and the affective in this book provides for a moving and yet scholarly account of real people engaging in real life activities in the Australian island state of Tasmania.

Ani Wierenga taps into first-hand narrative accounts of what it means to grow up in today's world. She gains knowledge of this social process by speaking with, and listening to, the young people with whom she interacts. She also lives in this world alongside them. She is no stranger to them or their families, but is a part of their community. She knows where they are coming from, and where they are most likely to be, now and in the future.

Being a youthworker had meant that Ani came to her 'subjects' as a practitioner and as someone who works with young people. The qualities of empathy, respect and professionalism were well honed before the study began. So too, Ani's relationships with the young people had been 'proved' – in her capacities as community worker, and as friend.

Yet, a social scientist simultaneously inhabits this universe. In this respect, Ani has managed to sense that what people experience and articulate is not quite enough if we are to adequately understand their stories. What they say and what they do must be analyzed and interpreted, if their stories are to find full purchase. There is no doubting that the accounts of the young people are 'authentic', but even authenticity requires contextualization.

We know from this study that 'what people mean' has to be considered in relation to the important cultural processes, local histories and social structures affecting their lives. No person is an island, yet the island is their home. The people in this book embody both the local and the global; their identity remains fluid yet fixed, malleable but somehow unchangeable. In short, they are who they are because of when and where they live. Their understandings and experiences of life generally, and their variable excursions and forays into the wider world beyond the immediate town limits, are shaped by family relations, school activities, peer friendships and the limitations and opportunities of growing up precisely where they have grown up.

In many ways, 'Making a Life' is as much the story of Ani Wierenga as it is about the place and experiences of young people in the contemporary world. Life is about complexity, growth, development, tension, networks and emotion. We find meaning, livelihood and social connectedness in many different ways, across many different lived dimensions. In the process of writing about these themes, Ani, too, has experienced them. She has made a life in the very moment of writing about others undergoing similar processes.

The biographical is not insignificant in moulding how we see ourselves and those around us at particular historical moments. The great strength of this book is that it provides a conscious reflection on young people and social change, but is not overly self-conscious in portraying this contemporary history. Ani is both there, but not there. We know who is talking with whom, who is observing whom, who is sympathetic with whom. But this never impedes upon the conceptual sense-making that allows us to better appreciate the great structural forces and shifts in the lives of these young people.

Thus, what is happening in the lives of these young people has local trappings but also has the features of the universal. For those of us 'not from here', there is much to acknowledge and appreciate in these tales from Down Under. The feelings of familiarity and recognition are understandable however. The dynamics of class, gender and localism permeate all of our lives, whether we live in Australia, the UK or Canada – we see ourselves reflected in the experiences of our geographically distant cousins. So too, global capitalism impinges upon all of our lived realities in ways that strike a chord of resemblance regardless of specific place or particular accent. This book has relevance regardless of which side of the planet we are on. For it is a social study of the human condition in general, as well as of local kids in a particular town.

Good longitudinal, long-term, qualitative analysis is rare. Institutional constraints on funding, and academic pressures to churn research projects through as fast as one can, tends to preclude this kind of long-term intensive work. Practitioner-relevant academic work is less rare, but it is seldom seen as well. These observations make the present book even that much more remarkable in terms of genesis, data collection and presentation.

Ani Wierenga's book provides valuable things to say about practice, about theory, and about how young people – in general – come to 'make a life'. It is a complete work. It is a work-in-progress. It is a book that has something to say. It is a book that leaves the door open for much more dialogue, discussion and debate. In short, it is a book that is as thoughtful as it is thought-provoking.

Professor Rob White
School of Sociology & Social Work
University of Tasmania, Australia

Acknowledgements

I celebrate the arrival of this book, and I am indebted to all those who helped to bring it into being. For the substance of my book, I am most deeply indebted to those who have been directly involved in the research process – the 32 young people whose stories are its focus. You have taught me so much, and are still teaching me.

I also wish to express my heartfelt gratitude to the families of these young people, and to the members of the Myrtle Vale community who so trustingly and repeatedly opened your homes and lives. And my sincere thanks go, too, to the staff at Myrtle Vale District High School. It was a privilege to work with you and your students.

My heartfelt gratitude also belongs to staff and fellow students at the Sociology Department, University of Tasmania for providing me with an academic home during the time I was doing the fieldwork for this study. In terms of quality of life and work, companions in the corridors have made all the difference. Collectively, over the life of this project (including my BA honours year, and my PhD) you shared so much. I would like to acknowledge the people responsible for very early input: Rod Crook, for help with isolating a very workable research idea; Jan Pakulski for help with framing those findings; Malcolm Waters for trust and patience when I disappeared into the field for years; Bob White who convened our reading group; and Gary Easthope who affirmed my ideas and encouraged me when everything looked too big, too connected and too unspeakable. I can hear each of your voices as I re-read these pages.

The early years of this research formed my PhD, and I would like to gratefully acknowledge my PhD supervisor, Rob White, whose advice and guidance brought insights into which ideas were worth pursuing, and how a good thesis can work, and ultimately helped me to do justice to the personal, idiosyncratic and globally significant raw material of this Myrtle Vale study.

More recently, I have been inspired and challenged by conversations with my colleagues at the Australian Youth Research Centre, University of Melbourne, who have been living with my growing impatience to finish this book. Thank you all. I'm particularly grateful to Johanna Wyn for valuable feedback and support over years of analysis, and for insight and recent care with editing. A heartfelt thank you also to Richard Eckersley for conversations over the last ten years, and new projects that have helped me to explore the wider implications of this research.

Most recently, I owe my thanks to my Commissioning Editor at Palgrave Macmillan, Jill Lake, and my Editor, Philippa Grand for their generous guidance through the process of transforming manuscript into book. Thanks also to Melanie Blair and Hazel Woodbridge, at Palgrave for their administrative support, and I am especially grateful to Olivia Middleton for email communication and encouragement during the completion of the final manuscript.

My deepest gratitude belongs to family and close friends for allowing me to be so engrossed for so long, and for your faithful care and support. Specifically I think of Mum, Dad, Dave and Kate; to Leah, for many lessons about courage; to Andy for helping me to remember why I do this; to Alice, for walking with me through days of drafting; to Natalie, Jacqui and Karen for the time you spent reading and giving detailed feedback, to Mandy for a home during fieldwork post-PhD; to David and Brenda for coaching and gentle generosity. I am particularly grateful to my Mum for your along-sidedness in this project, from being there for my first articulations of these stories in a foreign land, through to your engagement in the final chapter-edits. Finally, thanks to my husband Arnie, whose patience, humour and love continue to astound me.

1
Introduction

Near the end of the road south, at the southern tip of Tasmania, an island state (itself at the southern tip of Australia), lies a small rural town called Myrtle Vale. Arguably the most beautiful place in the world, this is also a place of considerable pain. It is in one of the areas where the costs of wider social changes are being acutely felt. Like many places on the planet, social changes are most clearly embodied in the challenges that the town's young people face as they grow up.

For some, this local life is clearly a life of abundance, *enhanced by* rurality, physical surrounds, and the bonds of community. Meanwhile, for others, day-to-day life seems far better characterized as a struggle, and the *burden is seemingly increased by* the same rurality, physical surrounds, and bonds of community. As an outsider to the community, I found that what began as my concern for the young people often turned into admiration and wonder at them and their families for their strength of conviction, resilience of spirit, and creativity of solutions. Yet there were many for whom solutions to the central issues of livelihood, meaning, and social connectedness clearly were a long way off.

I was a youthworker in the Lightwood Valley, which encompasses Myrtle Vale, from 1991–1994. In 1995, I withdrew from that role to do some thinking and some listening. This book is the result.

My own questions were many and varied:

- Why is life here so abundant for some and so tough for others?
- Why do apples swing unpicked on the trees while Ben has no job?
- What is happening to this town that makes some people so angry?
- How is it that some young people can make very contented and connected lives here, while the lives of others are so characterized by frustration and withdrawal?

- Why will some young people happily leave town to seek opportunities elsewhere while others have no intention of doing this?
- What helps and what gets in the way?
- (and stemming from my own role-struggle) What could a youth-worker or teacher most usefully do here? What would it look like?

There were some more fundamental questions lying beneath these:

- What is going on here?
- How could we know what is going on?
- How to make sense of it all; how to find and tell a story (or multiple stories) that do some justice to these lives, issues and struggles?
- What to do – in practice and policy?

Most of these questions can be encapsulated into a single research question: Why and how are these young people so differently 'making a life'? I am defining *making a life* in terms of livelihood, meaning, and social connectedness. I have framed this question quite broadly because, in empirical research, young people's lives often get fragmented into problems or issues that are studied discretely. Fragmented findings do not equip people in practice and policy settings to make holistic responses to current issues. Topics that resonate across sectors and disciplines include questions about young people's resilience, their well-being, and their capacity to live and to learn, issues of citizenship and young people's participation in, or exclusion from, their communities. A small local case study provides one way of exploring these global, pressing and inter-linked issues in some depth.

Questions about *making a life* also echo some familiar theoretical questions about social process: about the complex relationships between individuals and the societies in which they live; about how social differences and social inequalities become embodied and constructed in individuals' lives and choices; about transitions in young people's lives and how they are being differently experienced and negotiated.

The other questions (dot-pointed above) are really about research methodology and social process. The last 12 years has been about *living the questions*, and the book is a thematic gathering of the many stories that have made sense along the way. As an interpretive study, the research behind the book draws heavily upon conversations with respondents, in this case Myrtle Vale's young people. I also make use of other stories from within the sociological discipline, of bodies of social research, of material that helps to place these young people's lives within a social context. I draw upon the languages and concepts of sociological theory often, where they help to make sense of things heard and seen in the field. In return, through grounded research, respondents' lives and stories have the potential to expand the scope of sociological research, and further inform our conceptual understandings and our theories. Beyond this, the stories also have the capacity to speak powerfully to policy and practice.

This book shares the journey of a researcher, a longitudinal research project, and of 32 young people *making a life*. The project began when the young people were around 12 years old, and now they are in their mid-20s. The findings are a product of the relationships formed with young people and their families over years. Formally, data was gathered through essays, observations and mostly through focussed interviews with young people, although I also interviewed others (towns-folk, teachers and parents) to get a clearer picture of social context and process. Young people were interviewed every two years over the six-year period from early high school to their post-high school options. For the following six years, catch-ups and conversations continued to evolve the work. Now, over 12 years from the start of the project, I have lost contact with some of the respondents, but others have been centrally involved in the preparation of this manuscript.

This is a local story, but it reflects on some themes that are poignant around the globe. In terms of the sociological themes with global resonance, this study is essentially a look at young people in transition – many transitions – changing status, identities, passions, relationships, family structures, possibilities, geographical locations and living arrangements. Within youth literature, school-to-work has often been privileged as *the* transition of interest. Meanwhile, lived experience tells us that young people's lives are more complex and interesting than this. Other parts of their lives are also integral to understanding their work patterns and opportunities. The intersections between themes of wellbeing, learning and active social participation are of particular interest. Through the book I will explore some ways of writing more holistic accounts about young people's changing lives.

This is a story about subjectivities, the way people understand and respond to their world, about social change and human dignity. Equally significantly, this is a study about human agency and social structure. It explores individual lives being constructed in the midst of patterned opportunities and constraints. Many studies give information about the larger picture, the structural context in which young people grow up. Internationally there is a growing interest in how young people themselves are creatively making their own lives within that picture. This is one such study, based upon insiders' stories of lived experience.

Chapters 2 and 3 explore issues of growing up in a contemporary world, amidst conditions of social change and uncertainty. In this early part of the book I will also review the research which explains some of the reasons why young people in rural areas are having a particularly rough time. Young people's lives are deeply enmeshed in the issues of their communities, and so the focus needs to be on the changes that are affecting rural communities themselves. Then in Chapter 3, I will explain some more about Myrtle Vale, the particular, unique, local context for this study, and briefly outline the research that took place.

An interpretive framework for understanding the findings of this research will be introduced in Chapter 4. Rather than being generated from pre-existing theory, the model that I will present arose out of conversations with respondents. At that time of these conversations, narrative theory was not so prevalent, yet the data presented here brings a different stream of evidence about the power of narrative in the ways lives are constructed. Building on early findings (Wierenga 1999) this chapter particularly highlights the significance of individuals' different stories and practices of 'storying'. These are both reflections of their past (that is, their history and context) and powerful shapers of future possibilities.

Later interviews surround the time of respondents' transitions from Myrtle Vale District High School to elsewhere. Chapters 5 and 6 are processual accounts of the things that happen for different young people at this time, and how they are engaging, negotiating, and making sense of it all. These are cohort case-studies of particular moments: Chapter 5 as individuals plan to leave, and then leave, high school; and Chapter 6 as we find them nearly two years later.

Chapters 7 and 8 look at some of the most clearly emerging patterns in the ways in which these young people are making, and able to make, their lives. Issues of resources, and how young people differently access resources are paramount. Through close work with young people's stories it is possible to uncover much fuller accounts of the types of resources that they seek and access. Chapter 7 unpacks both the practical and symbolic aspects of social inequalities.

The focus for this work is well beyond school-to-work transitions. Based upon respondents' stories, the chapters present broad, processual accounts of how and why these individuals are making lives, and able to make lives, so differently.

As a whole, the book explores social processes by which different types of resources become available to young people. As respondents' stories reveal, individuals' networks are heavily implicated. Chapter 8 shows how, in *all* cases, flows of important resources depend upon relationships of trust (with individuals, groups, and/or institutions), that in turn depend upon individual and group history. Local issues, gender and class are still vital to these patterns. Story becomes a vital conduit – or not. Chapter 9 investigates the way in which individuals become centrally implicated in these patterns, and the twin workings of context and culture, of circumstance and subjectivity.

These chapters outline a process for mapping trust relationships through story, which might be useful to others. They trace the ways in which broader social patterns become part of the way individuals live their own lives, but also brings to the foreground and highlights poss-ibilities for change, or *methodologies of hope*.

Beyond the theoretical value of the analysis, it also holds some pointers for action. The implications of the project's findings for research, policy and practice will be discussed in Chapters 10 and 11. Although each of the young people's stories have emerged from one local, unique setting, together they also speak to global issues. Chapter 10 focusses in on the research findings about resources, trust, and nar-rative, linking these to growing international interest and evidence about the importance of these three foci. This chapter highlights learn-ings for policy and practice.

Over time, research often comes to embody the very patterns that it is aiming to explore. This project has been no exception: issues of power and powerlessness, voice and voicelessness, privilege and exclu-sion all make their appearances in encounters with respondents. The final chapter of this book examines research as social process, taking a long, hard look in the mirror, and a reflexive look at the research process itself.

2
Growing Up: Global, Local, Rural

When I started this project in 1995, it was relatively hard to find research about young people that looked beyond their problems, their physiology or their psychology. Part of the challenge, as I understood it, was to develop an understanding of young people making their lives, in context. As a youthworker, I had been particularly struck by two pieces of writing. One talked about social changes in Western societies and their unhealthy impacts on young people (Eckersley 1992). The second was from a Western Australian youthwork guru, George Davies, who spoke about so-called 'problem' young people and recommended that as communities we do not shoot the messengers, but learn to listen to them. 'Got to get trust to be able to do the listening, that means staying long term' (ABC 1999b). These early influences set the scene for this project.

During the lifetime of this study, the research backdrop has changed remarkably with the publishing of many significant bodies of sociological research about young people. This new research emphasizes the interplay of social and structural conditions and social change with young people's lives. Across continents there has been interest in rapid socio-economic change, and more recently particularly young people's experiences of social change. This issue makes visible some common patterns in the industrial world (Dwyer and Wyn 2001) but also highlights a diversity in research agendas (Furlong 2000; Helve and Holm 2005; Nilan and Feixa 2006; Ukeje 2006). Technologies have made gaining access to international research much easier. A significant body of youth research is now speaking to the themes of location in a changing world and amidst the peculiarities and uniqueness of place.

Globalization has received significant attention. From the perspective of industrialized countries it can be too easy to think of our own settings as the known world, and to forget that most young people today are growing up in majority world situations. At a recent session of the International Sociological Association in South Africa many of us from industrialized nations spoke from now shared understandings about young people's extended transitions and choice biographies, flexible identities and youth culture. Cutting through these narratives, a colleague from Nigeria, Charles Ukeje explained: 'In many African countries experiencing profoundly excruciating socio-economic, political and health challenges…children caught up in these circumstances find themselves literarily growing up overnight.' (Ukeje 2006). Ukeje highlighted that because of the extreme circumstances that surround them, many pass into the phase of 'youth' so quickly and then are stuck there, not making the transition into adulthood in the sense of age chronology that is privileged in the West.

At the turn of this century, in an issue of *International Social Science Journal* dedicated to global youth research, editor Andy Furlong noted that where young people have limited access to education and health needs, the themes explored in the West, like identities, biographies and subcultures tend not to be prominent. Instead the work has centred around survival and responses to threats of hunger, conflict and disease (Furlong 2000). It is also important to remember that in the twenty-first century the raw issues of survival cut across nations as well as between them.

I raise these issues at the outset for several reasons. Firstly, although I will make claims for the international currency of themes in this book, that will always be bounded by the social conditions and cultural frames from which the work comes.

Secondly though, others' work, and my own recent work in other countries, does seem to suggest that some issues transcend the borders of nation and privilege, particularly the themes of access to resources, trust relationships, and story. I will leave it to readers to ponder on the utility of these ideas in their own neighbourhoods.

Thirdly, class, gender and race have been fundamental structuring dynamics across societies, and the evidence tells us they still have a hold. In the face of contemporary sociological claims about the breakdown of social structures, one of the key issues raised in this book is access to resources, examined through young people's stories. They bring us firmly back to the knowledge that class is not dead, that gender shapes lives, and that race, acknowledged or not, continues to shape relationships.

One of the recurring themes readers will encounter in this book is the interplay of ordinary people's lives with social structures and social change and the so-called 'logic' of global capital. The failure of neo-liberal policies and promises is evident in the lives of young people. Under conditions of globalization, familiar axes of inequalities create new permutations of opportunity and hardship, with differential impacts across nations, within nations, on communities, and on folks within these communities. For contemporary social scientists it is important to document both the ravages and the creative responses. It is only by studying these closely that we can learn about methodologies of hope.

Herein lies the paradox: the issues that face young people are very global, but also very local. Social scientists sit somewhere between the grand narratives of the big picture and the peculiarities of culture and place. There is much more exploring to do. This awareness highlights the value of diverse voices, of international conversations, and of local stories.

Rural Australia provides one grounded setting in which rapid social changes, neo-liberal policies, globalizing markets and their imprint, and young people's creative responses can be explored.

This chapter will explore the impacts of these changes *vis-à-vis* growing up today, in Australia, and particularly in rural communities. As young people's issues are firmly embedded within the issues of their communities, particular attention will also be paid to the changes that have been affecting rural communities themselves. To create the backdrop, I draw on research literature from over the past 25 years, which is the period in time when the young people involved in this project have been growing up. Firstly I will explore the implications of growing up in different social worlds – particularly in relation to size of community and geographical isolation. Then I will draw upon research surrounding the changing conditions in rural Australia, and highlight the impacts of these on rural communities and their young people. In the context of making a life, one central issue for young people has been, and continues to be, about whether to stay in, or leave, their communities, and I will flesh out some of the implications of this dilemma. Young people have different experiences of growing up in a rural place, and the chapter concludes with some reflections on how social differences, particularly class, gender and race, can impact on individual lives.

Growing up in Australia

Young people growing up around the turn of the twenty-first century have been making lives amidst major structural changes in their societies. Like in other industrialized countries, in Australia over the past couple of decades technologies, rationalizations and global markets have led to radical changes in the labour market and the nature of work, the growth of 'precarious employment', the loss of the youth job market, and the disappearance of traditional stepping stones into work (Burgess and Campbell 1998; Dussledorp Skills Forum 1998; Polk and White 1999). It is becoming increasingly common for young people to combine work and study, starting from their schooldays. Peter Dwyer, Johanna Wyn and colleagues engaged in the University of Melbourne's 'Life Patterns' study have explored how this generation of young people are far less able to rely on established pathways and structures than their parents had been. Similar to patterns in other industrialized countries, lack of jobs and increased expectations of schooling have meant prolonged transitions to adulthood, a status which a generation ago had been linked to independence, getting a house, and family for-mation (Dwyer et al. 1999). As young people's transitions lengthen and fundamentally change in nature, post-1970s generations face new chal-lenges in terms of forming livelihoods, identities and meaning. The markers of adult status are effectively being denied to many (Dwyer et al. 1999; Dwyer and Wyn 2001).

In addition, some changes have been a direct result of national policy. Sociologist, Michael Pusey explains: 'We are living now in the wake of a forced 20-year-long, top-down, neo-liberal reengineering of a whole nation society.' Twenty years of economic 'reform' has entrenched this new free-market institutional order, which sits 'at odds with our longer historical inheritance of moderate social democracy' (Pusey 2007).

In the 1990s and into this century, Johanna Wyn and Rob White (1997; White and Wyn 2008) have provided useful commentary on these changes and their impact on young people. They explain that, at the same time as market-driven changes, a political climate of eco-nomic rationalism has meant a 'winding back' of the public sector, that is, of state resources available to young people and families. Particularly in the area of welfare this has meant the removal of tradi-tional safety nets for those who could not find a place within the labour market. This has been accompanied by a rationalization of ser-vices, for example in public education and health, from resources more freely available to user-pays systems, making them far less available for those with lesser means. These changes have happened across the board, but they affect communities and individuals very differently on the basis of long-standing social inequalities (class, gender, race). Restraint in the provision of services, together with neo-liberal policies that place great emphasis on individual initiative, have provided a recipe for expansion of social inequality and social problems.

As the next section of this chapter will highlight, although all are affected, changes are amplified even further by economies of scale and tyrannies of distance.

Living in rural communities

Rural young people are making their lives within social contexts that are often far removed from those of their urban peers. Both the lived experiences of growing up, and associated individual life-chances can be quite different. Distance and size of community can bring issues of *access to resources* into sharp relief. Social and geographical location determines which opportunities are physically available to individuals, whilst cultural location shapes how these opportunities can be perceived and made useful (Wierenga 2001). All of these things are mediated to individuals via their own communities, and have huge implications for the ways in which individuals' meaning systems and trajectories are constructed.

Although the changes mentioned above are felt as increased challenges across the board in Australia, they are felt nowhere more acutely than in rural places. People who, because of isolation, are dependent on local infrastructures suffer most when those things disappear. As part of this dynamic the differences between options for rural young people in deciding their own futures are amplified (Wierenga 2001). Significant numbers of Australian young people are affected in this way. This is a vast country with a relatively small population (just over 21 million people). Despite a national tendency to cluster around cities and on coast-line (ABS 2003), at the turn of the century approximately one quarter of the nation's young people (aged 15–25) lived in rural areas (Wyn et al. 1998). From rurality, however, we can not assume a commonality of experience; rural communities are diverse. Each setting is shaped uniquely by physical geography and regional differences, as well as settlement histories, indigenous relationships to the land, industrial development, sustainable production patterns and world markets.

Several writers from across continents have already commented about the problematic nature of 'rurality' as a concept and a framework for cross country comparison (see Cartmel 2004). In Australia, depending upon the focus of writers, rurality has been defined on the basis of different criteria, for example: demographic or social (population-based), or geographical (distance) or a combination of the two. For the purposes of this book, further exploring typologies of rurality and remoteness would be less than helpful. As Dianne Looker and Peter Dwyer (1997) have pointed out, rurality means different things in different social contexts. Smaller centres can be in close proximity to other larger centres, and distance may not be as fixed as it appears (for example, new highways, electronic communications). In their discussion of rurality, they point instead to other social characteristics: separateness and distinctness; patterns of relationships; concentration of social connections; fewer external connections or greater 'closure'. Each of these things will be the result of different combinations of size and distance. I see it as important to embrace stories from both small towns and regional centres within a definition of rurality, if for no other reason than the common impact of the decline in rural economies on young people's lives. Consequently I will also make use of a 'broad' definition of rurality offered by Barker and Milligan (1990) and Wyn et al. (1998), referring to 'all areas outside of capital cities and major urban conglomerates'. For reference, the Australian Bureau of statistics (ABS 2003) defines an urban area as a population cluster of 1,000 or more people.

Different social worlds

Rural young people live in different social worlds from their urban counterparts. Through distance and economies of scale they experience restricted access to certain services and resources. However, size and distance are also indicative of more profound social differences (Looker and Dwyer 1997). Through local community life, young people may have access to a whole range of other things that urban people cannot hope to understand. The lived experience of rurality varies with time, between communities, between families and between individuals. For some, growing up and living in a rural community represents a positive, viable experience. For others, it involves considerable struggle. Issues of class, gender and race are very significant, and will be examined later. First, though some common themes will be explored.

The strengths and abundances of rural communities are not well captured by statistics and indicators. They are often intangible but can be steeped in meaning. Amongst both indigenous and non-indigenous communities, individual lives may be strongly anchored to people or to place (Brady 1991; Wyn et al. 1998; Wierenga 1999; Bourke and Geldens 2007). The Australian Broadcasting Corporation has, for ten years, encouraged young people to tell their own stories through the

Heywire broadcasts and website: http://www.abc.net.au/heywire/. Their stories show how patterns of everyday practice often incorporate valued understandings that are shared across generations. Meaning systems can be structured around events, seasons and traditions in a way that cannot often be appreciated by outsiders.

Over the past 25 years, themes that have emerged strongly from Australian community studies are pride in the place, in the type of relationships that exist, and in the qualities of the people. Many people in rural places have explained that they appreciate fresh air and scenery, open spaces, lack of congestion, peacefulness, security from violent crime, and opportunities for recreational activities (Dempsey 1990). These themes are mirrored in some of the youth literature; rural young people have reported that they appreciate fresh air, clean, open spaces, being able to walk the streets safely and distance from the problems of the city (Hillier et al. 1996).

Rural communities, almost by definition, have strong cultural identities. Regarding the qualities of the people, young people often share communities' stories of what is good and honourable. Identities are built and maintained in the context of these understandings.

Attachments to communities may revolve around themes of continuity and belonging. For example, when talking about their town, inhabitants of Ken Dempsey's 'Smalltown' (Dempsey 1990) described qualities sociologists had earlier come to know as 'Gemeinschaft' qualities. A generation earlier, a classic community study by Bell and Newby had outlined these qualities:

> Intimate... enduring... in a community everyone is known and can be placed in the social structure. This results in a personalizing of issues, events and explanations, because familiar names and characters inevitably become associated with everything that happens. (Bell and Newby 1971:24)

Not surprisingly, over the same period these findings have also been mirrored by different research with rural youth. Young respondents have also reported that they appreciate the quality of relationships and levels of familiarity, and, in some cases, predictability and a sense of belonging were also appreciated (Hillier et al. 1996; Looker and Dwyer 1997; Wyn et al. 1998). Rural young people are more likely than their urban counterparts to have long-standing family ties to their communities (Looker and Dwyer 1997). Families tend to play a strong role in young people's lives, and are usually seen as very important to their wellbeing (Bourke and Geldens 2007). Some report that sport is a source of solidarity between generations. Significantly, also, young people in one national study reported that close-knit communities mean not just a greater capacity for emotional support, but also for physical support – 'the basics, food, wood and roof' (Quixley 1992:20).

However, the down-side of open space is distance, and the flip-side of close relationships is that non-conformity may lead to criticism, rejection and being stigmatized. The very qualities that are a positive feature for some are a negative feature for others. Family and community networks can, at the same time, be both 'close-knit and caring' and 'intrusive and controlling' (Glendinning et al. 2003). It is common in rural youth research for young people to mention that everybody knows everybody's business (Hillier et al. 1996). They know that their choices are made in the context of community reactions (Bourke 2003). Perceptions of gossip can lead to a desire to withdraw from their communities, and in small towns this leaves few alternatives for social contact. Ironically, a common issue for rural young people, even from within 'close-knit' communities, is the feeling of isolation (Wyn et al. 1998).

Economies of scale and tyrannies of distance

One study has suggested that rural young people see cities as a place of 'more'. More 'crime, more violence, more noise, more pollution', but also 'more jobs, more opportunities, more shops and more options' (Looker and Dwyer 1997; see also 15 year-old Freeman, 1998, in Heywire 1998). Rural young people also say that they experience lack of access to many things. Underlying most issues of access are two key factors: physical isolation from other larger settlements, and size of community.

Size of community is the determining factor in the development of local infrastructures, including those from both private and public sectors. Population determines, for example, the kinds of small businesses that can grow and be sustainable and, therefore, it also determines the numbers of families that can be supported and stay in town. Government expenditure is another significant factor. In less densely settled areas, real costs per capita rise when providing services such as education and health, electricity, phones, or sealed roads (Epps and Sorensen 1996), and specific youth services (Sercombe 2006).

Meanwhile, distance from other centres restricts access to external services, facilities, and infrastructures such as employment, health, and education. This is significant, as it leaves people in rural and remote areas far more dependent than others upon their localized infrastructures.

Access to resources

People in rural and remote locations cannot access many things that are taken for granted in larger centres. Some of these impact on quality of life now, others impact on future life chances. Research to date suggests that particularly salient issues for young people include access to entertainment, jobs, finance, education, health, and transport.

Young people frequently report that rural areas have limited recreational, leisure, and entertainment facilities. The issue of living in rural areas is met with some ambivalence. While many like living where they do, many perceive that there is 'nothing to do'. On the Australian Broadcasting Corporation's web page Heywire the themes most consistently raised by the young rural authors include the challenge of finding opportunities for interaction with people of their own age, chances to meet new people who did not know everything about them, and the need at times for something exciting and unpredictable to happen. The inadequate term 'entertainment', which keeps emerging in the literature, actually reflects rural young people's social isolation. Many young people feel that their needs and interests are not catered for within their communities (Wyn et al. 1998).

On a more tangible note, rurality has meant poor job prospects. At the turn of this century, unemployment rates were nearly twice as high for rural as for urban young people (White 1999). More than urban counterparts, rural students also experience a shortage of accessible part-time jobs. Naturally, then, combining school and work is more difficult for rural students (Looker and Dwyer 1997).

On average, rural people have lower incomes than other Australians, and higher levels of socio-economic disadvantage in rural than in urban areas (Haberkorn et al. 2004). While locally material disadvantage can be compensated by local barter and cashless economies, when individuals need to engage with different social groups, however, these systems may prove less transferable than cash.

Rural young people experience relatively poor access to education and training, and extensive barriers to participation. Research conducted by the Australian Youth Research Centre and the Human Rights and Equal Opportunity Commission elaborates this picture (Stokes et al. 1999; HREOC 2000). The equation of 'rural' and 'disadvantaged' has been a basis for much of the social, education and economic policy development in Australia. The reports are clearly not saying that schools in rural areas provide education of a poorer quality, than that of metropolitan areas. However, the quality local educational programs can also be bound up in, and constrained by, issues of access.

In many cases students have been involved with educational systems which were designed with urban students in mind. In order to respond to the particular needs of communities, many schools in rural areas have developed alternative and innovative forms of education. Distance education is suitable for primary aged students (although it places a strain on parents) but is a poor second option to an interactive high school. New technologies, such as the internet, promise much, but to date there has been an inverse relationship between remoteness and the use of new communication technologies. This is largely because of the associated costs. Aboriginal young people are less likely to access the limited options available and to consequently raise issues of cultural appropriateness, relevance, and language. Rural students are also more likely to be affected by material disadvantage than others, and the costs associated with distance education or school of the air, boarding, setting up two houses, transport, curriculum enrichment and technology have been issues for many families (HREOC 1999; Stokes et al. 1999; HREOC 2000).

The costs associated with higher education significantly affect students in rural and remote areas. The role of government policies is complex. Even whilst unemployment payments have been (in theory) restructured to promote continued education for all students, changes to fees, student loans, and means tests seem to have systematically ruled many rural young people out of the picture (HREOC 2000).

Earlier research also highlighted how a lack of immediate access to further and higher educational facilities can also limit the amount of information available to country students, many of whom have to rely on impersonal written documents when making choices about futures (Cunningham et al. 1992).

Some of the most pertinent rural issues relate to health. A recent publication (AIHW 2006) reveals that as the distance from metropolitan centres increases, so do mortality and illness levels. Despite this, rural people experience a widespread inadequacy of health services. At the turn of the century, this was *the key issue* raised in the Human Rights and Equal Opportunity Commission's current series of 'Bush Talks' (HREOC 1999) around rural Australia, and is still a regular source of media attention. The Commission heard that supply of primary care practitioners per head of population falls sharply in rural areas, as does the amount of spending per hospital bed. Restricted numbers of doctors and specialist services are only one part of the problem. Participants expressed concern at long waits for appointments with doctors (days, weeks), places where no doctor in town would bulk bill, the paucity of mental health services, lack of dental options, appropriate drug and alcohol services, counselling and psychiatric care, and especially of services suitable for young people (HREOC 1999).

Australian research with young people suggests that health services are being avoided by young people due to expectations of a lack of confidentiality or unfair treatment. In some instances young people are also unaware that services are available (Wyn et al. 1998). Meanwhile, health services for Aboriginal Australians are often rendered less useful by ignorance of cultures, high staff turnover (HREOC 1999), inappropriate modes of delivery (Quixley 1992; HREOC 1999) mistrust, or fear (Wyn et al. 1998). Services and interventions designed in cities may not be appropriate in rural areas. These issues have particularly come into renewed focus with the Australian Federal Government's less-than-consultative 2007 response to indigenous health issues in the Northern Territory National Emergency Response Legislation (see Commonwealth of Australia, 2007).

Transport is a key issue for young people in rural places. Without adequate transport, access to activities is limited and economic and social opportunities can be restricted (Currie et al. 2005). Public transport, if available at all, can be very costly. Other issues that limit young people's easy access to public transport include routes, safety, and shelter (Green and McDonald 1996). Workers with young people have reported that much of their time can be spent driving young people around (Sercombe 2006).

Changing conditions in rural Australia

A thorough analysis would have to look at the impacts of change on indigenous, mining, pastoral and fishing communities, and also the impact of tourism. The focus here will remain with agricultural communities for two reasons. Firstly, these are the conditions captured in most of the 'rural' literature, and secondly, Myrtle Vale, the geographical setting for this study itself, has an agricultural background.

Far-reaching and rapid changes to rural communities are being brought about by technological change, environmental issues, international affairs, private and corporate actions, as well as broader cultural, demographic and lifestyle shifts (Epps and Sorensen 1996). More recently, climate change, water shortages and ongoing drought have had severe impacts. Most profoundly affecting all areas of Australia, though, are the changes described earlier: the effects of global capitalism, changed economic conditions within labour and industry, structural unemployment, and the winding back of the public sector. Even though the same processes have been happening across the board in Australia, perhaps nowhere are the changes to social infrastructure more pronounced than in rural communities.

A shift from interventionist policy to market rationalism has been felt most profoundly in regional areas (Economou 2001). The globalization of Australian agricultural markets has increased some trade opportunities, but there also have been costs in the equation, and these costs have been felt first by rural commodity producers. Put simply: 'the prices paid by farmers for the inputs of agriculture are increasing at a faster rate than the prices which overseas and domestic consumers are prepared to pay for the products of agriculture' (Lawrence 1996: 332). With deregulation and the opening-up of markets has come the closing down of small businesses. Increasing scale economies in the farm sector herald the weakening of traditional rural enterprises. This accompanies a government reluctance to step in to support agricultural practices (Epps and Sorensen 1996), where rural operators have been claiming that this is appropriate, necessary, and even urgent.

Meanwhile, rationalization of both government and privatized services, prevalent across Australia, has been even more pronounced in rural areas. Policies that focus on economies of scale have led to the removal of many services from rural communities. Whether organizations retreat for a profit motive or to maximize service in other areas, the impact is the same: priorities clash with the immediate interests of rural communities and their people. The result has been reductions in infrastructure and service delivery in everything from banks to hospital care (Epps and Sorensen 1996).

The impacts of change on rural communities and their young people

These broad patterns impact firstly on whole communities, and secondly on individual life-chances. As towns lose key services and critical subsidies, cyclic or spiralling patterns are set up in both community life and individual trajectories. Links to the outside world may remain distant and tenuous, but, at the same time, self-sufficiency is dealt a hefty blow. As communities lose their own resource bases, they lose the ability to both provide for their young, and to protect them from external conditions.

The 'Bush Talks' (HREOC 1999) documented how keenly people of all ages in rural communities are aware of these effects. From all over Australia, both speakers at community forums and written submissions articulated rural people's 'deep concern' about lack of opportunities for their young (1999:20).

Communities' diminished ability to provide for their young has manifested in many ways. It is most evident in the loss of the infrastructures that sustain day-to-day life. Continued rationalizations and closures mean that young people have to go further to get access to the basic services that they need (Green and McDonald 1996; Currie et al. 2005) .

The infrastructures for building futures are also disappearing. Many traditional 'pathways' to employment no longer exist (Looker and Dwyer 1997). As traditional enterprises collapse and services are lost, there is less employment available (Epps and Sorensen 1996). 'Rural decline' also entails the loss of other viable roles – or ways of engaging and contributing to the community. In this way, lifestyle changes affect the young as much as the old.

These changes mean that young people lose ways of viably staying in their communities. In Quixley's national research (1992:16) she found that young people's questions about continued viable rural living very often came back to the larger question 'what is the future of this community?'. These questions are still being asked today by the young people on Heywire (McPherson 2006; Moyle 2006).

Unemployment has been both cause and effect of the withdrawal of services from rural Australia (HREOC 1999). Many people from rural communities leave, most notably the young, usually to seek education or increased future options. Declines in population are then matched by further declines in services. This places greater strains on the provision of support services for those who remain. So the cycle is perpetuated; when the greengrocer closes, this means one less job, and one less family that can continue to live in the town (Quixley 1992). It is in this way that unemployment contributes directly to the destruction of rural communities (Wyn et al. 1998:14).

Few people are keen to purchase property in declining communities, although economic hardship propels some families further out of cities to where housing is cheaper. Ironically, those who stay in rural communities, for example the aged and the economically disadvantaged, can often be the very groups who most need social services, welfare and health support (Lawrence 1996).

With regard to service provision 'a pseudo-Darwinian process' has been taking place for some time, in which some towns emerge as survivors, better able to win in the struggle for expansion (Epps and Sorensen 1996:156). Regional centres grow, but smaller towns fade. While the tyranny of distance has in some ways been eroded by substantial developments in communication technology, rural Australia has been, in other senses, moving further away. In particular, the contrast between inland rural and larger coastal centres has steadily increased.

Protection of the young

The above changes mean that the role of communities in protecting their young is also being undermined. The depletion in support services and the changing demographics in rural areas mean that families and their young fall through both formal and informal safety nets. The security that comes from a close-knit community is diminished, with unrelated newcomers moving in for economic reasons (lesser known and sometimes with less resources), while the young and the upwardly mobile (often seen as the community's future) are moving out. The image of haemorrhaging has been used to describe this pattern.

Regarding young people's futures, at this point even the expertise and guidance of previous generations is undermined. For both Aboriginal and non-Aboriginal communities, this means the erosion of intergenerational links to ways of living with each other and with place (see Quixley 1992; Wyn et al. 1998). As systems change and local options diminish, the young require more education outside their communities, in systems with which their local elders and experts are not familiar.

Cultural ways of life undermined

We have talked about social infrastructures, but communities also provide cultural infrastructures for making a life. These include ways of making sense of lived experience, expectations, shared understandings of who we are, what we are doing, and why this is important.

Alongside the onslaughts on infrastructure, rural communities have found themselves undergoing a process of 'detraditionalization'. Traditions, though, are intertwined with interests and with identities (Gray and Phillips 1996). People's health, in a holistic sense involves engagement in communities. Changes threaten not only livelihoods, but also people's shared ways of life. Whilst Aboriginal Australians have been experiencing attacks on tradition for several generations, for many more Australians this 'detraditionalization' has come into focus in the last generation.

Along with social changes, the ideology of rural-ness is undermined. Australian community studies describe a culture of 'countrymindedness' in that occupiers of certain rural towns define themselves in opposition to the city (Dempsey 1990; Gray 1991). They produce the essentials of life, which city people rely on for their own lives or for export. It is a notion of 'the bush' struggling with these problems, and without sufficient reward or recognition, that has been a catalyst for recent strain and tension, voter backlash, and the rise of new, conservative, political forces (Economou 2001).

At the same time, images of the bright lights in the city provide the young with alternative images of desirable lifestyles, and these remain quite disconnected from realistic understandings of options and their respective costs (Quixley 1992). Improvements in communications and technology may only serve to remind rural young people of the urban things which are not accessible to them (Wyn et al. 1998).

Indicators of social problems

In terms of young people's wellbeing, one of the most dramatic indicators of social stress is rural youth suicide. In recent decades Australia has one of the highest rates of youth suicide in the western world, especially among rural men (Bourke 2003). The number of deaths in Australia attributed to suicide rose from 2,197 in 1988 to 2,723 in 1997, an increase of 24% over that ten-year period (ABS 2000a), before beginning to fall again. Rural rates (17 per 100,000) have tended to be higher than capital cities (13) and other urban areas (15) (ABS 2000b) and substantially higher for young men than young women (ABS 2000b). In 1986, the rural male (age 15–24) suicide rate (per 100,000) was 24, and in 1995 it had risen to 34 (ABS 1997). Indigenous youth suicide rates have been as high as 1.4% times the non-indigenous rate (Department of Health and Family Services 1997). One comparison of metropolitan and rural trends in youth suicide (Dudley et al. 1998) revealed that while suicide rates for 15–24-year-old Australian young men have doubled since the 1960s, they increased by as much as twelve-fold in some (not all) towns with fewer than 4,000 people. While the suicide rates seem to be declining, they still remain unacceptably high in rural Australia (Bourke 2003).

Rurality means poor job prospects, with nearly twice as many rural, compared to urban, young people likely to report unemployment. Seasonal work is common and often does not provide adequate income for independent living. In areas where seasonal work is prevalent, these patterns serve to mask unemployment.

Rural students have tended not to stay at school as long as urban youth. This has been manifest in several ways. Firstly, rural young people have been less likely to complete education to year ten (HREOC 1999). Secondly, rurality hinders education past the compulsory mark. When compared to those in metropolitan areas, lower levels of young people complete year 12 in rural regions. The average year 12 retention rate for boys in rural and remote areas is only 54%, as compared to 63% in capital cities, and for girls it is 66% as compared to 74% in capital cities (Sidoti 2001). Non-completion is a significant issue; Australian students who did not complete year 12 in the mid-1990s experienced longer periods of unemployment (Lamb et al. 2000). Thirdly, more rural than urban youth take alternative, non-tertiary paths (Looker and Dwyer 1997). When compared to a decade earlier, at the turn of the century fewer rural young people were entering tertiary education (25% in 1989, 16% in 1997 (HREOC 1999:13)). These patterns are persistent, and low retention rates can be traced back to issues of access, and also to traditional rural pathways and expectations.

Staying and leaving

In the light of the issues above, choices about whether or not to continue education can become problematic or at least complicated (Looker and Dwyer 1997). One piece of research with rural young people (Bourke 1997) reveals that many more plan on completing year 12 than actually do. In high school, most are not sure of their future plans, and this is to be expected for most young people. It becomes problematic though, when options are cut off in ways that may be regretted in later life.

Decisions about whether to continue education are not made in isolation, but in the context of many other social factors. Rural / urban research in Australia and Canada demonstrates that transition paths are 'qualitatively different' from those of urban and suburban youth. The differences between choices are amplified for rural students, often entailing either severing ties or missing valuable opportunities. In many cases it can be a trade-off between perceived life-chances, and quality of life or living in ways that are known and valued.

Continuing education may mean being forced to travel long distances or leave home. This often involves tangible losses, such as in the costs associated with transportation or accommodation. Leaving may also involve the loss of less tangible things. In one national study (Quixley 1992), young people who left their communities reported in hindsight that they were ill prepared, homesick, hated city life, and many also said they believed that their choices had been made without a real understanding of options. A significant part of the challenge was that moving away involved multiple transitions at once; moving from small town to city; living independently; new school / learning setting; and new cultural setting.

Family and networks are often a major source of support. In research conducted in Australia and Canada (Looker and Dwyer 1997), young people identified that while some had found home ties suffocating and could not wait to get away, others felt 'lost and isolated' in an urban environment. In moving, the issue is not just adjustment to the changes, but that young people 'cut themselves off from the social support networks that they rely on to help with the multiple transitions to adulthood' (Looker and Dwyer 1997:14). It is important not to underestimate the significance of place and the proximity to established social networks, and the strain on this crucial means of support caused by decisions to leave. Respondents reported that living away from home creates problems for study, because it is hard enough simply to survive. Other research from Canada suggests similar themes; young people have to choose between improved prospects elsewhere and the things with which they are familiar. Regardless of whether respondents reported strong attachment to family or local community, plans to settle elsewhere after education were often linked to depression and unhappiness (Elder et al. 1996).

One young writer relates the lived experience of urban chauvinism against himself and other rural students, after moving to continue education. In order to accept and accommodate new experiences and ideas, he explains the felt need to reconstruct identity, beliefs and values (Irvine 1999). This involves hard work, especially when it is done in the absence of familiar supports and sources of identity.

Social inequalities in rural communities

Just as access to services, infrastructures and possibilities differs between communities, it also differs within communities. When making a life out of the limited available opportunities, some rural young people are far better resourced to do so than others. As in all other social settings, there are significant social divisions in country areas. These are historically based and structurally reinforced. Key axes of difference are gender, race, and class.

A recent overview of research into Australian young women's circumstances and aspirations (see Harris 2002) has suggested that although many young women now enjoy greater opportunities, greater rights and more choices than past generations, rural young women's local opportunities do not match those of their male counterparts.

Meanwhile, community-based studies indicate that in rural places the oppression of women has been, and continues to be expressed in many forms. The patterns are evident through community attitudes towards women in domestic labour and paid labour, in their exclusion from, and subordination within, spheres of leisure activity, and in the more subtle forms and expectations that are carried by specific cultures. Many young women discover that they have limited roles both modelled to them, and available to them personally in their home towns. Traditional gender roles which give domestic caring responsibilities to women are still strong. Married women have been, and in some places still are, perceived to be taking the jobs of young women, and local cultures often encourage little analysis of the systems that would exclude women, or of the interaction of patriarchy and capitalism. The phenomena of the 'auxiliary' which has been documented in past decades is still evident in rural Australia. This amounts to women's provision of free labour to support the public political world of men (Williams 1981a), their social lives, leisure and social causes (Dempsey 1990).

Repeatedly, rural research has shown how rural cultures also propagate and sanction certain forms of exaggerated masculinity that are centred around rugged conditions, sport, and hard work. In these cultural climates, social expectations leave little room for different expressions of masculinity (Williams 1981a; Hillier et al. 1996; Wierenga 2001; Bourke 2003). Gay and lesbian rural young people have reported that they are subjected to intolerance, discrimination, and harassment (HREOC 1999). Discriminatory attitudes and behaviour have been linked to rural male suicide (Green 1996; Wyn et al. 1998). Under conditions of economic change, loss of meaningful roles for men is also being considered as a contributing factor to suicide rates. Meanwhile, cultural patterns associated with working-class masculinity are also linked to poor performance in education. Boys from families with lower socioeconomic status are often the most disadvantaged in terms of schooling (Kenway et al. 2000; Wierenga 2001).

In Australia, indigenous people make up only 2.4% of the total population (AIHW 2006). Compared with major cities, people who live in rural and remote areas are more likely to be indigenous, and about

40% of the population of the more remote areas is Aboriginal (AIHW 2002). Demographic surveys of health and life-expectancy are particularly poignant reminders of differing life-chances between Aboriginal Australians and other Australians. Health inequality with the non-indigenous population appears to have remained static or continued to grow across a number of indicators. For example, life expectancy is 18 years shorter for Aboriginal Australians than for non-Aboriginal Australians (HREOC 2006). There is a higher birth rate among the indigenous populations and higher levels of mortality at younger ages (AIHW 2005). Indigenous populations are disadvantaged across a range of socio-economic factors, such as lower incomes, higher rates of unemployment, poor education outcomes and lower rates of home ownership (AIHW 2002). Only one in three Aboriginal students will complete year 12. This is less than half the rate of other Australian students (Schwab 1999).

Behind the indicators lies a history of dispossession, cultural suppression, and removal from land and family. With colonization, original 'oversights' meant that little attention was paid to Aboriginal patterns of land-use. Land rights issues have been of ongoing tensions with 'business' farmers (see Voyce 1996). Non-Aboriginal communities have shown widespread ignorance of Aboriginal history or declared it to be a non-issue (see Gray 1991; Friend 1992). Assumptions of a level-playing-field have meant episodes of backlash about 'special treatment'. Submissions to the 'Bush Talks' also suggest that short-sighted government programs, for example the simultaneous closure of schools and building of prisons, have acted as significant forces in the perpetuation of indigenous disadvantage (HREOC 1999:25). Regarding capacities to shape policy, there has been a history of Aboriginal estrangement from all levels of post-colonial government.

Beyond the tangible factors relating to Aboriginal life-chances, intolerance and discrimination have shaped indigenous Australians' experience of social participation (HREOC 1999). Australian research also relates accounts of lived experience of difference (HREOC 1999), of relationships that stereotype and make Aboriginal people 'other', and socially exclude them within their own towns. These cultural factors further constrain Aboriginal young people's opportunities.

These dynamics are overshadowed, further exaggerated, or compounded by socio-economic differences. Structured and historically based inequalities are very evident in Australian life, and no less in rural areas. Recent research reveals the impact of class on young people's lives. Different patterns of accessing health services is a prime example of this socio-economic influence, with people from more socio-economically disadvantaged areas far more likely to use doctors and outpatient or casualty services, but less likely to access preventative health services (ABS 1999). Often it has been socio-economic status, rather than rurality itself, that has been most important in shaping whether young people go on to higher education (James et al. 1999).

Community studies across the decades (see Wild 1978; Williams 1981a; Dempsey 1990; Wierenga 2001) have shown how small town egalitarianism and class differences are forces which work in opposing directions to create complex and contradictory interaction patterns. Differences are revealed in many ways, including patterns of housing, in the education of children, work habits, and social practices. Socio-economic differences are perpetuated across generations, with a wide range of structural and cultural factors contributing to current patterns.

In rural areas the young people who can access the limited occupational and educational options are also those who have greater reserves of personal or family economic resources. Patterns of association tend to serve to reinforce other more formalized distinctions. For example, employment is found through the formal labour market, but also via family-based social and occupational connections.

Implications

In this chapter we have looked at some of the issues pertinent to growing up today in a changing world, particularly drawing on research from rural Australia during the past two decades. As they go about the business of making a life, there are substantial differences in the ways that young people can negotiate the challenges that face them. These depend upon the availability of certain social resources, which in turn are grounded in social divisions such as race, gender, and class. Geographical location adds yet one more level of complexity to this picture. Social changes and specific policies have stripped resources from some communities, facing young people and their families with new challenges. The picture presented by past research serves as a backdrop. The research on which this book is based looks at how these things happen amongst one group of young people in one rural community. Chapter 3 will introduce that community.

3
Making a Life in Myrtle Vale

In this chapter I will explain a little more about Myrtle Vale, which is the particular, unique, local context for this research, and the setting in which the young people in this book will make their lives. Like some other localized studies, this research seems to be exploring the site of a global-local paradox. Myrtle Vale is as unique in geographical setting, history, economy, and culture as any other town. At the same time, over the past decade I have been surprised that as I describe this very local research to people in UK, Europe and Asia, Pacific and the Americas, they have recognized the patterns all too well.

Part of this familiarity is a recognition of the patterns caused by social inequalities. Another is a recognition of patterns in biography, choice and life opportunities. Another point of familiarity is about the struggles of those on the margins under conditions of globalization and particularly, global capitalism. I am learning from these conversations that rurality can serve as a kind of metaphor for other bounded communities, be they cultural enclaves or city blocks. Yet another point of familiarity is the shared human challenge of maintaining a sense of meaning, control, connectedness or even human dignity under conditions of rapid social change.

In the sociological literature which focusses on social change, considerable attention has been paid to globalization, and some writers (for example, Giddens 1994a) have suggested that under conditions of late modernity, place becomes irrelevant. It is true that information now travels in different ways and that this can transform possibilities for practice. For example, as I write this paragraph I am working on a home computer, checking the university library on the internet and downloading articles from my colleagues overseas. Local and international research reveals that, for many young people, globalization is a genuine force and technologies like these have also revolutionized the process of growing up.

At the same time, youth research indicates that local relationships and cultures are still salient features of many young people's experience of making a life. These findings are borne out not only in Australia (Wierenga 1999; Geldens 2005), but also in the UK (Hall et al. 1999; Jones 1999; MacDonald et al. 2005), Ireland (O'Connor 2005), Canada, (Corbett 2006) and Europe (Yndigegn 2003).

Young people's own stories are enmeshed in the stories of their communities. Local relationships are powerful in the ways that they mediate individuals' access to social goods, to other relationships, and to social reality. They can be particularly powerful in isolated communities where it is the same relationships that mediate *everything*.

Arturo Escobar (2001) explains that place is central in the everyday concerns and political struggles of ordinary people. Raewyn Connell (2006) also points to the way in which, when embracing grand narratives about late modernity, it can be too easy to erase history, difference, and to deny the gritty realities and diversity of people's experience.

Along with others, I would like to suggest that, under current conditions, small scale local explorations become not *less*, but *more* important, as sustained local activity holds many of the keys for restorative social change (see also Hawken 2007). In this context, the links and the conversations that can be shared between local places across the globe also become vital.

So let me tell you a story about Myrtle Vale...

At the outset it seems important to explain that Myrtle Vale has changed. In this chapter I will share an ethnographic description of the town that was written in 2001, from data collected primarily in the 1990s. I do this for two reasons: firstly, it creates a picture of the social world in which the young people at the centre of this research were growing up, and when they were making some of their most significant life-choices. Secondly, in many ways the story is still current. This is a picture of community life which parallels that of many other places today.

I have just come out of a self-imposed five-year embargo on completing and releasing this book. This gap of silence has allowed for change, for forgetting, for re-visiting respondents and checking interpretations, and for protection of those same respondents from the possibility of recognition in a small community. With this knowledge, readers might approach this chapter as a diary entry.

It is important that the stories told by researchers do not bind communities too tightly to the past. Near the end of the chapter I note some of the more recent changes, and Chapter 10 reflects on what can be learned from this community to support young people making a life.

About Myrtle Vale

The Lightwood Valley is beautiful. Nestled in the southern tip of Tasmania, The Valley follows the Lightwood River down to the sea. Apple orchards and European trees line green hills, proclaiming every season. Cut off from the rest of the world by an arc of purple mountains, Myrtle Vale is a landlocked island. The Valley even has its own climate – surreal from above and mysterious from within. A commuter will often drive down through heavy curtains of fog to get there.

For some, Myrtle Vale is the perfect place to live. Seventy-nine years ago, 'Old Mr K' came down to do two weeks' work, and at the time I started this research he was still there: 'Gets to you, this place' (Fieldnotes, October 1997). 'Sydney-side' commuters and retirees like Beryl and Steve have recently been attracted to the rural lifestyle: 'and it's less than two hours from the airport!' (Fieldnotes, May 1999)

The Valley's physical beauty belies some of its social conditions, which can be harsh. The Valley has some real poverty issues. In the 1990s, when these young people are in high school, it is one of the districts of lowest (personal, median) incomes in Tasmania. Tasmania is in turn the state with lowest personal median weekly incomes in Australia. Incomes in the town of Myrtle Vale are lower still. Unemployment in The Valley is high, as is the number of people in receipt of Government benefits (ABS 1996; ABS 1997a; ABS 1997b; Centrelink 2001).

Distance, culture, identity

Issues of isolation and distance are central to the challenges that face local young people. On one hand, Myrtle Vale is hardly remote. It is around 70 kilometres from Hobart, the capital city of Tasmania, and so most services are available within an hour's drive. On the other hand, with 800 people and less than 300 houses, the town is small, and it *is* a long way out. As much as anything else, the distance is cultural and ideological. Several historical and cultural factors are important here.

Firstly, a history of distance is significant. Before the Lightwood Highway was opened, trips to Hobart were long. In the 1930s a coach trip to Hobart took eight hours, and symbolically it still does. Wider social changes have been significant in shaping the meaning of distance. Most of Myrtle Vale's population has lived there for generations, and, ironically, as the city gets closer by road, it also gets philosophically and politically further away from its rural neighbours. We will return to this issue.

Secondly, there is the issue of Tasmania and distance. On an island only 400 kilometres from bottom to top, Tasmanians are not used to either driving long distances or spending hours in traffic. From a Tasmanian perspective, an hour in a car is a long time to travel.

Thirdly, there is the issue of Tasmania's own isolation. Until very recently, the state had a shrinking population, high unemployment, particularly high in rural areas, and was showing clear signs of its own rural decline (ABS 2001a; ABS 2001b). In a small population of half a million people, service delivery and critical mass have been prevailing issues even for Tasmania's largest cities. Any distance from urban centres exacerbates these issues.

Finally, and related to this, is the town's location near the end of the road south, on the southern tip of the 'Island State', at the bottom of Australia, itself a sparsely populated island continent. For Myrtle Vale this has far-reaching implications. A lack of flow-through traffic has meant a lack of interface with the 'Stranger' (see Simmel 1950; also Schuetz 1944), a homogeneity in the expectations and stories that circulate, and a self-contained and self-referencing local culture. The town is ethnically and culturally homogenous. Census data only records 20 people that are not of Anglo-Saxon / Celtic / Australian heritage. In the early 1990s (but less by the end of this study) the 'Strangers', some of the 'City- folk', the 'Gays', the 'Greenies' who moved into town also moved straight back out. 'We learned quite fast that it was not the place for us.' (Conversation with a 'Greenie', 1992).

A proud history, an uncertain future

The town of Myrtle Vale was settled by Methodists. One result of this is that no pub was ever built within the town boundary (although several clubs now have liquor licences). This sits in stark contrast to Swanville, on the other side of the river, where the Catholics settled and there are three pubs. Other results of the Methodist heritage include a 'puritanical streak' (Conversation with a local clergy member, 1993). This means firm convictions about personal and public morality, frugality, and a rigid work ethic. With or without religious adherence, these other cultural qualities have remained strong.

Myrtle Vale's written histories are built upon tales of pioneers, hard work and internationally recognized excellence. History books explain that 'piners' (woodcutters of native timbers, and particularly Huon

Pine), were first to settle Myrtle Vale. The George Valley, beneath the town, borders the great South-West Wilderness areas where unique and renowned tree species grow. Huon Pine is particularly good for boat building, and Myrtle, Sassafras and Blackwood are craftwoods prized for furniture. These resources meant the growth of a rich timber industry, which at its height employed 1,500 men. Because of its cool, temperate climate and good soils, The Valley was also ideal for fruit-growing. Earlier this century it was the richest orcharding district in the Commonwealth. The port was busy, and ship-building boomed.

Since World War II, the rise of global markets, rationalizations of business and government alongside industrial, technological and labour market changes have unsettled each of these 'boom' areas. In the 1970s, because of competing international markets (African), the apples (primarily golden delicious, which had been sold in British and European markets) became less viable. In order to keep people on the land and redirect their energies, the State Government paid a bounty for fruit trees to be ripped out of the ground. When the local pulp mill closed down in 1982 (and closed again after 18 months' operation in 1988), the port also quietened.

Meanwhile, native timber harvesting in Tasmania became economically devalued and political. The southern forests provide around 60,000 cubic metres of eucalypt veneer log and sawlog per year, and this contributes significantly to Tasmania's economy. Forestry Tasmania, however, claims that much of the timber from old-growth forests is only suitable for wood-chipping (see Forestry Tasmania 2001). At the same time they pay their tree-fellers per cubic metre / tree (depending on whether it is harvested in a way that makes it suitable for pulp or saw-milling, or not), and it is in contractors' interests to provide volume rather than quality timber. The result of current practices is that between 1.4 and 1.8 million tonnes of hardwood, including old-growth-forests, become pulp and woodchips every year (see Forestry Tasmania 2001). This is a devalued resource that sells for very little. The returns to the local community are now very small. Since the introduction of wood-chipping in the early 1970s, there has been an inverse relationship between Tasmanian forests logged, and jobs provided in both logging and downstream processing (Greens 2001).

In a town where the primary industry had been the main employer, the 1996 census records 72 people working in agriculture, forestry, and fishing. This is an improvement on the previous census, and correlates with the growth of the local aquaculture industry. The other major employers are retail and manufacturing. Much of this work is seasonal and casual. A report by the Tasmanian social services peak body on poverty in The Valley is aptly subtitled: 'All the jobs I've ever worked in have gone' (Just Tasmania Coalition 1999).

These changes have happened within the context of a national and global context of towns undergoing similar changes. New technologies, rationalizations and globalized world markets have undercut primary industries, and many small towns find themselves in crisis as a result.

From the 'centre' to the 'margins'

Rather than being a naturally occurring phenomena, 'rurality' and 'remoteness' are relational concepts. Places are rural compared *to* an other, remote *from* an other. Even size and distance become problematic standards for understanding rurality when small towns make up larger centres or when travel routes are improved (Looker and Dwyer 1997).

Shields (1991) offers a different and more processual conceptualization, suggesting a focus on 'places on the margins'. 'Places on the margins' become 'marginal' in three ways: geographically, economically, and in terms of identity. Myrtle Vale is all three. In fact, most of The Valley's problems could be traced to its movement from 'central' to 'peripheral' status along each of these three axis. (I will elaborate on this further, but paint a broader picture first). As Shields explains, marginality is the state of being 'left behind'.

Each of Myrtle Vale's changes has happened in the context of an island state that has been undergoing similar movements – from being central to being marginal in terms of geography, economy and identity within Australia (Lenehan 2000). Tasmania was one of the earlier places in Australia to be colonized, and for a time it was the hub of economic and cultural activity and population growth (Rimmer 1989). After dramatic industrial and economic shifts and related population movements in the mid-1800s, Tasmania has found itself geographically and economically marginal in relation to 'Mainland' Australia. Now Tasmania's identity and its tourism appeal is based almost purely upon promoting itself as being 'other' to mainland Australia – for example through images of rainforest, wilderness, and colonial heritage (see also Morris 1974; Lenehan 2000).

The decades since World War II saw Myrtle Vale *become* marginal in terms of population and geography. In terms of Australian history, the Lightwood Valley was also colonized early (1830s), and it fast became both a geographical and economic centre. Markets and populations are now centred elsewhere, and the same social forces (globalization, rationalization) that feed large city centres also starve Myrtle Vale. In 1996, Daily Bread left town to centralize operations in Hobart, and Daily Bread people like the Wells family left town at the same time. As if symbolically, the Apple Pie Factory also left town in the late 1990s. Reflecting changes in employment opportunities, Myrtle Vale's population had been slowly shrinking. Over a five-year period, the age groups 10–14, and 15–19 shrunk by one third and one quarter respectively (ABS 1994; ABS 1997a). Population shrinkage has savage implications for the sustainability of many aspects of town life, from small businesses to netball teams.

As shown above, Myrtle Vale's economic marginality is a direct result of changes in world markets. Forestry Tasmania's old-growth forest logging programs have become increasingly debased in purpose, and absurd in economy, being both unsustainable and heavily subsidized by the State Government (Marsden Jacob Associates 2001). International market competition continues to make 'doing the apples' a struggle. The apple industry is contingent upon fickle international markets, and it has been common to see rows of mature and productive trees removed from the ground and burned as new varieties, more fashionable to Asian markets, are planted. Like other rural places, Myrtle Vale has been hit hard by rationalizations of both government services and businesses. When the banks leave town, even faithful local people start shopping in larger centres, which has more implications for local businesses.

Under these conditions, identity, too, becomes marginal. Whereas for years, 'Tasmania: The Apple Isle' was *named after* the activities of The Valley, the symbolic power of this is now diminished. Equally powerful, with wider public sentiment apparently stacked against them, forest workers feel vilified for 'just trying to do our job'. Ruth, a forest-worker's wife explains how hurt she feels when she listens to talk-back radio: 'I just can't listen to it any more – turn it off' (Conversation, 1993). As log trucks make their way through Hobart and up to the East Coast with their controversial cargo, they are often hissed at by an urban population of people who are considerably 'greener' than their rural neighbours.

This, then, is the central conundrum: although rural communities have a destiny that increasingly depends upon their relationship to the outside world, they develop cultural identities that are alien from it. In a town built upon a strong ethos of 'progress', the last few decades have been full of 'undone deals'. Local stories about social change are usually stories of loss and betrayal, of partnerships repeatedly dishonoured by the other. Of paramount importance is the issue of autonomy or the 'agency' of this little community. So much power resides outside the community in wider social structures, in big business and a distant government.

While old businesses leave, new players will make promises but rarely deliver, such as the promised processed wood factory in the 1990s, or the fabled 'new mill' which would re-appear as a prospect each decade. The aquaculture farms, which at first looked like the new saviour for The Valley, have a strong voice when any other polluting business idea is proposed. Meanwhile, city bureaucrats in government departments change rules and redirect resources, gaining a (resisted) control as the proportion of the town's people who are dependent upon welfare increases. Decisions which simply involve pragmatic options for those outside the town (for example, raising the standards that apply to apprenticeships), can become body-blows to local operators. Meanwhile, a new road (to a neighbouring valley, making a ring-route out from Hobart through picturesque forest and rural districts) could make all the difference to Myrtle Vale's fledgling tourist industry, but it is vetoed by successive governments (and 'the greenies'). Each of these things has become both a point of moral high-ground and of wounded 'other-ness' to 'them' – to people who live in cities.

For Myrtle Vale, at the point of entering the twenty-first century, geography is marginal, economy is insecure and identity is very much 'other'. Activities which were honourable work have become vilified and politicized, and practices which were careful and sensible are becoming senseless and wasteful. From here stems both the heartbreak and the fury. It is *these inversions* that are the 'flashpoints' – when current realities differ so greatly from private and collective stories of 'what was' and 'what should be'.

Apples in the wind

At the peak of Perrins Rd, promising spring apple blossom gives way to summer apples bobbing, and then to drying autumn apples swinging idly in the wind as they wrinkle and desiccate on the tree. Locals explain that it is not worth Zac's time or money to pick again this year. They know why: 'It costs more to have them picked than he'll get back for juicing apples.' They still criticise: 'Sitting inside doing nothing...'; 'Such a waste...' (Conversation with community member, April 1999). Within the district, in the absence of a tangible embodied 'other' to blame, wider market conditions have become reasons to throw (verbal) rocks at each other, and scorn is often turned on insiders.

The ever-widening division that runs through this community is 'the working' and 'the not working'. This newer picture of social exclusion sits in contrast to the more traditional working class / middle class divides of earlier community studies. Numbers of middle-class families shrunk when the businesses and banks left in the 1980s and 1990s. Meanwhile, the number of families on benefits or compensation increased.

Hard work does not always equal the good life, and some know this too well. Manual occupations are often repetitive and dangerous. Larger companies that have moved into the district are focussed upon export dollars and can have few local and personal allegiances, investing little in their workers. John (mid-20s) has been battling the same 'compo' case (workers' compensation) with one company since I first interviewed him in 1997. Meanwhile, Phillip (mid-30s) explains his own reluctance to work. After being injured, repatriated, redeployed, re-injured: 'What – do I want to be employed again so that I can go and lose another bit of my body?' (Fieldnotes, April 1999).

Many of the people I spoke with were either claiming some sort of workers' compensation, or had parents who were doing so. Some townfolk suggest a high correlation between 'compo' and depression or mental health issues, and between unemployment and loss of meaning. More general statistics (ABS 1997c) lend support to these ideas. Some working locals also suggest a high correlation between 'compo' and 'laziness'. Again, the problem resides in the way that labour and industry are structured, but the local effect is to 'divide and conquer' a fragile community.

A good wood stack

In this town, work is not only about employment, but also about a respectable way of life:

> People judge each other very harshly here. Big ideas of what other people should be doing, not very forgiving if you don't fit in with that. You're judged on whether you work hard, and whether you're providin' for your family. Whether you work hard and whether you got a big wood stack in the yard. And if you got those two things, it doesn't matter what else you're doing – whether you even talk to your family – whether you're beating your wife or anything – what happens behind closed doors – they say that's none of our business. But here – if you got a good big neat woodpile and you're providing for your family – as long as you're providing for 'em – then you're a

good bloke – and people are judged like that. (Reconstructed conversation with 'Brian', 1999)

Brian, a born-and-bred-local who lived out of town for several years, now finds himself in a position to analyse his own old habits. It is in becoming, or coming into contact with, the 'Stranger', (the 'other') that one is forced to question assumptions and normal ways of doing things (Simmel 1950; Schuetz 1944):

> That's how people are judged – we used to laugh at them – 'cos they were 'out there getting their behinds wet'. On a wet day they'll be out there trying to get wood – and of course it's not going to burn – these people just won't plan ahead – won't think about tomorrow – sort of people who aren't employed and that – because they don't think ahead, they're judged by everybody else. (Brian, 13 April 1999)

'Providing for' the family is a gendered activity but the concern is not limited to males: 'My mother always felt secure – coming up to winter – when the cupboards were full and there was a good big neat wood stack.' (Brian, 13 April 1999). A domestic woodpile of generous proportions, all dry and neatly stacked, becomes a shared symbol of a man's worth:

> AW: (later) Is it really true about judging each other and the wood stack?
> Brian: Oh yeah – its prob'ly the best example of it, and you'll see 'em everywhere.
> AW: Yeah actually I did – I was looking for a kid's place and he said: 'It's the house with the wood stack!'
> (both laugh)
> Brian: You got to have 'em out there, and you got to have 'em on show.

Brian laughed as he went on to tell the story of his own indignity and wounded pride when his new 'outsider' bride: '...wouldn't let me keep the wood stack out the front'.

Scrutiny and stories

As an outsider, when in town I had a strong sense of surveillance – of being watched. Insiders also claim being watched as central to their own lived experiences. In a small town like this, there is shared owner-ship of individuals' identities, and of their stories.

While I was interviewing Dale, a car drove past (fast), turned, and sped back down the road. Dale smiled knowingly. 'What?' He explained that last week at work they had been 'hassling' him about 'the blonde' he had been seen with (me). He also explained that any story takes two days to get right around the town: 'Then it stops, 'cos everyone's heard it before' (Dale 1997).

Locals explain that this can be a frustrating but endearing feature of town life:

> Myrtle Vale has friendly people. They know too much about every-one else's business, but it's part and parcel. But if there's anything wrong there's always someone asking: 'Is there anything I can do...?' (Teacher, 1995)

But growing up under constant scrutiny can also be claustrophobic: 'Especially down here cause if you do something, the next five seconds it's 'round' (Elizabeth). From time to time, scrutiny and critical morality combine to erupt in savage public outbursts. The sign on the stripped shop-window of 'Country Meats' reads: 'Due to the lack of support within this community this business has been forced to close...', and some packing tape, stuck across the top, says: 'Our high prices and poor quality didn't help either.' (Fieldnotes, October 1997).

The ways in which things are publicly storied can be quite political. 'Official' storying (local press) can be empowering for the powerful, while 'unofficial' storying (public gossip) is further disempowering for the less powerful.

Good news

The Lightwood News consistently and publicly proclaims the commun-ity's prouder moments every week: sports trophies, business invest-ments, public contributions, children's events and youth achievements. The paper-staff take seriously their role of morale-building, and report-ing 'positive things' as well as the more familiar issues and struggles (Conversation with paper staff, 1993). Definitions of good news favour respectability, traditional values, and progress.

There are other pockets of 'good news' that are not privileged and not being publicly re-told in the ways that the protagonists would tell them. Mike moved from Sydney nine months ago and he believes that he is 'in heaven'. He is unemployed but he sees this as a peaceful, viable lifestyle here (unlike in Sydney). He points to the ease with which one can 'get together the basics', for example collecting firewood, and the cheap price of housing: 'Y' just don't need more than that here.' Living in Myrtle Vale increases his options for a 'good life':

> Look, here if you've got $5 in your pocket then you're the richest man in the world. You can get some fish 'n' chips, and a bottle of something to drink and then go fishing all day... She's beaut. Fresh air and a bit of quiet, couldn't ask for anything more. (Fieldnotes, October 1998)

Like fishing all day, there are other activities that will be storied in contrasting ways, depending upon who is talking. While the 'hoons' (teenage recreational car riders) are 'the only thing wrong' with the district for Jenny, for Brett 'hooning' is the only thing right with it.

'My Myrtle Vale': different voices, different stories

When asked about Myrtle Vale, nearly everyone talks about clean air, space, beauty and a community that 'look out for each other'. Beyond this, depending upon who is asked, Myrtle Vale is actually the name of many different towns. For Sandra, the community represents 'one big happy family'. Everyone shares Myrtle Vale – it's everyone's place (Sandra, 1995).

By way of contrast, Angela's lived experience centred around social divisions and fear. She tells the story of needing to pick up the young people from school in the car, despite the distance being less than five minutes' walk, so that they would not get 'roughed-up' or 'hassled' on the way home (Interview with a parent, September 1995). Another teenager explains how one early dispute has led to a situation where he and his 'outsider' family are being 'frozen out' of town – their house is now on the market (One-off interview with 'Andrew', May 1999).

The relatively harsh social conditions described throughout this chapter are being felt more acutely by some individuals than by others. Those with more resources to draw upon outside that community, and/or more power within local arrangements, also tell more positive stories about living there. They are living there 'by choice'. Interviews indicate that this is true of parents and their young people. As they plan to leave so that the young people can further their education, Helen explains tearfully:

> It was a deliberate strategy, a lifestyle choice to stay here... It is a good place to raise a family... We like having close neigbours... I like the people down here – they're friendly and caring, lots of community spirit. Down here people gather around (tears)... We feel a part of the wider community. We know most people and where they live. There are some negatives – some times you feel people know too much. But if anything goes wrong there's always someone there to help, and if something good happens, they share it with you. If one of the young people is in the Lightwood news, they will come and congratulate them, and the phone rings lots (more tears). (Parent interview, 1995)

Conversely, the less power locally and/or the less access to outside opportunities, the worse are the stories about the place, and the more imposing and invasive become the sanctions and scrutiny of others: 'None of our parents would have told us to get on out of here but that's what we're telling our kids – don't ever come back down here – except to visit us.' (Parent interview, 1995).

The more that families are subject to what happens locally, the more they are disturbed by difference: 'It used to be nice – then the druggies moved in – rif raf – never had half the burglaries before.' (Parent interview, 1995).

There are significant links between people's sentiments and the economic resource base on which people can draw. Relative economic comfort coincides with the propensity to regularly travel in and out of the city. Those who can do this on a daily basis (for example, commute, or have a family member who commutes) seem to be less caught up in local criticism, can afford to be more generous with other subcultural activity, and are more affectionate and humorous about the town's peculiarities. Meanwhile, to those who have everything invested in earlier forms of town life, alternative activities and social changes can easily (both subjectively and objectively) become a threat.

Lived experiences differ along the lines of gender as well. Although young men are likely to report a sense of contentment with living there: 'It's OK', Myrtle Vale is rarely just ok for girls. Unlike male counterparts, who can 'middle' through (at neither end of the spectrum), the lived experiences of young women appear to be much more intensely analysed and/or critically negotiated. They are polarized, and the place is either a haven or a prison (or both at once). These gendered patterns will be picked up in later chapters.

Aboriginal stories

Despite a high Aboriginal population (13% where the national average is 2%, ABS 1997a; ABS 1997b), Aboriginal history sits like an awkward sub-plot on the town's written histories and is rarely featured in conversation. Generations of Tasmanians have been educated to believe that Tasmanian Aboriginal people had died out with Truganini in 1877. A compilation of local Aboriginal oral history is aptly called: 'We who are not here' (Friend 1992). Like the rest of Tasmania, where dispossessions occurred, here Aboriginal claims on land and culture have been disrupted, but European-based information sources are very limited regarding what has happened. Oral histories link back to a few tribal women who never left the land (Friend 1992).

Individual Tasmanian Aboriginal descendants explain to me that skin colour disappears within about two generations, making Aboriginal descent easy to deny. One older woman explained: 'I didn't see myself as any different, and I didn't *want* to be any different.' (Reconstructed conversation from Swanville, 1993). A desire to 'blend in' meant her family denied their own heritage. The gathering of the descendants of one Aboriginal woman in recent years has led to a process of discovery and rediscovery. Much of the history of other families has been lost but the people remain a strong presence. As Jim Everett, Tasmanian Aboriginal educationalist, stated in an ABC TV documentary: 'We were never lost, we just didn't know that they were looking for us' (2001).

Within this context, it is understandable that the two respondents in this study who identify as Aboriginal *see it as neither a major point of identity, nor a significant source of difference*. Wider cultural processes ensure that it stays this way.

Recent changes and challenging futures

By the beginning of the twenty-first century, a glorious past and an unsettled present leave Myrtle Vale with the challenge of creating a sustainable future. Natural resources are abundant, but the contemporary challenge is about using them in a way that is valued both by locals and by the outside world. Local stories are also abundant, but there is often a lack of dialogue with the outside world. Although the school and a younger generation have embraced tourism, it seems to have been very much externally imposed on older community members as a solution. With Federal Government funding related to the

Helsham Inquiry (1980s), in 1991 the Myrtle Vale Town Hall was converted into a 'Forest and Heritage Centre', visited by tourists, but seeming, in its early years, to be worked-around by locals. Initially, the ecologically-based sentiments that are appealing to tourists have been often less than appealing to locals. Older community members explain about the Town Hall:

> And the greenies. They bugger it up every time you want to start something up. They even took our town hall. Now it's used as a haven for greenies and their artifacts. (Parent, 1995)

> 'We used to have our dances and films there, before they took it over.' (Parent, 1999)

At this time, this disparity of understandings puts Myrtle Vale at odds with the very thing that could save it. The only significant development funds that the town is likely to access from state and federal governments will be in relation to tourist dollars. A new project, for which both local and outsiders have high hopes, is the 'Treewalk', a viewing place from which to see the southern forests. Its construction (by Forestry Tasmania) is creating considerable short-term work.

New industries have moved in to The Valley, for example 'the fish' (extensive aquaculture farms and a huge processing plant). These are owned by outsiders and create substantial casual employment, but do not seem to create meaning and purpose for locals.

During the fieldwork for this study, the sight of houses sitting empty by the side of the road was common: 'I think I just drove past six houses in a row with "for sale" signs on them.' (Research journal, 1997). Later in the study these same empty houses are attracting low-income families from around Hobart. Their presence becomes part of stories about social fragmentation. Still later, in the background but not often storied, the Sea Changers begin to move in. (Sea Changers are a new-ish phenomenon, being recognized in the popular press across Australia. Often, professionals with significant resources, they move to coastal and rural areas for lifestyle purposes).

The passage of the 1990s sees significant changes in people's day-to-day movements. At the start of this study, few would have considered commuting for school or work. Increasingly, they do. Because of this, the distance to Hobart is shrinking markedly, but it is only shrinking for some. For others who have lived in Myrtle Vale all their lives, their own town is increasingly becoming a place of strangers while the city is still alien. This is problematic when futures, both corporate and individual, may actually depend upon close links with city.

Throughout my time in the field, I heard considerable differences in the ways that young people storied their experiences of growing up in this town. The desperation I heard in the early 1990s was replaced in the late 1990s and early 2000s by significant pockets of hope. As I concluded the fieldwork for my PhD thesis in 2001, I wrote: 'A few significant individuals with stable networks may well be changing the course of history'. In hindsight, they were. The school has been very intentional in what it is doing, not just with young people in terms of options for their own futures, but in fostering a community culture where creating confidence and links to the outside world are central. The Lightwood Valley Youth Service has been involved in creating extensive resource bases and community networks – and in this way has been a quiet shaper of opportunity and culture. The well-targeted activities of trusted facilitators can have a big impact in a small community.

Meanwhile, as I write, the town and its folk continue to construct their own stories. To change the course of history (personal or shared), this research has taught me that it takes the sustained interplay of three things: the resources, the narratives, and the trust relationships. The resources initially came in through government and business, and an inflow of people. However, the provision of external resources alone will not make lasting change. Stories of hope are important too. These narratives have come from people both reconnecting to the past, and beginning to imagine different possible futures. The trust relationships are testament to the faithful and to the generous, in community, business, civic organizations, parents, young people, artists, teachers, leaders and ordinary citizens. Life in the town has not suddenly become easy, but for many it looks more hopeful.

I returned in 2003, 2005 and 2007 to find an increasingly different landscape. There is more work to be done documenting these stories… exploring beyond the dynamics of *making a life* to *making a village*. However, that is another story, for another time.

Being young in Myrtle Vale

The conditions described through this chapter are felt by everybody in the town. Being young, though, accentuates all sorts of issues, like distance, transport, privacy (others talk). Young people explain that in a community of people who are very familiar to each other, individuals' stories are scripted by others' expectations, which can put extraordinary pressure on teenagers making a life.

A small number of young people leads to some other issues. The sense of: 'all pull together or we go under' is felt, even when individuals decide which sport to play. A struggle for critical mass means that if there are not enough players, there is no football team. In a small town, the issue of finding a reference group is complicated by low numbers of teenagers (around 60 on the census and 80 in the school). As they explain: 'We are all kind of forced in together.'

Options for making a life are limited for some more than others. For example, growing up in Myrtle Vale can be hard if you are a girl. One young woman points to a lack of meaningful options among her peer group, explaining it makes early motherhood more appealing: 'By the time I had finished grade 12, two of my old class were pregnant, and one had a baby.' (Conversation, 2000).

Like every other small town, the needs of young people to be drawing on a broader resource base *clash directly* with issues of local sustainability. As families move out (for example, for education), the critical mass of the town is lowered again.

The end of grade ten is a particularly significant time in Myrtle Vale young people's lives. Though most students from the area attend the Myrtle Vale District High School, the nearest secondary college, incorporating grades 11–12, is about 60 kilometres away. International and Australian research is telling us that, in industrialized countries, urban young people are increasingly creating biographies out of overlaps, zigzags and shuffles between life projects, including education and work (Du Bois-Reymond 1998; Côté 2000; Dwyer and Wyn 2001). However, the work of other researchers (reviewed in Chapter 2) reveals that choices, and the related costs of decisions, are qualitatively different for rural students. Young people who do not continue education, but stay in Myrtle Vale, face limited job opportunities and/or long-term unemployment. Older role-models (including their parents) mostly finished their own education early, with two thirds of the adult population having left school before the age of 15. To continue further education is one of the biggest single life-choices that a Myrtle Vale young person can make. To stay or to go, and who to travel with, is another.

About this research

The Making a Life study incorporates material from three distinct pieces of research. From 1991–1994, I had been employed as a youthworker within The Valley, and I focussed my BA Honours project there (1995) on a study of young people's aspirations. Following a long PhD (1996–2001), a more relaxed research project involved intermittent conversations with respondents (2002–2007) about changes and developments, but more specifically about analysing and drawing on respondents' stories. The material contained in this book, then, is drawn from research that spans 12 years, and represents a culmination of 17 years' (intermittent) focus around one community.

Background

An earlier action research project, with a local youth group (1993) also informs the Making a Life project, and it deserves a mention here. In its most basic form, action research is about two different kinds of outcomes: research in the form of understanding, and action in the form of change (Dick 1995). It should be a collaborative effort, and the issue under scrutiny should stem from recognized community need, rather than the interests of the researcher (Voth 1979). As a regional youth-worker, at the time employed by churches for The Valley (150 kms to drive around the town centres), I was employed to resource groups who were interested in doing projects themselves. A Myrtle Vale church youth group made contact because their peers had 'nothing to do'. They felt that the town was quite hostile to 'the youth problem' after some particularly rough (vigilante) activity against a group of young people, and they wanted to do something about it. Supported by youth leaders, school teachers, community members, and the council youth-worker we started our work with information gathering. The young people interviewed their friends about what it was like for them to live in Myrtle Vale, and what was needed. We all interviewed community leaders, members and parents. Information was compiled and analysis continued in meetings (over home-made biscuits), and adults finished the draft. The finished report 'Myrtle Vale youth: gateway to our future' (Myrtle Vale Youth Outreach 1993) was launched to the community, local politicians and media, at a youth performance event. The findings led to a series of youth activities the following year. Retrospectively it is clear that this project met most of the key criteria for action research. At the time, though, we were not even aware that there was a name for what we were doing.

My BA Honours project (1995) marked the beginning of the Making a Life research. This research focussed on Myrtle Vale young people's aspirations, and mapped the different ways that they were thinking about their futures. Fieldwork involved essays, interviews and observations. With school co-operation, and through their health class, all 41 year seven and eight students wrote three essays: 'Who am I?'; 'Who do I look up to and why'; 'What will I be doing in five years, ten years, fifteen years...'. Interviews were theoretically sampled according to emergent categories: male/female, working class / middle class, and whether or not individuals had lived in the district all their lives ('movers' and 'non-movers'). At the time I also selected these respondents from among older (year nine/ten) and younger (year seven /eight) students, in order to get a sense for what was happening at different ages. Although age ceased to be a key consideration in the study, this starting point meant that the cohort already spanned cliques and specific year group dynamics. Within this panel there were also two brother-sister dyads, which helped to create a feel for some family dynamics. Parents and teachers were also interviewed for the purposes of triangulating data and better understanding social context. In this initial year of what would become a much longer study, a model of different aspirations, narratives, and maps of resources had begun to emerge (Wierenga 1995).

Respondents

Respondents who were interviewed and wrote essays in the 1995 research also made up the panel of 32 for my longitudinal PhD research. This meant that the different dimensions from earlier theoretical sampling (class, gender, 'movers' and 'non-movers') were well represented. This maintained some age differences in the cohort that tempered the dynamics and specific group culture of the (by then infamous) 'year eights', and also helped to veil the identities of respondents.

Time spent with Myrtle Vale's young people before doing this study had revealed that access to social goods – to resources – had great bearing on the ways that individuals approached their futures. Class was an issue. I adopted socio-economic status as an indicator of difference in class situation at an experiential level. Describing the key household income earner, there are clear status differences. At the level of common sense these are best captured in the language of middle class, working class. Within the working-class group, one third came from families who were not currently working.

Time in the field before the study had also clearly demonstrated that gender was an issue. Around the town there is a lot of attention paid to gendered practices at the level of everyday theorizing. One working-class mother explained the differences that she had observed: 'Girls seem to find jobs more and apply themselves better to what they're doing. Boys don't worry – then end up unemployed.' (Parent, September 1995). As they go about the process of making lives, local young women and young men are actually doing quite different things, and I wanted to understand this better.

From conversations with young people, and from the stories of others, it was also becoming clear that a very significant difference in these young people's ways of being in the world was based around whether they had spent all of their lives in The Valley or grown up elsewhere. This seemed to be shaping both their outlooks and their willingness to engage outside The Valley. The categories of 'moving' and 'non-moving' were a reflection of this.

Theoretical sampling (Strauss 1987; see also Charmaz 2000) also meant selectively interviewing other individuals from time to time, as new issues arose and needed more clarification than I felt I could get from within the cohort.

Approach and methods for the longitudinal study

For the longitudinal study, fieldwork again involved focussed interviews and observations. A grounded theory approach provided the methodological framework (Glaser and Strauss 1967; see Strauss and Corbin 1990; Glaser 1992). Research followed an inductive process, that is, driven by emergent themes from fieldwork rather than by theory. The interviews, in particular, formed an 'iterative spiral' (see Minichiello et al. 1995). This means that early findings inform later data collection, patterns are found and verified over time, and negative cases or surprises in the data lead to more intense inquiry surrounding those surprises.

Interviews are more staggered than is suggested by the neat year-by-year descriptions that I will use throughout this book. Although working in a small town meant that respondents were usually easy to find (everybody knows where everybody else has gone), at times, and for different reasons (people were away, or respondents did not want to talk now) interviews did not happen and were re-visited later.

Over the six years from 1995 to 2001, I closely followed the stories and trajectories of 32 young people. Included in this number are four young women who withdrew *during* the re-interviews (agreed and then quietly subverted the process). Their practices of resistance, the dynamics between us, and their silence became a significant part of the study. The issues raised by their (partial) involvement will be explored in later chapters.

Conversations with respondents

From 2001–2007, some other equally significant work was happening: less formal, less structured, and still involving respondents. This was about use of the stories. Wherever possible, respondents have given feedback and pointers on how their material is used, and the substance of those conversations underpins this book.

In this book, some details (names, places, jobs, hobbies) have been changed. Characters have sometimes been split in two, to separate more recognizable stories from those of a more sensitive nature. One of my biggest regrets is the fragmentation of individuals' stories, and even how incorporation of stories into themes is a poor acknowledgment of individual contributors and their rich lives. Ironically, I have needed to cut up stories in order to render them unrecognizable, and at the same time also keep the story's integrity (not change every detail to the point where they were simply not the same story). Fragmenting people's stories might be a 'violent' act but far less so than exposure in a small town. This is also an issue of purpose and objectives. Good interpretive (thematic) studies have the potential to usefully critique social structures and processes. Social change requires good critique.

Some opportunities and limitations of chosen methods

Through its qualitative methods, this research focusses on one small group of young people in a certain place and time. Statements will be made about his group, but they can not be generalized to whole populations. The concepts may be useful elsewhere, but the model is strongly local.

Rather than drawing out one feature of young people's lives to examine (for example, continuing education), the scope of the Honours and PhD processes looked like an opportunity to engage more fully with some local complexities. There were both advantages and disadvantages to this approach. From a period of immersion in a community, it takes time to claim back any sense of conceptual clarity. The hardest part of the study involved sitting with the data, reading and scribbling until chaos became (relative) order. This took years. Everything becomes relevant to the subject of making a life – it is a task with no edges. This type of work does not usually fit within usual funding constraints, or the rigid candidature periods now set for postgraduate students.

Longitudinal fieldwork is good for exploring social process – and the research is 'film' rather than 'snapshot'. With interviews, returning again and again meant not just a chance to clarify stories, but a chance to hear different stories from the same authors (prospective and retrospective). Reliability in grounded theories is about corroboration of data; concepts *earn* their way into these studies by being constantly present (or conspicuously absent) in interviews (Strauss and Corbin 1990). Repeatedly going back meant the chance to re-check stories, to compare the stories of others, to test interpretations and concepts / constructs, and to test and clarify understandings about social process. Returning also meant opportunities to check discrepancies in the data. 'Saturation' of some ideas came early, and for others it is still elusive. There are still some unanswered, or unanswerable questions, particularly about doing this type of research, which are the substance of the final chapter in this book.

Making sense of it all

In this chapter I have touched upon some of the issues being faced by young people who are growing up in Myrtle Vale. I have highlighted some specific changes – many of them negative – that have become particular challenges for a generation of young people growing up in this community. Finally, I have introduced the research behind this book, which explores how these young people are differently going about the process of making their lives within this particular social context.

We have seen that Myrtle Vale's young people's issues are intertwined with the unique history, geography, economy and cultural identity of the area. The shift from 'centrality' to 'marginality' in terms of geography, economy, and identity has featured strongly. In amongst local issues, there are many echoes from the research about other places, for example changes in industry, rationalizations, population decline and the issue of young families and young people staying and leaving. When local stories are set within a wider national and global context, we can get a sense of why apples may be swinging unpicked on the trees while there are not many jobs available, and the reasons lie well beyond The Valley.

Having gained some sense of the social context, we can focus our attention on the young people making a life within these circumstances. To watch any young people making a life is to observe something quite mysterious. Examining this mystery can be likened to examining a jewel or gemstone. Each facet of the stone frames a new view of the whole, and a different view into a much more complex reality. Although each facet reveals something unique, each also hints at things that can be seen more clearly through other facets. Rather than aiming to be exhaustive, the chapters that follow are thematic. There will be many gaps and some overlaps. On the basis of these young people's more poignant stories, I have chosen only six themes, six 'facets' that reflect different views into some fairly complex realities. These are: about 'storying' (see Chapter 4); 'negotiating changes' (Chapter 5); 'practices of engagement' (Chapter 6); 'resources' (Chapter 7); 'resource flows' (Chapter 8); 'familiar patterns and transformation' (Chapter 9).

4
Storying: Towards an Interpretive Framework

To ask a young person about their future is not just to inquire about some isolated goals, but to seek directions into the world in which they live. Where there is a relationship of trust, a listener may be given a tour of a whole universe of meaning. In 1995, after three years of being around the town, I started to ask young people: 'What do you want to do with your life?'. The young people responded with abundant and varied stories about *past, present, future and me.*

This chapter starts exploring some of the most significant differences between young people's stories and practices of *storying*. In the following pages, I will present a way of thinking about how Myrtle Vale's young people are differently orienting themselves towards the project of making a life. Rather than being theoretically driven, this conceptual scheme arose out of these early conversations with respondents. This scheme would also become central to subsequent data collection and analysis throughout the project. Insider accounts, and the patterns in these, make good sense of local practices. Examples are issues like: staying in this small rural town or going; staying on at school to finish year 12 or leaving school early; or sticking alongside the familiar faces of peers and families to maintain a sense of wellbeing, or even leaving them. Of particular interest in this chapter are insights gained from the earliest interviews, when most of the young people are in year eight (early high school), but a few of the older ones are preparing to finish year ten (the last year of high-school offered locally).

Back then, and still now, it seems as if the most profound differences in young people's stories are between those set in *global* worlds or *local* worlds, and also whether these stories themselves are *clear* or *unclear* (fragmented).

Known worlds: global or local

A sense of place is of utmost significance in the stories told by respondents. From one respondent to another it is the shape of that place that differs. Noah's world consists of Myrtle Vale and nearby towns. His family has lived locally for generations, and his relatives have settled around The Valley. Daily activities also occur within the context of The Valley: 'Footy, take m' bike up top paddock, work on the bikes with Col, collect wood with Uncle Merv…' Like his grandfather and uncle, Noah wants to be 'a truckie'. He does not see much sense in continuing education or broadening his options: 'All my friends are here.'

Chloe's world is a little larger. She wants to be a nurse:

> That means I'll have to go to Uni in Launceston and I'll probably have to live in Hobart for a while. That would be hard, getting to know new people and everything, but Julie – she's my friend from netball – she's trained to be a nurse and she says at the college it's easy enough to get to know other people.

Chloe plays on a state team and gets to talk to Julie when they practice in Hobart.

The main difference in these respondents' plans is a focus on, or engagement within, The Valley, versus a focus on, or engagement in, a world beyond The Valley. Respondents are basing their stories on *known worlds*. To some extent all respondents have an *awareness* of the world outside Myrtle Vale, but not necessarily a *working knowledge*. (This is why the District High School runs an annual 'city orientation' program in the nearby city of Hobart for senior students.) Engagement in local or global worlds also correlates with respondents' intentions to *stay* in town or to *go*; that is, to move even for a short time, or leave to complete education (Wierenga 1999).

The significance of geography, locality or place in the structuring of young people's lives has already been a source of sociological interest. Social theorists like Giddens (1994a) have asserted that in late modernity, place becomes unimportant, and the role of locality is usurped by mass communication systems or globalized options. By way of contrast, other theorists (for example, Furlong and Cartmel 1997:94, 113; Geldens 2005) argue that individuals' opportunities and life-chances are structured through *lived* rather than simply *mediated* experiences. Even if Myrtle Vale's young people are exposed, for example, to more universalized media input than ever before, they are receiving these other stories into lives that are grounded within local circumstance and possibility. Further, more globalized stories about social reality are received into the context of local history, conditions and relationships, and so individuals are making use of this input quite differently to one another.

Among the young people in this project, a sense of 'place' or a sense of the 'known world' very strongly underpins stories of past, and stories of possibilities. Within respondents' stories, real-world spaces are actually functioning as boundaries on their imaginations (Wierenga 1999). Individuals' 'known worlds' are being mapped out through their lived experience. The known world sets the parameters of where the individual realistically sees themselves travelling. These young people are constructing their stories by using the cultural resources (ideas, meanings, practices), already on offer. They glean and appropriate this cultural material from others (family, peers, school, community, mass media), but are piecing it together idiosyncratically. Every idea encountered and assimilated in history (or herstory) becomes a resource for imagination about futures. In this way, future plans are autobiographical. To ask about the future is to hear about the past.

In interviews, we also jointly explore the distinction between individuals' future plans and impossible dreams. I ask: 'If you had everything you needed, and could choose anything to do with yourself, what would it be?'. Individuals' stories about of their dreams also reveal the limits of their known worlds. Chloe explains: 'I want to do something that changes things – war, fighting, there's so many people in the third world.' Meanwhile, Noah's dream is to: '… go on unemployment and drive a truck occasionally'.

Clear and unclear stories

Individuals' stories, as told in interviews, vary not only in content but also in form. While some respondents quite clearly articulate some things that they might do, and how they might go about doing them, others do not. In their stories, individuals show a marked difference in their ability to project themselves into the future. Bronwyn speaks clearly about an area that excites her:

> I first started wanting to do this in grade eight. I looked up career options and the subject levels I needed. I looked up 'early childhood

teacher' – and when I saw that I had a high level in most of the subjects I needed, I thought: *'That's just me!'*

By way of contrast, when I ask Beth what she wants to do with her life, she grimaces, shrugs her shoulders, sighs and apologetically explains: 'I dunno.'. Beth and I have spent some years doing Friday lunch together, but the conversation rarely moves beyond a commentary about the task at hand. An inability to clearly talk about 'me and my future' corresponds with an inability to articulate stories of 'me and my history'. *Beth cannot say where she wants to go, because she does not know where she is, nor where she has come from.*

These ideas have been raised before within the social sciences. In 'Sources of the self' Charles Taylor suggests that orientation within the social world has two aspects: 'I can be ignorant of the lie of the land around me...' or '... I can be lost in another way if I don't know how to place myself on this map' (Taylor 1989:41). Here Taylor is not talking about physical space but *moral space* (or a space of meaning and of time). Individuals grasp the meanings of their lives in narrative: 'In order to have a sense of who we are, we have to have a notion of how we have become, and of where we are going' (Massey 1994:47). These meanings are open to revision, just as individuals are ever changing and 'becoming'.

Narrative theorists suggest that within individuals' stories, progress is charted in relation to 'the good' (Gergen and Gergen 1988; see also Taylor 1989) or valued goal states. Examples of respondents' valued goal states would be 'a happy family life', 'a good career', 'helping people and easing animal suffering' or 'peace and quiet, footy on Saturdays, and good mates'. For these respondents, having a language (or multiple languages) with which to orient themselves towards valued goals states, is effectively the difference between *life as quest* (like a hero or heroine in a novel) or *life as chaos*.

Within the Symbolic Interactionist tradition, Anselm Strauss (1977) pointed out the centrality of language and story to individuals' understanding of identity and action. Individuals' accounts provide a symbolic ordering of events: 'If your interpretations are convincing to yourself, if you trust your terminology, then there is some kind of continuous meaning assigned to your life as a whole' (Strauss 1977:145).

Contemporary writing suggests much more fragmented and changeable forms of individual identity within biography. Kevin McDonald (1999) points to new challenges for young people growing up in postindustrial societies. For young people confronting dramatic social and cultural change, the lived experience can be one of social fragment-ation and corresponding struggles against the fragmentation of self. Also, within this same changing world, he highlights actors' struggles to make sense of their world, of their subjectivity, and of their relation-ship to other actors. In the context of weakening socialization and institutions, norms and roles, and the increasing complexity and mobility of social life, McDonald sees the young people involved in his research as involved in particularly intense forms of struggle: '...for connection, for presence and relationship, for dignity, coherence of subjectivity and body, for communication and integrity, for memory and possibility' (McDonald 1999:218).

Within this project, respondents' stories reflect not just a difference in ability to make sense of, or find meaning in, their own lives, but a pro-found difference in the ability of individuals to make sense of the world around them, or a 'struggle for subjectivity' (see McDonald 1999). The stories that they tell embody a sense of coherent, trusted and trust-worthy subjectivity (*or not*) with which they can make sense of their own actions and of the situations in which they find themselves.

Beyond the study of struggles or subjectivities, other sociological work is highlighting a connection between social change and the new challenges individuals face in order to negotiate social life more gen-erally. Social change (for example, increased geographical mobility, loosened institutional ties, 'risk-society') heightens the need for indi-viduals to be 'reflexively mobilized'; that is to be self-reflexive man-agers of their own lives (Giddens 1991; Beck 1992; Beck et al. 1994; Beck and Beck-Gernsheim 2002). In societies where youth transitions are protracted and de-sequenced, adulthood can be elusive (Côté 2000), and it can be harder for young people to sustain coherent narratives of the self (eg Furlong and Cartmel 1997). A sense of control is at stake for many young people (eg Evans 2002). Young people's effective negotiation of conditions of uncertainty seems to depend increasingly on their capacity for reflexivity, which involves their capacity to make coherent sense of their circumstances for themselves.

There is also a sense in which the stories that individuals told in interviews were some of the many that could have been told by the same respondents in a different interview, or on a different day (see Yates 1996). However, the stories represented here were respondents' preferred offerings in this time and place, constructed and shaped within the context of our encounters. They are the different resource bases on which they are drawing as they make their lives.

I would like to build on these ideas and suggest that in a context of rapid social change, beyond the particular narratives or stories being told, it is individual and cultural practices of 'storying' that are most significant (Wierenga 2001; 2002). Storying is the act of listening to, telling, re-telling or revising a story. Rather than being completed products, stories can most usefully be understood as ongoing creative endeavours. This is a collaborative process which is differently available to people. I suggest that it is the social *practice*, rather than the product, which is most interesting and deserves more attention (Wierenga 2002).

Following Garfinkel (1967), who, 40 years ago talked about individuals being 'inquirers' regarding the social world around them, perhaps the young people in this project could be cast as ethnographers or researchers of social life, asking 'what is happening in this setting?', 'what are the rules?', both creating and drawing upon other plausible stories. However, it is not so simple. Their accounts during interviews actually show them to be quite differently engaging in, and very differently equipped for this task.

Although almost all of the young people seem to be developing accounts about their own meaningful paths through the known world – or storying – a sizeable minority are clearly concentrating their energies elsewhere. For some, to story is *not core-business*. Rather than creating any narrative of progress, it seems more likely that negotiating the world is a matter of survival. It looks as if life, through the cultural practices of those around them, has served notice that all available energy belongs in risk-management. In a conversation with Nell, she is ducking and weaving as if to avoid the blows. Both the content and form of her story suggest that she is expecting to have to defend herself:

Nell: Myrtle Vale is stupid. There's nothing to do. It's a big hole. In Hobart you're right next to Kentucky (Fried Chicken).

AW: (Later) Would you go up to town and do college?

Nell: I'm not livin' in town *by miself*! I dunno, all the drongos. My friend was walking through town an' at daytime she got belted up.

AW: What do you want to be doing in 20 years?

Nell: I don't reckon I'll be alive in 20 years. I'll die. Underwater. I don't know. If I get old shoot me. That means that I'd have wrinkles. Yuk!

AW: (Later) Where would you like to be living?

Nell: I'd bring up my family anywhere but 'ere I guess.
AW: (Later) So are you going to have kids (children)?
Nell: Nuh. I 'ope not. Don't want 'em. Nuh. Can't be bothered. *I'm tired.*
AW: How much is enough education? When should you stop?
Nell: Right now is enough. At least the end of high school.
AW: Why do you say you might continue then?
Nell: I have to. Dunno. Be better. Probably. (Nell 1:1–2)

The issue here is not only about exposure to different geographical and social worlds, but about a different *cultural orientation to life*, and about ways of approaching new options. As well as being a qualitatively different way of being in the world, this becomes sociologically interesting, in terms of implications. *When individuals' stories about 'past, present, future and me' are not clear, they have neither the full benefit of backwards references (building on history) or forward references.* They miss out on some of the most significant tools with which to pro-actively and/or creatively (imaginatively) engage with the future (Wierenga 1999).

By clear and unclear stories I mean relative coherency and consistency of individual narratives. Individuals live complex lives in complex spaces, and as a result, all stories seem to be inconsistent to some extent. They are ever dynamic, clashing in some places and hazy in others. Also, different roles and settings mean that individuals carry multiple, even conflicting, stories about selves and identities. All stories are also works-in-progress. By 'clear story', though, I mean *a comparatively high* degree of consistency in what is being said, and that, in interviews, an individual's stories often integrate with each other.

The clearest stories are the ones where individuals make use of 'thick' descriptions (see Geertz 1975; Denzin 1989) about both themselves and the world around them. These are dense and multi-layered stories. They present paths through individuals' universes of meaning that have been well travelled, and which have multiple exits and entry points. These stories are full of possibilities: plans, contingencies, past experiences, hopes, anecdotes, beliefs and impossible dreams. Not coincidentally, thick stories tend to have multiple points of connection with the stories that other people tell. These might be in their community, the institutions with whom these young people must engage, or with the parents, teachers or friends who know them well. Both in my own fieldwork and in the 'fieldwork' of these young ethnographers, these points of connection show up as triangulated data, or as effective *reality-checks* on the stories being told.

Thick stories also appear to leave respondents more flexible. Should circumstances change around them, they have contingency plans, and alternative ways of understanding their situation. Closely related to this issue, Michael White (1995; 2000), psychotherapist and pioneer of 'narrative therapy' with young people, explains that individuals equipped with 'thick' stories about themselves and their lives are also the most robust in times of crisis.

Practices of storying: four ideal-types

On the basis of these contrasts in respondents' stories (global/local reference, clear/unclear stories), four ideal-types of cultural orientation emerge: *Exploring, Settling, Retreating* and *Wandering* (see Figure 4.1). Although ideal-types can never capture complex realities, they can make social patterns and processes much easier to understand (see Weber 1969:250–3). (For a further reflection on the politics and purpose of using ideal-types in this type of research, see Chapter 11). Rather than claiming to be about types or qualities of individuals

		Clear	Unclear
Focus	**Global**	**Exploring** Middle class and female working class	**Wandering** Working class, non-working working class Mixed gender
	Local	**Settling** Working class, more male than female	**Retreating** Female Working class + non-working working class

Stories of Identity

Figure 4.1   Four ideal-types of cultural orientation

or the psychological essence of the bearer, the following types refer to social practice, at a given time and place. Over the years that follow, a few respondents' stories will shift in relation to these types.

Exploring entails global references, plus telling clear (if multiple) stories of 'past, present, future, and me'. *Settling* revolves around a local world, and also telling clear stories about identity. *Retreating* relates to The Valley only, but with fragmented stories, and *Wandering* is about the intention to go into a bigger world, explained with unclear stories.

Figure 4.1 shows how, in early interviews, some interesting patterns have already emerged in relation to class and gender. At this stage, all middle-class respondents (except two – see stories about 'crisis' and 'losing the plot' in Chapter 10) are *exploring*. However, not all those who are *exploring* are middle class. There are children from working-class families represented here also, and overwhelmingly these are young women. Those *settling* are from working-class background (and one 'non-working' working-class family), and they are predominantly male. They are engaged in a localized world, and also tell clear stories (if less thickly worded) about identity. Those *wandering* and *retreating* are respondents from working-class and 'non-working' families. *Wandering* individuals are of mixed genders but all of those who are *retreating* (four people, by far the smallest representation) are young women.

Far more often than their brothers, the young women say that they intend to move out for a time, if only to complete education. In this research, young women tend to use both a more global reference, and tell clearer, more elaborate stories about identity. This finding correlates with reports from their school teachers that the young women are (on average) much more interested in the outside world, adept at written work, and articulate in class. This pattern is also anchored in relationships (see Chapter 8).

Some interesting developments will happen later in relation to these stories. Not all of those who want to leave town will go, and two of those who are determined to stay will be unceremoniously moved-on by changed circumstances. Again it is the patterns of practice to which I seek to draw attention, rather than the stories themselves.

Planning destinations and routes (goals and means)

These individuals are travellers in time and social space. Their 'trajectories' are the courses which they will chart through the social world (see Berger and Berger 1975). Zig-zags and loops can be part of these trajectories. Over the last two decades youth research from industrialized countries has highlighted the increasingly non-linear and contingent movements that make up young people's lives. Despite new life patterns, against a backdrop of uncertainty, individuals' stories are a little like travel plans. These travel plans have distinct qualities.

In order to have a travel plan, one needs to have firstly, some sense of *goals*, and secondly a basic understanding of the *means* (ways, routes) necessary to reach these goals. These are being drawn from the individual's known world. For those *exploring* and *settling*, the goals have become relatively clear: 'I feel pretty good about my future' says Tony. 'Living in Myrtle Vale, getting a good job, settling down... become a builder ... one day be self-employed.' Meanwhile Sandra is planning to become a vet: 'in a rural sort of area'. Among respondents who are *exploring* and *settling*, the means to these goals are also clearly stated:

(Sandra)

> Something like six years at Uni. I think you actually have to go to Melbourne to do it. And umm, yeah you have to have really high percentage for school work when you leave college, I think.

(Tony)

> I reckon I'll get a job, fairly soon after I leave school – perhaps by February... I know a couple of builders. First you need to go to college and get a proper apprenticeship. Or you can start as a builder's labourer and learn as you go along. I think that I'm more likely to do it that way. I already know a bit 'cos I helped a bloke from around here to build a whole house.

Those *exploring* and *settling* are usually armed with multiple storylines and contingency plans:

(Sandra)

> They tell me you have to be really smart for that, so if I can't get through that, what I'll actually do, is I'll be a veterinary nurse, and you only have to go to college and then you do TAFE and then you sort of learn on the job.

(Tony)

> If those things fall through, then there's forestry, or the fish-farm...
> or the sawmill. I'm going there for work experience – driving
> machinery and stuff. Got some good friends there too... Also Mum's
> dad – go out with him some weekends for abalone. I could work
> with him.

It appears that the amount of effort put into pondering options,
detailed research, or planning is directly related to the individual's
sense of their own agency – their relative autonomy, power, or ability
to make things happen:

> I'd do the courses that I needed to, to like get (my scores) up...
> 'Cause I really, I don't want to spend six years at uni just to find out
> I can't do it, so I'd give it all I could to like make sure I got there.
> (Sandra)

The converse is also true:

> If you want to get a job you might as well kiss the moon. (Lisa)

> No, I don't really think about my future much. Because it's weird.
> You're planning ahead but you don't know what's going to happen.
> So you get disappointed eventually. (Phoebe)

These latter sentiments are revealed in both *retreating* and *wandering*
stories. *Retreating* young people are not telling stories about goals
and means. Rather, in their stories, avoiding disappointment, pain
or risk, appears to be the good. 'I'm staying here 'cos it's safe here'
(Lisa, same conversation). The student who said these words had
been ostracized by her peers for years, but moving outside her known
world was an even bigger threat. *Retreating* stories often also involve
a collective and stationary sense of 'we'. Articulation of individual
identities is not strong, but there is safety in numbers. These are the
students who ask to be interviewed in pairs, and who will later leave
the project.

Finally, *wandering* young people will tell of destinations, but be
unable to provide detail about how they will get there. William
hopes: 'to become a computer operator'. How? William does not
think much about his future: 'Nup. Fair while yet.' He is in the final

weeks of year ten. 'What are your chances?' 'Not good.' This story is a fantasy or pseudo-plan, with ideas that are not at all grounded within the individual's social context. In fantasy, ideas have no real-world connection with articulated means or with social networks – because perhaps the story is serving another purpose. It almost looks like the periodic entertainment of other-worldly ideas (opiate for the masses?). Or is it a smoke-screen, because I am asking questions that are not core business in his world? Regardless, this pattern seems to have a dialectic operation, as both a response to individual powerlessness and a cause of further powerlessness. The role of mass media in the maintenance of this pattern will be explored later (in this chapter and in Chapter 8). The politics and purpose of speaking in such a blunt way about another's story is discussed further in Chapter 11.

The uses of networks

Networks shape individuals' ideas about the world. Social interactions enrich the individual's stories with shared meanings and thicken stories with new ideas. Social relationships both supply ideas about goals, and supply ways of attaining them (for example practical help, ideas). Even weak ties are fulfilling this role. Network theory explored these ideas in the 1980s (for example Granovetter 1982), and more recently extensive bodies of work around social capital has touched on these same themes.

Among these young people, broader networks are linked to broader world-views (Wierenga 1995). Many of those *exploring* are young people who have moved into Myrtle Vale, or first generation migrants from elsewhere in the country. They or their families have external contacts, whose ideas they are accessing. These are classed patterns. For example Pete's networks extend globally, linking with his family's recreation patterns (that is, they travel). Observations in homes and interviews with parents reveal that those parents (usually, but not always) have similar cultural orientations to their children. Parents who commute to the city also make family friends there. Mel's elite sport involvement (and networks) in the city means her parents need to have the resources to support her in this. The role of families in resourcing their children will be explored further in Chapter 8.

Myrtle Vale's young men and young women have quite distinct networking practices.

The girls are very active researchers of the other women around them. 'What did she do?' 'How did she do it?' 'Is it working for her?' 'What does this mean for me?'

> I want to be just like my step-sister... she works part-time but she has a family and she's got time to spend with the family... I think office administration is the kind of job where I could do that too. (Bronwyn)

Young women are also active researchers of future options outside Myrtle Vale. This is related to a dislike of local options and cultural definitions of both good work and femininity. Note, though, that they do not mention gender or being a young woman, but they talk about the things that are valued and valuable, and the things that are to be avoided (see below) and it is *these* definitions that differ on the basis of gender.

Work within Myrtle Vale, as in studies from other places (Willis 1979; Connell et al. 1982), is closely linked with definitions of masculinity, and is a source of identity or 'vocation' for young men. As an early part of this research in 1995, all grade seven and eight students at the local high school completed an essay titled: 'What I will be doing in 20 years time.' Overwhelmingly, young men expressed manual work as *the* main feature of their imaginings. By way of contrast, the young women's essays are more likely to feature friends, careers, families, and lifestyles.

A different cultural orientation in women is driven not just by parents but by everything they see and hear. Cultural messages are carried not just in words but in action. Although 'politically correct' ideas have infiltrated the town (I could only find a couple of young men to tell me that housework was women's work) day-to-day practice is different. Statistics from the census of the time (ABS 1997a) reveal that 'skilled vocational' qualifications relate to men (34 out of 40), and 'basic vocational' relate to women (11 out of 11). Here, as in other places, women are still domestic servants. The message and role-modelling that young people receive is that in Myrtle Vale, men can work for identity, but that women have paid jobs out of necessity to supplement family income. If they stay in town, messages from school and media to empower women are potentially rendered powerless by the limited local options available.

However, girls actively respond to the social conditions which they experience. They are, corporately or separately, constructing other interpretations of this picture, and resistance to the patterns that they see:

'No, I wouldn't work at (Fish Place) – Mum wouldn't let me. She says it's not a good job, I can do better. Anything I can git apart from that.' This comes across strongly, irrespective of class: 'They've (my parents have) encouraged us to keep away from the apples – thought that we can do a bit better.' (Kelly), or 'Bullshit, no way! Nuh, I wouldn't work over there!' (Nell). Among the few *settling* young women, working in a shop looks 'Ok' – and there is no analysis of the precarious nature of this position. In contrast to their male counterparts, the young women are overwhelmingly intending to go on to complete their education (year 11 and 12).

It is interesting that in our conversations, the mantra: 'there's nowhere to go and nothing to do' only comes from the mouths of young women. Superficially, we could take this as applying to recreation options. It is, though, a 'good call' on the existential plight in which they find themselves. Some delight in the idea of motherhood and find it the most meaningful thing in the world. However, this does not appeal to all, and in terms of employment options, and in terms of cultural expectations, barring friendship, motherhood and family life there *is* no vocation for them in Myrtle Vale.

Networks and access to ideas

As explained earlier, information and ideas are gathered by individuals on a *'need to know'* basis, depending upon what they are doing.

Respondents who are *exploring* are drawing on a wide range of sources (family, school, peers, community, mass media). Because they, family members or mentors, have moved in, their networks stretch well beyond 'The Valley', and contact with new and diverse ideas is frequent.

Those *settling* are also drawing from many sources, but their information is locally bound, and more homogenous. Teachers are sources of ideas from outside The Valley, but because these young men are focussed on staying here, any information about the outside world is understood but shrugged off as 'not relevant to me'. Ross will tell me that he knows that the best way to get a job is to go to college, but that it makes no difference to him because he is going to drive a 'fork-truck'. Definitions of self are anchored here, and engaged only in narrowly defined information-searches.

Narrow definitions of 'people like me' reinforce the boundaries, sharply demarcating what information becomes relevant.

Retreating individuals seem to be not so much seeking information as protection. The peer group can be useful to this end. Shared stories are highly effective defences to external attack. Such stories involve themes of possible danger and 'why we're not going to risk it'. Nell's interview earlier was an example of this.

Respondents who are *wandering* seem to be making use of mass media as the key or sole sources of their own stories (this will be explored further in Chapter 8). Perhaps images of cities and the promise of a glamorous existence provide a welcome contrast to current conditions. Whatever the reason, this has some serious implications in terms of capacity to follow through. Laura is in grade ten and delighted to recount that: 'there's only 55 more days of school! Can't wait. Never going back to school again…'. Laura wants to be a model. 'So how do you go about becoming a model Laura?' 'S'pose I should think about it a bit.' She does not know anyone who has become a model; her acquaintances are all local but estranged. All of the interactive social sources of information mentioned earlier are useful in that they can provide ideas, both about goals, and about the social means (practical help, contacts, ideas grounded in circumstance) to attaining those goals. TV, as a non-interactive source, does not do this. A goal with no means will remain a fantasy.

Most respondents make statements about 'me' (the type of thing I could do or not do) about 'us' or reference-groups, and about 'the kind of thing that people like me do'. The content of these statements corresponds to broader and narrower world-views or life-experience. The ability to do this at all, though, corresponds to a clarity in stories about 'past, present, future, and me'. Both of these practices have an impact on the individual's ability to absorb different possibilities into their own understanding of the future.

Different histories of trust

Individuals' stories and practices of storying are autobiographical. In other words, individuals have learned these specific ways of operating amidst the socially located conditions of their own histories. Three factors are important here: firstly, trust of their own narratives; second, trust of significant others and their stories; and third, the availability of coaches, mentors, and translators. These ideas are explored below.

One important factor is the individual's trust in some stories about reality, and their own ability to make sense of the things that they experience. Chapters 5–9 explore this idea in more detail.

Trusting certain significant others and their stories is critical. If, in early years, young people have learned that they cannot trust family members or significant others, then they will not readily place trust in generalized others (that is, other social sources of ideas and information). Laura, ('model') does not spend much time with anyone after school: 'Just keep to myself, mostly, watch TV and sleep.' Her siblings all live locally but she's lost touch with most of them. Significant others include: 'Mick (boyfriend), cat, dog, sister, horse.' Where there are few trusted sources, there are often corresponding fragments of stories of betrayal. Laura used to ride a lot but: 'Dad sold my horse when I was at school one day'.

As much as anything else, teenage networking is about accessing the stories of 'people like me'. If relationships are trusted, these become useful sources of ideas. If alienated from social sources, the related information is not useful, and not used. As they talk, individuals provide possibilities for new insights about this. Storytellers cite their sources as they speak, and, through a close reading of their narratives, it is possible to map their trusted sources (Wierenga 2001). Figure 4.2 shows the sources that are 'referenced' by young people when they tell their stories (for example, 'My Mum said...', 'at school we did...'). It shows how those *exploring* and *settling* acknowledge a wide range of social sources, the former more diverse, the latter more localized.

		Exploring	**Wandering**
sources of idea	**more diverse**	(family, school, peers, local community, non-local communities of interest, TV)	(TV)
	more homo-genous	**Settling** (family, peers, local community, TV)	**Retreating** (peers or isolated family members)

high   **low**

Trust of social sources

Figure 4.2   Mapping respondents' social sources of information

Retreating respondents are mentioning few social sources. *Wandering* ideas are globally sourced, but quite disconnected from real-world networks and possibilities.

Beyond their own stories, and 'people like me', the third important factor in the practice of storying is the *availability of coaches, mentors, and translators*. These are the people who *translate* ideas so that they can be understood in the child's language. They are the people who say: 'this is relevant to you', or encourage engagement: 'you would be very good at this'. They provide a consistent source of ideas about the world and, probably more importantly, these relationships help to shape and define the young person in their own eyes. Individuals use conversation in order to construct an understanding of the world and the self (Berger and Luckmann 1967). Young people who do not converse cannot construct.

Not surprisingly, these patterns – of high and low trust of social sources – are also echoed in the themes of the stories. Clear narratives, crafted with supportive others tend to reveal themes of hope, of best options for me. Meanwhile, among those who have learned to trust less, the stories highlight *least-worst* options for individuals' lives. These stories are most powerfully characterized by fear.

A story like Laura's demonstrates the absence of trusted others, or mentors. Sometimes, though, the limitation is not the absence of mentors, but the limited world-views of these mentors. So when the next door neighbour tells Ben that: 'You should be able to get a job as a mechanic without going to college', he is believed. The young people in this research are more likely to listen to someone trusted than someone qualified. This hits the young men the hardest as they are more likely to be networking locally, and conversing less.

Implications – what does all of this mean?

Stories are political, and they involve power. How people tell the story shapes action. In the creation of a future, so much rests upon people's abilities to draw on a history. Scattered dots do not make a line. Individuals' stories, and their different practices of storying, pave the way for life-choices, negotiations, and engagement with future options. Already it looks as if these things may be exponential in nature. These dynamics might still be thought of in terms of a career, with each choice requiring further investment into particular identities (Becker 1963). Conversely, each choice potentially removes the individual further from other options, other social networks, and other definitions of self. Even in a new era of flexible 'subjectivities', concepts from classical sociology still make good sense. Later chapters will continue to explore how these things unfold in a contemporary society in the lives of these 32 young people.

Storying is social practice. Differing practices are both a function of social structure, and a daily re-creation of same. In the lives of these young people this is clearly the case. It is cultural patterns, like the ones highlighted in this chapter, that reproduce and re-construct social inequalities in a new generation. In a classic longitudinal study of young people, Robert Connell and associates explained that gender can be best understood not as two categories of people, but as ongoing relations among people. Likewise social class can be seen, not so much as about social categories or ownership of certain things, but as intrinsic to patterns of practice – what people are doing, and are able to do, with resources and relationships (Connell et al. 1982).

The patterns replicate themselves within lives but also within the community. Young people are not just absorbers of local culture, but co-creators of it. Leaving Myrtle Vale, or not leaving, will have a significant impact. Those who leave will take their optimism, networks, new learnings and *exploring* cultural practices with them. Those who choose not to go on to further education become role models for younger people. In a small local community this is a self-perpetuating pattern.

Exploring respondents are the ones who are talking about availing themselves of the highest number of different future options. By leaving The Valley, even for a short time, they will further increase their networks, contacts and ideas, but also increase their geographical understanding and the resource-base from which they can tell their stories of past and of future. In short, they will expand their cultural universe.

The situation of *settling* respondents looks more precarious than that of their *exploring* sisters. In their stories they have expressed a profound sense of connection and commitment to the local world. By planning locally only, these young people make themselves *subject to local conditions*. *Settling* respondents are aspiring to the traditional, male, working-class rural jobs of their fathers and grandfathers, which are fast disappearing from rural towns. In this way, they are playing by the local rules of the game, but the rules are being changed without their consent. This generates heartbreak and hostility. Those who have placed trust in the old rules are locked in and may quickly lose a sense of control. In the face of globalizing markets and rapid social change, this pattern has great social significance in many places. Small rural communities are a crucible. The rise of ultra-conservative political parties demonstrates a similar element of despair about social change, rural decline and mistrust of the outsider. More broadly, some parallels could probably be drawn between the upsurge of religious and racial fundamentalism in many communities around the globe, and resistance to the more displacing elements of social change. There is a deeply felt injury when externalities shift, and when the stories that hold day-to-day life together stop making sense.

Wandering and *retreating* are both unhelpful strategies in that they are *re-active* rather than *pro-active* about future options. *Exploring* and *settling* respondents have (albeit with limited scope for some) claimed 'captaincy of their craft' and are making plans for the journey, while those *wandering* and *retreating* are at the mercy of social forces, blown about by wind and tide (Wierenga 1995; 1999).

The dynamics of hope and fear are powerful, and we will return to them in later chapters. Those who have a basic working assumption of a benevolent world are searching for *best practice* ideas. Meanwhile, local experiences of a hostile world are leading others to search for *least-worst options* – ways of hiding (*retreating*) and escaping or fleeing (*wandering*). Later chapters will reveal how this is not helpful in terms of individual life-chances, learning, social participation or wellbeing.

Finally, these patterns, these four cultural orientations, may be both exponential and political, but they are *not determinate*. As later chapters will show, young people's lives change. However, re-interviews with the same respondents two, four and even six years later reveal just how deeply individuals' stories, and their practices of storying, have been enmeshed with other significant patterns in their lives. That is, understanding respondents' practices of *storying* is integral to understanding the ways that they *negotiate* significant changes (Chapter 5); their different ways of *engaging* with the institutions that manage their trajectories (Chapter 6); the different types of *resources* that they are able to draw upon as they go about the process of making their lives (Chapter 7); and how this all happens in the context of ongoing *relationships to self and to others* (Chapter 8). The conceptual scheme introduced in this chapter offers a way of making sense of each of these significant themes over time.

5
Negotiating Changes

This chapter explores important questions about young people's choices, decision-making and human agency. Because of the high impact of choices made at certain biographical moments, teenage decision-making comes under a lot of scrutiny at a variety of levels: not only their educational and occupational trajectories, but also where they live, who with, how they spend their time, how they engage as citizens of a wider community, how they support themselves, lifestyle choices, health choices, help-seeking behaviours at times of crisis, and the kind of everyday assistance they access along the way.

Conceptually, the dynamics of free will and determinism, agency and structure, opportunity and constraint have been a preoccupation of social theorists for decades. Researchers across the globe have been tracking the social structures and forces that shape opportunity and constraint. At the same time, internationally in the youth literature, a strong body of research has developed around the notions of biography and choice.

Some of us are also interested in these questions at a practice level. How are choices being offered and constrained? How does it work? Until we understand the dynamics behind young people's choices, we as communities and workers are poorly equipped to assist them at critical moments (Wierenga 2001). A growing number of other studies with young people share the news that the traditional approach of loading them up with information, to prepare for all these choices and return to in a moment of decision or crisis, may not be useful. Often we will educate, inform and broadcast information without much sense of the dynamics of how information is used, or can be used, by the recipient. Young people at times report feeling overwhelmed with information, or having trouble relating information to their own lives (Stokes et al. 2003; Cahill et al. 2004).

October of 1997 marks the end of year ten for our cohort at Myrtle Vale District High school. The 16 students in this class have been involved in this research project from the beginning. Leaving year ten is a moment of truth, or a particularly significant moment in time. Drawing on a critical moment in these young people's lives, this chapter will explore some of the social processes around their decision-making.

In the following pages I will set the scene both practically in terms of the significance of the choices which face these young people, and conceptually in terms of the language of 'choice' and question how we might more usefully conceptualize the things we can see. In the lead-up to finishing high school, interviews with respondents reveal that this moment means different things to different individuals, and that, as a consequence, it is being approached in a variety of ways. The chapter continues as a case-study, to document the activity taking place over the summer of 1997–1998, and explore how members of this cohort are negotiating this time through a complex set of changes. Their movements, and the stories that they tell illuminate some significant contemporary issues, including the diverse working of human agency, the dynamics of young people's decision-making, how different choices are being made, and how they draw in support for these movements.

What happens at this moment of leaving school is very significant in terms of individuals' lives and life-chances. Firstly, where individuals go now shapes where they can go next – opening up or closing down other options. Secondly, education and work are pivotal ways in which young people are connected to their communities. Thirdly, young people's practices of engagement in work and education are both shaped by, and shaping, their other social engagements; these are interconnected. As such, the shift from compulsory schooling to other commitments is centrally enshrined in the whole process of making a life. I am seeking to present a holistic picture that does not ignore these other transitions, and other significant relationships (or the absence of them). Later chapters will also broaden beyond a school-to-work focus.

Staying on at school

Around two decades ago, in Australia, the Finn report (1991) set the target of 95% of 19-year-olds finishing year 12, having a post-school qualification, or being in formally recognized education programs. As in other countries, in recent decades the notion that young people should stay on beyond the compulsory years of education to year 12 has been a policy pushed by governments of either traditional persuasion. Through the 'Working Nation' white paper, the Labor Government of the 1980s and early 90s claimed: 'We will never again return to a world where large numbers of jobs are available for unskilled young workers' (Commonwealth of Australia 1994:89). Under the Liberal (conservative) Government of the era (1996–2007), The Common Youth Allowance Scheme meant for this cohort, receiving ongoing support also entailed being open to continuing education.

There were good reasons for this emphasis. Some Australian research has continued to indicate that young people who did not complete year 12 in the mid-1990s experienced longer periods of unemployment than their counterparts a decade earlier (Lamb et al. 2000). Meanwhile internationally, recent OECD research has again linked early school leaving to difficult transitions to work (OECD and Canadian Policy Research Networks 2005). However, policy measures are usually quick to establish the responsibility of individuals to be trained and job-ready, rather than the responsibility of other parties to provide work. Education and training now play a significant role as 'holding tanks' for the young unemployed, and welfare payments are essentially tied to an education and training agenda (Wyn and White 1997).

In the context of a lack of local work, Myrtle Vale's young people have been encouraged by their teachers to continue education. Respondents' interpretation of this message depends very much on the kind of understandings about education shared at home. These young people grow up in a town where a minority of people have 'gone on'. However, this cohort is growing up in a changing climate. Each year a few more go on, and each year a few more plan to go on.

Australian research shows that rural and remote students have lower participation rates, less consistent attendance, and poorer academic performances than their urban peers. The average year 12 retention rate for boys in rural and remote areas is only 54% compared with 63% in capital cities, while for girls it is 66%, and 74% in capital cities (Sidoti 2001).

For rural Tasmanian students, decisions about whether to continue education beyond year ten have been complicated by two things. Firstly, within the public (government) school system in Tasmania (unlike some other states) year 11 and 12 have been known as 'college', and separated from years seven to ten as a different institution in a different location, with different rules, social dynamics, staff, subjects and expectations.

As earlier commentators insightfully suggested, Tasmania's comparatively low retention rates beyond year ten may particularly be a result of rural students being unprepared for this different world (see Abbott-Chapman et al. 1992; Cunningham et al. 1992). Secondly, until recent developments (year 11 is now offered in some district high schools), going on with education has typically meant either long daily travel or leaving town. Practical considerations are significant but, as respondents' stories will indicate, there are other far more salient factors influencing individuals' movements.

Young people's choices

The framing of young people's choices is important because of its intersection with popular debates and policy. Emerging from social theory and some extremely solid bodies of youth research, though, are caveats warning that an uncritical acceptance of the notion of 'choice' can be far more problematic than useful. Issues of free will and determination, action and constraint, or agency and structure have been traditional areas of debate in the field of sociology. Tensions exist between focus on individual volition and broader social patterns, and many theorists have tackled the sociological struggle of finding appropriate ways to describe both (see Evans 2002).

Over the past decade or so (following the early work of researchers like Connell et al. 1982; Jones and Wallace 1992), these foci have also been a central feature of youth studies. Youth researchers appear to have wrestled with this topic more than most. Perhaps this is because working with young people has continually sensitized researchers to the social stakes underlying these debates. Policy debates constantly reinforce the need to revisit and re-group, and to temper arguments with empirical material about the lived realities of young people (for example see MacDonald and Marsh 2001).

White and Wyn (1998) have pointed to the predominance of either 'deterministic' or 'voluntaristic' understandings of youth. At one end of this spectrum, ideas about normal transitions, deviance, normality and abnormality can ignore questions about social context and young people's agency, becoming patronising and disempowering when they are used to justify interventions that are designed to simply control young people. At the other end of the spectrum, within discourses around choices, futures and pathways, young people are often seen to be powerfully constructing their own realities, but with scant attention paid to the ways they are positioned materially within the social world

(White and Wyn 1998). The contemporary 'paradox of youth' lies in the relationship between the choice or agency of the individual and the structural conditions which for many 'preclude the attainment of adult social goals' (Wyn and White 2000:1).

Social change, transitions and eroded pathways

Jane Higgins and Karen Nairn (2006) point to the skill-deficit discourse that surrounds young people's transitions, conflating the notions of post-school qualifications with labour market power. The young people in their study expected that if they gained a qualification, employment would follow. As Higgins and Nairn point out, this may be a costly assumption to make.

Through recent decades the notion of 'pathways' has framed education policies and the study of young people's movements from school to training to work. Young people have been seen as responsible for 'choosing' different pathways. Alongside this, policy and rhetoric has increasingly constructed young people as consumers (Bessant 1996; Wyn and White 1997), once again describing outcomes as a matter of individual choice.

Youth researchers around the globe have noted that emphasis on the individual making the right choices or choosing the right pathways has political implications in a time where some pathways resemble '...the road to (no)where' (Holden 1992) and many other alleged pathways look more like 'mosaics' (Abbott-Chapman 1999). For both early school-leavers and those who continue, pathways is no longer an adequate metaphor (Dwyer et al. 1998).

Where research emphasis is placed only on individuals and their choices, it is easy to overlook the fact that much of what is happening for young people is the result of wider structural and social changes. Many of the difficulties encountered by young people who are negotiating futures with work are linked to broader patterns such as changes in economies, labour and industry, technology, broader patterns of economic rationalization and the globalization of markets. A focus on the individual as responsible also removes the focus from the economic and political processes by which large numbers of young people are being marginalized and excluded.

At the same time, young people know that they continue to have and make choices. In fact, often when they make decisions about school and work, they feel a huge burden of personal responsibility (Dwyer et al. 2005).

Choice biographies

Andy Furlong and Fred Cartmel (1997) argue that a cultural ideology of 'individualism' suggests to young people that they alone are responsible for their circumstances. Following Beck (1992; Beck and Beck-Gernsheim 2002), they suggest that in late modernity risks become individualized. That is, crises and setbacks are understood as personal shortcomings and problems to solve on an individual basis. Individuals, however, are being forced to negotiate risks that are not individual but collective in nature (for example, unemployment). Their circumstances are more likely to be socially structured and outside the control of the individual, than a result of individual action. This is the 'epistemological fallacy' of late modernity. As such, late modernity does not mean the disappearance of class distinctions, but rather obscurity and lack of recognition.

As Furlong and Cartmel have suggested, there is a real need to recognize that, although an ideology of individualism prevails, the real material conditions in which people live continue to structure their life-chances.

Individual young people's choices are qualitatively very different from one another. The nature of the options available to individuals varies greatly across different axes of social inequality, depending on structural conditions like class, gender, race, and on the different resources which individuals are able to access.

Negotiating changes

White and Wyn (1998) have advocated a 'contextual approach' which focusses directly upon the interplay between young people and society. By placing social practice and the development of social practices at its centre, this approach allows the researcher to explore how agency is played out within particular structural conditions. In this study a contextual approach is being claimed. That is, the research gaze is directly upon respondents' different practices at a significant moment, and also upon the histories and social conditions which surround their different practices.

For our purposes, the most useful conceptual framework in which to understand young people's choices is to see them as ongoing negotiations between individuals and their social world. A picture that comes back both from fieldwork and from other literature is one of 'negotiated realities'. The concept of 'negotiations' makes sense in two ways. Firstly, it is about respondents' movements in different directions, for instance when negotiating meaningful paths or negotiating obstacles. Secondly, it is about power imbalances in the construction of different arrangements between social agents. Instances of this include negotiating relationships or contracts with significant others and institutions (Wierenga 2001).

This chapter will show that young people are active negotiators, but also that they are very differently placed to engage in these negotiations. Due to the different life-histories and family contexts of respondents, they will be quite differently equipped to negotiate. Having re-framed the issues this way, we can shift our focus to one moment when respondents' trajectories diverge, and then onto some of the different negotiation strategies involved.

The moment of truth

In terms of understanding social process, it is important to understand what the end of year ten means to respondents. Some of their explanations will set the scene first, and a more analytical scheme will be developed later.

For the class of '97, this moment is a turning point or crisis, in that a large part of 'life as normal' ceases to exist. This might sit alongside what other authors have also discussed as 'fateful moments' where external events force individuals to take stock (Giddens 1991), or 'critical moments' as identified in the narratives of respondents (Thomson et al. 2002).

For respondents, leaving year ten coincides with other significant life-changes, such as having friends leave town, the emergence of partners, moving out of home, or families moving out of town. It signals a time where respondents find themselves faced with multiple choices, including what to do next, how to go about doing it, and who to do it with. *Some* of them say that they are confronted by these changes, but, as with all decision points, the unfolding events will catch others less prepared. The meaning of the moment is most clearly framed by respondents' understandings of what they are leaving and where they are going. These understandings, in turn, have been framed by the context and content of each individual's biography.

The class of '97 have lived with the blessing and curse of having an intimate home-group, and now they face the blessing and curse of leaving it. The stories about this movement vary between students, depending upon how encircled they felt themselves to be by the group-life, and where they have been in the social pecking order. Several, though, reveal the complex push and pull associated with branching out beyond the familiar. Alyssa sums up some common themes well:

> Oh I guess it's probably like a second home to me this school, I've been around here so long, ….I think I'll make a heap of new friends and that, but they won't really be as good as what I've had here, I mean I've known Mark since we started – we were in play-group together – we were this big, and how we're all grown-up and he's been like my brother and everything. (Alyssa)

To a point, less intimacy would be welcomed at times:

> I really wanted to be, you know, get away from this, and one of the bad things about being at such a small school is that everyone knows what you do, everyone knows every little detail about you no matter how embarrassing or horrible it is, like so at least going to college is going to get away from that. (Alyssa)

As the end of year ten approaches (only weeks away) this grows as a source of ambivalence:

> … hmm and there's all these faces and you can't put names to half of them… yeah, sometimes, sometimes people need to get away but at least they're there for you if you need them. (Alyssa)

In their own way, others are echoing these sentiments:

> But we all grew up together and that, got in trouble together… (Simon)

Amongst other school years (the class of '95 and '96), interviews are pointing to respondents' quite different lived experience of school. A minority, those *retreating*, say that they are simply relieved at the idea of having no more school. This small group (female, working class) fit Holden's (1992) description of school 'refugees'. Some others are seeing this as a good opportunity to shake off those that have been 'in my face' for too long. In a small community, antagonisms and patterns of group oppression are hard to escape.

For these young people, meaning is constructed not only in terms of what individuals are leaving but also what they are going towards, and what comes next. Among those who want to continue their education, as well as planning and dreaming, many are simply grappling with the sheer unknown-ness of what they will encounter on the other side:

> Alyssa: Yah I reckon it will, it'll be so strange going to college next year – it's such a big place and such a small person.
> AW: What do you reckon will be the hardest thing of that?
> Alyssa: Yeah, um, probably finding my way around. (Alyssa)

Going to college evokes fear for several reasons. For example – going from a small and intimately known world to a larger unknown one, and leaving familiar people:

> It's really like that's kind of like oh God I've got to go without my friends – it's a bit daunting but I know I have to go .... (Nicolette)

From this vantage point, thinking beyond college is even more daunting. 'Scarey' is defined in terms of the unknown: an unknown place, unknown people and unknown demands awaiting them. I ask Nicolette what is 'scarey' about going on to university:

> I don't know. Maybe it's the four years or the six years of more learning or something, I don't know. It's just everyone says it's hard. Like schooling and stuff, like that. Like people have parties there, but if you want to get like a good job and a good education, you have to work. And that is way different from high school. So, it's scarey. (Nicolette)

Fear can be a blockage, until there is an over-riding story to which it becomes subordinate:

> But I don't know if I could do that... but if I want to do that job, I know I have to. (Nicolette)

As the more articulate students explain, a large part of what is holding them back from college and other education systems is fear. Less articulate students do not explain in terms of fear, or anything else for that matter. They simply do not explain. As Nicolette shows by her movement over the next two years (through college), some respondents can and will, by virtue of their own significant projects, be propelled through the barriers created by their fears.

At this point, those with the most abstract (non-local, not directly experienced) ideas (those *exploring*), are also articulating the most uncertainty. If some of the best resourced and most articulate students are dogged by these fears, how are the others managing the shift? Figure 5.1 contrasts the varying patterns, in terms of respondents' cultural orientations. Those *settling* are facing the moment by naming only the things which are familiar as their future options. For those who plan to stay, familiar things, and tasks they can already do, are most important. Uncertainties are tackled by the naming of familiar industries and jobs in specific workplaces.

In their second interviews, *wandering* students are still not very specific about futures. The mantra 'you need college to get a job' has made a surprisingly regular appearance. Most interesting here though was the mantra being uttered amongst those who could not or would not elaborate on this further and were quite clearly putting their energies elsewhere (more on this later). As in Chapter 4, not all are able to talk clearly about where they are going. For some (especially those

<table>
<tr><td rowspan="2">Focus</td><td>Global</td><td>Exploring

Specific but abstract: launching into the unknown. School and work plans anchored to occupation or area of interest, not specific industry</td><td>Wandering

Vague – Going to college: 'you need college to get a job'; Looking for work: often glamorized but ungrounded ideas</td></tr>
<tr><td>Local</td><td>Settling

Specific and locally grounded: local jobs and local industries</td><td>Retreating

No plans

'I couldn't really say'.</td></tr>
<tr><td></td><td></td><td>Specific</td><td>Vague</td></tr>
<tr><td></td><td></td><td colspan="2" align="center">Stories about what I'm doing</td></tr>
</table>

Figure 5.1   Facing the moment of truth – different cultural orientations

retreating and *wandering*), this is over-shadowed by what they are leaving and the idea of being free of it:

> Being at school is like being caged. (Laura)

> Glad to be rid of the hassle... getting up in the morning and that. (William)

Probably just as significantly, the meaning of the moment is framed by another set of factors. Respondents' different understandings about what was required of them at this time were significant what the end of year ten means in terms of their own futures; what they themselves should be doing or worrying about; and the particular onus on them to individually *get it right*.

As they approach the end of year ten, some feel that the stakes are particularly high:

> Oh I freak out, the idea of choosing a career and I am going to stay with it all me life.... I got to think about how much money I earn and family and wo!... Yeah. It's hard, it is really hard. Yeah and then what subjects you choose are based on that, so you need to do it now and all that. (Max)

By way of contrast, in the last week of year ten I ask Ben why he wants to go to college:

> Ben: Um, just give me more experience.
> AW: Yeah. Any particular areas that you want to do extra study on?
> Ben: Ah, not really just anything I need I s'pose. At the time. (Ben)

Vague notions about futures do not offer much sense of immediacy and direction about what needs to happen now. Clear stories do. Sonia, confessing that she hasn't always been a vigilant student, explains:

> See now I'm just starting to wake up and think: 'Oh now, I've only got two years left.'

'Now' only becomes significant in the context of her clear story about what she wants to do in the future. The relevance of her move to college, in the terms of her own stories, leads her to resolve:

> I've only got year 11 and 12. I don't really want to go to [further vocational education] or anywhere like that, I just want to do the best I can at college...

Now (the end of year ten) is framed quite differently by respondents because of the different stories about the future that they bring to this moment. Respondents' stories and 'the meaning of now' will be explored in greater detail in Chapter 6. Here, it suffices to say that for some this is a time of intense activity; for others it seems no more intense than usual.

Different negotiating practices

The focus of the last chapter was on aspirations, and it dealt only with those who had clear goals and means (a plan and a project) and those who did not. From this vantage point it could have been argued that only two of the four cultural orientations (*settling* and *exploring*) exercise *any* kind of agency. A question was left hanging: so what are the others *doing*?

The class of '97 prided itself on its togetherness and its abilities to group-think and respond. These qualities made them, at the same time, very inward-focussed and hard to handle as a group (infamous). The end of year ten was 'A Moment of Truth'. From the outside it seemed as if everybody must make their *own* tracks, ready or not. At the Leavers' Dinner, which was organized by the group, for the group, an emotional speech by the class captain declared that this was the best class ever, and galvanized the sentiment of everybody. From that moment there was no going back.

Talk gives way to actions. When different negotiation practices are embodied (lived out), some other forms of agency become visible. Over the summer of 1997–1998, individuals were employing some very distinct negotiation strategies or patterns of practice. These included: Plan and Project; Negotiation by Proxy; Flee; Social cluster movements; and Default Movements.

Respondents' patterns of practice can offer some insights into the complex and differentiated social processes taking place, and the diverse manifestations of human agency, help-seeking and decision-making. Each pattern is worth exploring in turn.

Plan and project

'Plan and project' is a new name for an embodied pattern that will look familiar from Chapter 4. Its characteristics include clear goals, and clear means (global or local). Since these individuals already have some ideas about what they want to do, emphasis is not so much upon goals, but getting the means right. Choosing the right school:

> Mel: Oh, I'm just gonna look, look at all of them and then decide which one offers me the best courses for what I want to do. So … if I can get three courses that I want to do in one school then two at the other, then I'll choose the one that offers me the best.
>
> AW: Even if it's further traveling?
>
> Mel: Yeah.

And the right courses:

> I think I am doing Maths, English, Physics, Electronics, Information Technology and Auto Maintenance… I'm not really good at English, I'm [in] standard Maths and the job that I want to do has high demands on Physics and Maths. So I've got to do them. (Max)

At the point of leaving year ten this *plan and project* pattern involves the young person in directly interacting with representatives of employment or education systems. These could be either 'global' (outside The Valley) or 'local' (within The Valley). The *individual is negotiator*, although they almost always have *allies* who *coach* them in decision-making and *facilitate* the process in other ways (for example, going with them to enrolment day, driving, research). On the part of the respondent, any anxiety at leaving the familiar places and faces is funnelled into *researching* options (networks, web-sites, newspapers, agencies, course-counsellors, pamphlets), into *anticipating* obstacles, *stock-taking* their own position, resources, abilities, chances (as above), and into *imagining* possibilities.

This is one way of negotiating futures. It is very *active, cognitive and verbal*. It involves the individual in being *engaged* with the whole process of *making their own future*. Central questions, self-directed, are: 'what are my best options?' and: 'what should I be doing now?'. Allies assist by asking and re-framing these questions in the light of their own wisdoms and their own histories of exposure to the world. For the respondent, the answers to these questions are central to lived experience. They become priorities and are articulated as such. Other more peripheral questions are answered in line with them. To paraphrase Sonia: 'I'm not down at the beach with my friends this summer because I'm getting a part-time-job, so I can get a car, so that when I finish school I can go to work in town.' In the light of their plans – where they want to go and the real-world options for getting there – *life is about time-in-motion projects. The key issue is therefore one of accessing and making use of resources to those ends.*

But what are the others doing?

Negotiation by proxy

This pattern of social practice presents some direct contrasts to the one above:

> Mark: Um, Dad drives an oil truck and it's at Lightwood [nearby town]. This fella rang up Dad and asked him did I want to do an apprenticeship with a month's trial? So I said yeah. Give it a try.
>
> AW: Yeah, so you didn't even have to do anything?
>
> Mark: No, I didn't even know anything about it. (Mark)

It is only at the time of leaving year ten that *negotiation by proxy* is becoming visible at all. This is because it does not manifest in and through respondents' own narratives or action, but within *group practice*. As such, it is far less individually-driven or self-contained, resting entirely upon the goodwill, creativity and reliability of family and local networks. This is different from the previous strategy. Allies take a far more front-line role in negotiations, sorting it out for the kid. Within this culture, emphasis is on less talk and more action. As one mother explained: 'You have to give them direction.' Allies are usually parents or family friends. Central questions involve 'what are his best chances?' (This strategy seems to mostly involve young men) and 'what can *we do* now?'. Often these strategies will exclude continuing education because this is not one of the worlds familiar to these networks.

Negotiation by proxy is a different kind of agency, a collective process, a *clan-based* creativity. It is a different cultural prototype which has worked very well for generations. It contrasts starkly to the more individually-centred, self-contained, system-familiar model discussed above. This is also a class-based difference in family practice, which will be explored further in Chapter 8. Initially, rather than individuals engaging in making their own futures, this strategy involves others engaging *on their behalf.* The rationale for action tends to be in clan-and-community-based stories rather than simply individual ones, like: 'They're alright.'; 'We are doing alright.'; and 'We always look after our own.' Referring back to earlier interviews, comments that had initially looked like respondents' vagueness and ineptness at planning and talking about their futures, can now be seen in a new light. *The key issue in this strategy is not personal project management, but solidarity and social connection.*

Flee

This pattern will look familiar from the previous chapter. While some are very engaged in negotiating their way *towards* certain options (for example, a chosen vocation, career, or lifestyle), others explain retrospectively that their movements have been very much structured by the need to *get away from* certain situations (for example, a violent home-life): 'Got me out of there, anyway' (Beth). At the time there is not a lot of language for what is going on, but central issues are about harm-minimization. Leaving school can be about keeping the peace at home (fitting in, helping out) or getting the resources together to get away from home (money, boyfriend or pregnancy). *The key issue, therefore is safety and survival.*

Other research with early school-leavers has found that movement can be fuelled by desire to get away. In the cases of such 'refugees' there is often little thought for what comes next (Holden 1992). Lack of forward projecting means these respondents are some of the least equipped to make sense of their next set of arrangements. As with other patterns of crisis management, this *flee* pattern often involves a rapid sequences of changes (for example, leave town or come back; leave home or come back; working or not working; at school or leave school). As such, it sits in direct contrast to the strategies listed above, which can develop more orderly and cumulative sequences of action. This pattern is also characterized by the young person's *lack of allies.*

Least resistance/default

Some respondents are following similar patterns of practice, but neither now nor later is it clear in their stories from what they are fleeing. For whatever reason, these respondents have little desire or available attention to plan where they are going. Central questions revolve around 'what do I have to do' and 'what is going to be the least uncomfortable'. From outside, this looks like the most passive way of negotiating futures. This pattern is characterized by either a lack of adult allies, or a lack of shared understandings or consensus with those adults who say that they are trying to be allies. *Negotiating futures* is actually beyond the point, because the key issue seems to be about responding to life *now*, which is a lesser understood form of agency (see chapter 6 for a further exploration of this). However, in terms of institutional demands (such as schooling) this usually involves a *re-active* rather than a *pro-active* stance. Directions are found on the basis of what is left when the worst options are ruled out, or whatever just happens anyway. So Phoebe chose her smaller college on this basis:

> Hobart's for druggies, Elizabeth [college] is I don't know I don't like it there (you been there?) No I just don't like the people there, Friends [private college] and that are too expensive... (Phoebe)

Rather than a path of best options, this becomes a path of least resistance. Often it entails just ending up somewhere without an articulation of what could be valuable or relevant in that move.

Social cluster movements

At the moment of truth, this is the third pattern which only becomes visible through praxis (in practice rather than in conversation). It looks a little like *Least Resistance*, but it has a *collective* element that seems to be central:

> Simon: I hate holidays, there's nothing to do.
> AW: Really. You prefer school?
> Simon: ... No, I hate school, but I would rather be with my friends and that every day. (Simon)

At the point of leaving year ten, *social cluster movements* involve going to great lengths to stick together with certain key others, usually peers, but sometimes particular family members. Colleges and course details, or job arrangements are sorted out in this light:

> I want to go there 'cos Sarah's going there. (Kylie)

This is one pattern of practice that is probably most likely to be criticised as short-sighted or illogical by teachers, parents or other well-meaning outsiders. Sonia, in a later interview, is being insider-ethnographer among her peers. She makes sense of it in this way:

> It's like with um, one friend, she's always had somebody with her like she won't do anything on her own – like she's always got to have someone with her. She won't even ring up somebody to ask about something like – [social security] – she wanted to get a job at Woolworths in summertime – and she said: 'Do you want to come, do you want to come?' and I said: 'No I don't want to work there 'cos I've got this other thing lined up' and, she didn't go. She didn't go 'cos she didn't have anyone to go with. (Sonia)

This pattern does not seem to be simply about high levels of trust of these significant others. Rather it is related to respondents' low levels of confidence in their ability to go alone, to interface with the world and/or its institutions on their own. Kylie later says emphatically of her own negotiations: 'I trust no one.' But like geese who can fly in the slipstream of the other, young people who are less certain of their own next moves can move in tandem. This seems to take far less energy than the investment required to go-it-alone anywhere else. There is also a lack of adult allies that are (avail)able to make sense of these things with them. *The key issue, therefore is peer connection.*

Although social cluster-movements are collective practices, they are unlike the *proxy* pattern in that they function without the traditions, wisdoms, networks or inter-generational life-experiences (grounded stories) of the clan and community-based practices. This pattern also does not necessarily equate to high levels of engagement in the *formal* task at hand, such as schooling or securing a livelihood. Again, while some others have found for themselves the *best* options, these young people appear also to have sought out the *least-worst* options. *Unlike their peers described above, the worst thing for them is not uncomfortable options, but being left alone.* Reasons for being at school are couched in vague terms, and those engaged in both *social cluster* and *default* movements (see above) were most likely to simply say:

> You need to go to college to get a job.

This statement is superimposed on their other stories, and has few or no points of connection with their other day-to-day activities, focuses or dreams.

Negotiation practices and youth agency

The patterns listed above are the cohorts' visibly different embodied practices for negotiating a moment of significant change. As already mentioned, some patterns had not been evident in previous interviews, or in conversations *because they happen not in cognition and conversation or abstract reasoning but in individual and group practice*. This, then, is one of the limitations of biographical narrative methods.

Not all of the patterns could be called strategies (entailing personal deliberateness), and by some sociological definitions not all could be said to entail agency, if agency is 'the exercise of will and conscious action on the part of human subjects' (White and Wyn 1998:315).

However, the *proxy* model in particular serves as a useful reminder that agency manifests in different ways. As middle-class urban outsider-observers it would be easy to only recognize the agency of self-aware and self-mobilizing articulate individuals, the type who can fit contemporary organization culture (*plan and project*). To simply measure more or less of these qualities could lead us to overlook other significant manifestations of agency.

Last century, Paul Willis (1979) suggested that amongst the group of working-class 'lads' he has studied, it is *only* at the *group level* that creativity happens (in this case, the claiming of alternative meanings, resistances to school, and early work-patterns). In the case of The Valley, a narrow analysis of agency is potentially disrespectful or dismissive of other significant and powerful and historically useful cultural patterns of practice. The problem though (also as captured by Willis), lies in the connection and intersection of these cultural patterns of creativity, these different expressions of human agency, with education, with the available jobs, with the directions of wide-sweeping social change, with future life-chances, and with the institutions that manage young people's transitions. These findings have some resonance with other contemporary youth research which explores conditions of social individualization, or the shaping of neo-liberal subjects in the social contexts in which contemporary young people find themselves.

Some of the patterns of practice that have been detailed above are far more portable, flexible and adaptable to new social settings and circumstances than others. Social clusters cannot always stick together. Stories that are practised only within clans and communities remain intact only within that group. The implications of this will be explored further in Chapter 8.

In the Myrtle Vale study, young people's practices point to significant differences in history and context. We will explore these below.

Patterns of practice, everyday alliances, and young people's different histories

How are we to respectfully make sense of this diversity in practice? The biggest challenge is that the less articulate, less 'plan and project' oriented respondents also provide many less verbal clues as to what they are actually doing.

When these patterns are overlaid on the two-by-two diagram of cultural orientations, some other things show up.

Figure 5.2 shows the different sources that respondents are *referencing* when they talk about what they are doing, who travels with them, or who is assisting them. Even when talk gives way to action, the patterns

		high	low
sources of ideas	**more diverse**	**Exploring** (family, school, peers, local community, non-local communities of interest, TV) {books} plan & project	**Wandering** (TV peers {isolated family members}, {isolated teachers}) default social cluster
	more homo-genous	**Settling** (family, peers, local community) most by proxy 1 plan & project 1 default 1 social cluster	**Retreating** (peers {or isolated family members}) social cluster default

Trust of social sources

Figure 5.2   Histories of trust and negotiation patterns

look strangely familiar. Over time, between interviews one and two, there have been a couple of additions to the lists of social sources accessed by respondents (indicated in the diagram by 'curly' brackets) but patterns have stayed basically the same as two years earlier (see Chapter 4). Some of those who were reacting against families in earlier interviews have now found allies within them. Those *exploring* are still drawing their world-view and ideas from a variety of global sources. Many have now discovered books as authorities in their own right. Those *settling* are engaging with, and listening to, a wide range of local sources. Those *wandering* and *retreating* have again found reason to extend their trust in much more limited ways. Here, engagement with social others is still happening far more reluctantly.

The most significant pattern among all respondents is that within the crisis and the dramatic changes of leaving year ten, respondents' strategies and other patterns of practice are closely reflecting their *everyday alliances*. They are drawing upon the relationships that already existed well before the crisis. Put simply, *individuals are negotiating futures with, and through, those who have already been helping them to make sense of the world*, and drawing only on their assistance.

To *plan and project* via school or jobs is a natural option for some (primarily those *exploring*). This is because they are used to listening to and hearing these sources, and because what the system is say-ing already rings true for them and their allies. Earlier, Connell et al. (1982) pointed to the ways in which parents' own histories with school shapes the ways in which their children can make sense of their com-munication with the school. In middle-class families, the messages of this source come to them in ways that are familiar and understood. In short, they can be heard, they are accessible.

Meanwhile *negotiations by proxy* are as natural as breathing for others (those who are *settling*) and are simply one extension of functioning within the mutuality of that small community.

For some, *social cluster movements* are quite literally the few reliable real-world options that they know. In this light, they are not illogical, but extremely sensible. Practices represent a tenacious attachment to allies (usually peers) and a scramble to hold onto those that they already have. There may be connections between this pattern and the lack of clear pathways that young people find themselves facing. Respondents have just demonstrated that confronting uncertainties and risk 'alone' is just too costly. In the context of a culture and ideo-logy of individualism (Furlong and Cartmel 1997; Wyn and White 2000), and in a situation where young people can bear a huge burden of personal responsibility for their own decisions (Dwyer et al. 2005), these practices among less advantaged respondents are illuminating. They speak of survival through collectivity in the midst of some fairly hostile conditions.

To *flee* reflects the will to live, which, if it is an issue, is the *only* issue that matters. *Default* practices are for those who ran out of options. In the context of these different histories of trust, each of these patterns of practice can be recognized as rational, understandable, and to some extent, explainable.

In these ways, the diverse embodied practices for dealing with the current decision-point or crisis reflect the biography and cultural milieu of each respondent. They are about histories in families, about relationships with school, with peers, and with communities that are already in place. They are about established patterns of rapport, but probably most significantly, they are about *trust*.

The young people in this study are negotiating this moment of upheaval only with and through those who have already proved to be their allies in the day-to-day process of making a life. As in chapter 4, lived experience of safety with significant others (or the lack of it) is framing the meaning of relationships with more generalized others. Those whose social world has proved to be full of allies can exercise a freedom of movement and extend trust further, going beyond the boundaries of where they have been before. This is enabling some to venture right out into unknown territory, even negotiating alone. For those who live within a world that has offered them few allies, the practice of clutching on to those that they have is all the more pronounced. Despite being understandable, this finding has *significant implications*.

Respondents' practices show clearly that *to offer something to this population of young people does not render it accessible* to all of them. If these findings can be understood more broadly, they may have implications for interventions into young people's other turning points and life-crises. Short-term outsider-designed programs that are issue-specific (for example, youth suicide) and outcome-based, about providing information rather than trust or community-building may not be the best use of resources. Without a history of trust, any service on offer to young people may well be rendered inaccessible to those who most need it.

Different negotiation practices meet the real world

Not surprisingly, the world comes to meet respondents in different ways. What happens next reflects the intersection of these different cultural practices with some broader structural factors that are way beyond respondents' control. All respondents find themselves in a world where social conditions are not ideal, jobs are sparse and entry-level jobs are not what many are looking for. Their experiences reflect wider social patterns, and particularly the disappearance of the full-time youth labour market.

Negotiating risks and uncertainties is a messy business. Even good strategies do not mean success in terms of what was planned (two of those *exploring* find themselves in trouble early). What happens may not be predictable, but it follows some time-honoured patterns. Those *exploring* move via the *plan and project* pattern into jobs and schooling, even if not quite in ways they had anticipated. Those *settling* have been hit by both the collapse of the youth job market and rural decline. Using the *proxy method,* only half of these move into the jobs that they wanted. Most of those *wandering* end up at college via *social cluster movements and defaults*. Those *retreating* flee – they make sure that they do not go to college.

The capacity of rural groups to look out for their own has been severely eroded (see Chapters 2 and 3). On the community's part this does not reflect a lack of commitment to their young, but rather the shrinkage of their own resource base (jobs, services, population etc.). Consequently, communities, particularly rural ones, have a reduced ability to deliver jobs via either the *plan and project* or the *proxy* methods. This means that *default* options and *social cluster movements* become a reality for individuals who thought that they had other quite realistic plans. This undesirable set of circumstances also represents a savage assault, for all involved, on their sense of ability to plan and project, or to look after their own.

For young women, pregnancy is one reliable and meaningful option. Although three older respondents have taken this path, none of this year's school-leavers followed.

In the year 1998, changes to the Federal Government's Youth Allowance scheme mean that *school becomes the main default option.* Young people need to stay in formal education to access financial assistance. This has some interesting consequences in terms of crises and their own meaning systems and stories, and in particular for respondents' negotiations with education systems (to be explored next chapter), as well as for said education institutions' capacity to cope.

Nearly all of the class of '97 'make the choice to go on' to college. These are qualitatively very different choices. Respondents are also very differently equipped to make use of what they find there. *Social cluster movements* work quite well whilst groups can manage to stay together. One social group has had a falling-out, and one student has found herself leaving school and having to re-think her career plans as a result. The practice of *negotiation by proxy* leaves individuals very poorly equipped in a local world where their allies are losing their resources, or in a world outside Myrtle Vale where these allies are neither present nor experts.

What we see here might be the collision of collective practices with a contemporary social context, which seems to demand mobile and flexible individuals. This disjuncture raises questions about *collective practices*, and the practicalities of maintaining them, or their portability or transferability, and the powerful implications here for individual mobility and individual trajectories. It also raises questions about whether being a flexible, mobile individual is the only way to be. Perhaps social advantage does not necessarily equate to long-term social good. I will hold that question for further thought.

Meanwhile, much has depended upon where respondents are putting their trust and whether it has been able to come through for them. It does not always come through. Private enterprise let a few respondents down. Some have planned to work in local industries which have not made or do not have any room for them. To have one's overtures knocked back is a rude shock. Brett re-frames and re-stories his own let-downs as we speak: 'I've changed me plans a bit.' While some are holding tenaciously onto their dreams, others change their plans to fit the reality that faces them.

To have one's plans stolen is a crisis. Crisis often involves the further loss of story (Strauss 1977). This leaves individuals in a changed position from which to function in the world. It messes with world-views and it messes with trust. Unemployment and forced school-retention both become structural blockages to those who are *settling*. These few respondents (perhaps representing many other young people) are experiencing blockages to, and separations from, their stories, particularly when these have been community-based. When the individual is not the keeper of his or her own story, removal from the community means dispossession. (Issues of the separation of children from their roots, from the custodians of their stories, in the name of improving their life-chances recur in history yet again. And as before, there are no simple answers). While some others have held onto their stories and will still talk in interviews about their frustrations, one more (*settling*) respondent, at this point, will not be re-interviewed, he is not engaging at school... . He is now in a story crisis. Away from the keepers of the story, he loses his voice. No, he is not interested in talking about it, and it will be a year before we resume contact.

Rethinking agency: you and whose army?

Respondents' negotiation practices are structured by the different ways in which they are able to make sense of what is happening around them. Beyond understanding though, beyond cognition and the things that young respondents will explain in interviews, negotiation *practices* are expressions of agency which reflect individual histories and social contexts in very powerful ways.

If youth agency is 'the conscious actions of young people in relation to the world around them' (Wyn and White 1997:140), to some extent, agency is embodied in both ends of the spectrum – both in the striving for excellence and in the will to live. The agency of the individual seeking what is best, or seeking what is least-worst, is there like a stamp on each pattern of practice. Among the most oppressed, survival skills are impressive. However, it is the intersection or fit of agency with social conditions, the level of ability to act meaningfully, creatively, and effectively that varies. These factors impact significantly on life-chances.

What is most clearly differentiated is the individuals' power to negotiate from within the context of their relationships to the social world. For this reason, young people's strategies, and for that matter, young people's agency, should not be seen as simply an individual phenomena but also anchored, via their social and historical relationships, to their context. Agency cannot be reduced simply to self-concept or self-esteem, personal efficacy, resilience or even individual and group consciousness-raising and empowerment. It is about knowledge and understandings, but also about the capacity to activate resources.

Agency only partly relates to the ways that individuals understand themselves in the context of the social world. It also relates to their different, culturally learned *patterns of doing* (see Connell et al. 1982; White and Wyn 1998) and social practices of drawing on different alliances (in this case examples are using books or on-line sources, using networks, using education). Individuals bring with them to these negotiations within their different world-views, understandings, and, *embodied within their practices*, the full weight of all of their different social alliances. When negotiating their futures, the social isolate or the respondent with few allies comes to the negotiating table very poor.

Qualitatively different choices: reviewing the choice to go on

In February 1998, and for the first time ever, most of the Myrtle Vale school-leavers will start college. Their 'going on' reflects a number of social factors that cannot well be teased out: wanting to; the closeness of the group who have finally attained a critical mass at college and on the bus; the paucity of other options; that messages about continuing education from their school have been taken on board, and changes in government policy mean that unless they have secured a job, or unless their families intend to support them, they have to go on.

Statistically in terms of retention into year 11, this class rates well above previous years. At face value, this represents a victory for government retention policies. Also, as statistics indicate (for example Lamb et al. 2000) it may provide a boost for individuals and their chances of employability. To compound this ideology further, in later interviews each respondent who goes to college, even for a few weeks, will retrospectively claim the choice to be there as their own. And if researchers or policy makers were to ask them, all would say that they were there: *'because you need college to get a job'*. However, qualitative interview data has shown that this means very different things to different individuals. Interviews reveal that respondents' choices are qualitatively very different, and for some they have become extremely limited. While many individuals have *laid claim* to their post-year ten options, other individuals and groups appear to have *been claimed*. The forethought and planning put into these manoeuvres locates individuals very differently in terms of whether their next set of arrangements with institutions are meaningful and safe.

Thus the 'choice to go on' is made by the deliberate, the distracted, the desperately hanging on, as well as the confused and the broken-hearted. This raises some questions about what it does mean to be going on in the current educational climate, not only for those who would rather be elsewhere, but also for those who are trying to do their work (staff, students) amidst resources and facilities that are now being stretched further and further. What we do know is that, on the basis of what is meaningful and who is trusted, individuals are equipped very differently for these transitions. All are being stretched, but for a time some people are operating well beyond the places where they are used to functioning effectively.

Thinking beyond the moment

In this chapter I have focussed on respondents' movements and stories at a particular, significant moment in time. Their stories reveal that this moment is not isolated in time, a before-after experience for which individuals need to be given a lot of information (on a level-playing-field). Rather the moment is part of biography, and framed by ongoing understandings, social relationships and different alliances. Rather than being simply a matter of choices, crises and decision points, the things that happen in these stories are far better understood as part of respondents' ongoing negotiations with the social world. For each individual, the moment is being handled with already familiar, already differentiated patterns of social practice.

How the young people deal with this moment in their lives gives some clues about how they might be dealing with many other moments. Indeed, later in the book we will see these patterns manifest again, across other arenas that impact on health, wellbeing and social participation.

6
Practices of Engagement

As I write this chapter, there is (another) debate raging in the UK over school retention and proposed legislation about the legal age for school-leaving. The arguments and themes are familiar in Australia and elsewhere, touching on themes like increased demands for skills and being work-ready, early school-leavers being 'at risk' of long term unemployment and other ills, providing appropriate options for disengaged young people, systems' capacity to cope, and suggestions of education and training being used as holding tanks to manipulate unemployment rates. Meanwhile, in part as a way to address these questions and inform policy, there is a growing international interest in studies which track where young people go when they leave education. Qualitative components are not always present in such studies, which is puzzling. Young people are not simply being processed. They negotiate. This chapter will dig beneath these topics as they play out in the lives of the cohort from Myrtle Vale.

Some of the most challenging questions for rural young people are whether or not to continue education, and whether to stay in their rural hometown or go. In 1999, nearly two years after leaving year ten, respondents are again being interviewed. Topics include what has happened, as well as future plans. Propelled by different understandings and steered by different opportunities, at the time of interview they have fanned out in terms of their geographical location and their social relationships. Their lives differ enormously from each other in terms of both everyday practice and the sense that they are making of it all.

This chapter will look at what is happening for the respondents. It will explore some of the challenges of conceptualizing what has happened, in the context of social change and young people's complex lives, and reflect on some implications for tracking studies more generally.

I will then propose an alternative way of conceptualizing what has happened, based not on the notions of a school to work progression, or on tracking young people through categories of student to worker (and so on), but placing the focus on the young people's own practices of engagement.

The chapter highlights the need to listen more closely to those who are seen as marginal, for the evidence suggests they are not a small minority. It is not only their life-chances that depend on this capacity to listen, but also the effectiveness of the very institutions which are designed to shepherd them.

What happened between interviews

In contrast to earlier years, at the beginning of 1998, nearly the whole class of '97 started college (year 11 and 12) in Hobart. This is a break-through for school retention. The unusual development can be attributed to multiple factors. Other options for local work are diminishing. High school teachers have instilled the idea: 'You need college to get a job.' There is a critical mass of students, and the young people in the cohort bring each other along. Probably most significantly, though, Australian Government policy changes. With the introduction of the Common Youth Allowance in July 1998, unless these young people have a job, or their families want to financially support them, they simply have to go to college.

After only weeks the shuffling starts. Several from the class of '97 are leaving college. The reasons they give include: getting a job; looking for a job; couldn't get into it; other life priorities or crises. But the most significant change is that some of those who earlier would probably not have been at school, have stayed on for the duration of year 11 and 12. However, as this chapter will later demonstrate, retention in schooling has not always resulted in meaningful engagement.

Overview: for those who left The Valley

At the time of this third interview, two thirds of the respondents are now spending a large part of their week outside their rural hometown. Some have moved up to town alone or with families. Some are there for weeknights, whilst others have continued to commute daily. Because of higher levels of school retention, there is significant postponement of other kinds of 'outcomes' for most. Two have secured jobs outside The Valley that offer significant future career prospects.

Most clearly at this point, respondents' lived experiences are polarizing. For some this is a time when the issues of livelihood, social connectedness, and meaning are being addressed, while for others it is much more about becoming lost or set adrift. This – being set adrift – is happening either outside arrangements with school, work and job-seeking institutions, or within them.

Simon's is one such story of being set adrift. By the time of our third interviews, almost two years after school-leaving, he has moved to another suburb. He has just quit a casual job in retail that he found meaningless, or rather, as he explains later, he was sacked after not showing up for work too many times. Unemployed and lonely, he rocks gently backwards and forwards and asks: 'Who've you caught up with from the group?' For confidentiality reasons, he cannot be told. Trinkets and ornaments are sparse in his basement flat, but the leavers' dinner group photograph, dog-eared from inspection, sits in the middle of the floor.

Overview: for those who stayed in The Valley

For most of those who stayed within their rural home-town, the dust has settled faster, but not always in the ways that individuals had wanted. For some, staying has meant compromise of other priorities. Being with the family represents a huge 'pull factor', and two who had intended to go opted to stay instead. One has found a full-time job.

The young women who had said that they would work 'in a shop' were indeed in retail, and three others from the group are there too. Reactions to retail jobs are diverse: from Ellen, who had a real drive to learn and get ahead and be promoted, to Todd, and his lacklustre: 'Not getting me anywhere.'

Two respondents encounter occupational closure. One of these, a young woman had sought an apprenticeship in a typically male career, and had been denied access. Another explained that he felt that his inability to get the job was the result of an ongoing inter-family dispute within a small town, and effectively he had been 'blackballed'. These complications added to an already diminished local job market, mean that both have struggled to make alternative plans.

As in other rural areas, work options in The Valley are mostly in primary industry and food-processing, or service industries (for example, in retail). This prevailing situation limits the quality of most available entry-level jobs to the routine and mundane, or the physically exhausting and the dangerous. For some of the respondents these jobs are both meaningful and fully appreciated. Dale enjoys his very physical work, and wrestling with the machinery. Several of the young workers interviewed, though, highlight work-hours, working conditions, and trying to retain some control of one's own life as key issues. As in Holden's much earlier (1992) study of early school-leavers, seasonal work presents both a safety net and a poverty trap. A minority of the local jobs offer clear future prospects. Two individuals have created back-up options for themselves (Navy, small home business). However, among those who stay, for every worker with a future there is one anticipating that the job may soon dry up.

Overview of patterns for different cultural orientations

By the time of the final interview, those who were *exploring* at the time they left school are disproportionately involved in both school (over two thirds) and work (over two thirds) and many are doing both. All of them have commitments outside The Valley. Two students have part-time hobbies that are in fact, promising second careers. Only two clearly articulate not being where they had planned to be.

Those *settling* are mostly occupied, either in school or work. However, only half are where they had wanted to be. Two are at school, which has meant moving outside familiar networks and ideas. Over half are working, which considering rural youth unemployment levels is a tribute to good strategies, good local allies, or both. One family even went to the extent of re-mortgaging the house to set up an agricultural business 'for the kids to work in'. As explained above, two have also made significant inroads into second careers.

Of those who were *wandering*, significantly *none* are where they said they wanted to be. Their interests have limited connections with the world of real possibilities of school and work, so half of them are at school and half are neither in school nor at work. They have not been able to make use of entry-level jobs and education options to further the glamorized aspirations of earlier interviews (although I suspect these were never really their agenda). The common pattern for this group is that their movements have stalled. Some will now snicker at their own transcripts: 'I can't believe that I said *that*', but few have tangible plans which replace them. Those who are attached to school or work are there primarily because they are forced to be (by parents or by economic circumstances), or because their friends are there with them. At this time over half of those who were *wandering* are now on job-search or other benefits, and one is raising a family.

Retreating young women are living in Myrtle Vale, working in retail and raising children of their own. The women in retail are part of a fearsome small group, fortified against the world, watching each other's backs and no longer willing to be interviewed.

Conceptualizing what happened

Around the turn of the century, using data from these interviews, I attempted to conceptualize what had happened. A much earlier body of literature, the status attainment literature of the 1970s and 80s, presented some interesting contrasts. Those early studies identified outcomes in terms of people's passage through school, possibly training, and then into workplaces and careers. By way of contrast, with these respondents it was interesting to see fast-changing strings of commitment, in and out of school and work, and other life-projects.

Of course, the patterns described above could not properly be called 'outcomes'. These are early days yet for this cohort. Another five or ten years of following respondents' movements might yield some interesting results... or not?

It was a relief to discover a fast-growing international literature which places these findings in a broader context. A significant body of research reveals how, in industrialized societies, wide-sweeping social changes mean that young people's transitions to adulthood have been extended in time, increased in complexity and changed in nature (Côté and Allahar 1994; Furlong and Cartmel 1997; Wyn and White 1997; Dwyer et al. 1998).

Peter Dwyer and his colleagues have noted that school-to-work transitions have traditionally been thought of as binary, and adulthood is still often positioned as an unproblematic status into which young people will arrive. However, in industrialized countries, research is documenting that, rather than the linear pathways of earlier generations, young people's patterns are characterized by movements in and out of training and in and out of work, in and out of home and other commitments (Dwyer et al. 1999).

One commentator writes: 'even after 10 years, it is difficult to see an end point' (Semmens 2000). Meanwhile, from Australia, after 14 years tracking their respondents, the youth researchers in the Life Patterns team have proposed that, in the post-1970s generations, they are seeing evidence of a 'new adulthood', where there may be no settling down into careers as traditionally framed, but, instead, continuing change (Dwyer and Wyn 2001; Dwyer et al. 2005). It seems that the days of claiming 'outcomes' may be past.

Correspondingly, even years after this third interview, what has become clear from most of the Myrtle Vale interviews is the open-endedness of the individuals' arrangements, even for those who have things 'sorted'. We are now watching just one group of young people who are engaged in a process of ongoing negotiations and re-negotiations which may be life-long.

A second observation from looking at the data is that categorical or static approaches do not work. In this study, as in others, when attempting to classify individuals' movements, nearly every category becomes problematic. Where previous generations of young people could be classified as 'students' or 'workers', many of these young people are now both students and workers. Again, a significant body of international literature now places these findings in a context (see Dwyer and Wyn 2001; Dwyer et al. 2005). Other researchers are also asking questions like: In an economy where part-time jobs are replacing full-time ones, should a part-time worker be counted as a worker?; What makes a 'career' in a market of part-time jobs?; Is it appropriate to speak about careers as being a marker of having 'arrived' at adult status in a market-place which increasingly offers short-term casual jobs?

Further, 'worker' is also hard to define in a rural market with its seasonal work patterns, its 'feast and famine cycles' (Holden 1992). The respondents in this study demonstrate that it is even becoming a moot point to talk about young people becoming integrated within a rural labour market that is itself dis-integrating. Whilst one respondent is secure within his apprenticeship, another apprenticed respondent is not sure whether the business that employs him will stay afloat long enough for him to complete his training. It is not just particular jobs that are tenuous, but whole workplaces, and, as Myrtle Vale's recent history with apples and logging demonstrates, whole industries.

It will be important to keep exploring alternative ways of conceptualizing what is happening in the twenty-first century. If we view the commitments in young people's lives by 'objective' or categorical methods, we cannot see that: while some are gaining a position of strength via their movements, others are losing strength; while some are gaining options, others are fast losing them; while some are being empowered, others are progressively becoming worn down and disempowered in their interactions with the world of work and education.

In this chapter, close examination of interview data leads to a focus on one central conclusion. *The most significant patterns are not in respondents' formal institutional attachments per se, but in the kinds of negotiations and re-negotiations that are taking place between young people and those institutions*. It will be important to understand the ways in which young people are engaging with the social others that shape their life-chances. How did they get there? What are they doing? What sense are they able to make of their circumstances? What can they do with these? If we are interested in better understanding differentiated processes involved in young people's transitions, what is important, in a time of enforced retention and limited options, is not to document where young people are attached, or the sequences of their commitments. Rather the need is to document what they are doing with these relationships, and what they are *able* to do with them. It is these dynamics that are making a difference so powerfully in respondents' lives.

An alternative focus: patterns of engagement

The young people in this study do not think of themselves as 'integrated students' or 'integrated workers', as if at some point they become somehow assimilated safely into institutions and cease personhood. From our conversations, as in other studies, a much richer picture emerges. Respondents indicate that there are different ways of doing college, doing work, doing unemployment. They make it clear that these are two-way negotiations, which are complex and loaded with meanings.

There are different ways of doing college. Sonia explains how she is making full use of the formal program at college:

> I went on all different work placements and I enjoyed that. And I wanted to do that to know whether I actually wanted to be a secretary, or whether to back out of it while I could, but I decided it was good. And then I um, and this year I'm studying 'Secretary in Business... (Sonia)

By contrast, on a school day, Sarah is just as likely to be found at the bus-shelter smoking dope with her friends. She explains that she has trouble getting motivated to do her school-work or to go to classes. It just does not interest her:

> AW: So why go to college?
> Sarah: There's – school's a – its hard to explain 'cos its something that I do every day and I suppose I really live for it, you know like um, I haven't skipped a day...

AW: So school is where a lot of your life happens now?

Sarah: Um oh – it's not where a lot of it happens but it's where it's created.

AW: Tell me more about that.

Sarah: Well if I didn't go to school a lot of other aspects, parts of my life wouldn't be there, I don't think, and they've only showed up since I've been going to college. So it's a really good place (laughs) and you have to keep on going, to gain a good social life and all that.

AW: Yeah, so it's kind of in your interests to be there?

Sarah: Yeah, and also to learn things, I guess.

These stories highlight some quite different approaches to being at school. Likewise, there are different ways of doing work. Respondents who have secured entry-level jobs are articulating their different levels of investment in them. Ellen is enjoying her job in retail:

Ellen: It's about the pay-check but it's about other stuff. I really like doing new things. I love training new people when they come on, and they've been getting me to do that a bit....

AW: So you put a bit of yourself in there?

Ellen: Yeah I do, I do – and they know that. (Ellen)

In contrast, Todd's job in the same service industry is a daily violation. Days at work are approached with reluctance. Time on the job is made bearable, sometimes interesting, by workmates, but the tasks are not something that he cares to think about. They are boring. He's waiting for the day when a 'real job' will come along.

There are also different ways of doing the job-search. Andrew has been pounding the streets earnestly looking for work for months. The search for paid employment is sincere to the point of being soul-destroying, and he feels that it is really 'messing up' both his life and his confidence in himself. In the absence of a real job, he's committed himself to a program of unpaid work experience: 'just so I can keep busy, keep out of the house, keep on track.' (Andrew).

By way of contrast, Nigel's approach to being unemployed is far more resigned and pragmatic. He has not really thought about what type of work he would like: 'just anything really', or what he could do now to help prepare himself for work. Having discovered that there is no work around for him, and checking the options as best he felt he could, Nigel spends most of his days: 'eating, sitting around watching

TV and sleeping'. He describes the process as making him: 'not happy but not really miserable – bit of both – just getting along'. Nigel finds the requirement to get out and look for work 'pretty harsh', because he knows that there is no work about: 'You don't feel like getting out and doing it.' He explains his rationale to keep doing it:

> Nigel: Just the fact that if I don't, I'll have no money.
> AW: Ok ... so it does work on one level 'cos you get your money?
> Nigel: Yeah – enough money to live on – depends on what I've got to do with it.

What we see here is a skeletal and pragmatic commitment to going through the motions, because it sustains him financially, and, for Nigel, to do anything else does not make much sense.

Engagement and disengagement

The most significant differences in all three institutional settings (college, work and job-search) are seen in individual levels of *engagement* in the *formal* task or program. In their interviews, these young people are talking about different levels of engagement in the daily process of becoming educated, in day-to-day work and in finding a job. *Engagement* is about a connection with a social other or project. Engagement allows flows and exchanges of information and resources. It requires openness, even to the point of being able to be changed through the relationship. Individuals' different levels of engagement in projects and with social others are shown by their investments, most obviously by the willing investment of *time*. However, time on its own is a particularly unreliable indicator, especially for those who have limited power over time-commitments, as do young people in compulsory schooling. As Sarah, Todd and Nigel have just demonstrated, it is quite possible to be present in body while not in spirit. More reliable indicators relate to investment of *attention* and *energy*, and of *self* and *identity*.

Investment of *attention* and *energy* relates to having really thought about the project. It is shown when the young person is researching options (what's going on here?); stocktaking (where I am in relation to desired goals and how my different achievements and assets are significant or useful); means to ends calculations ('storying' how it might be and what I could do now). Conversely, lack of engagement is shown when minimal attention/energy is put into the project, when respondents have not really thought about it, or when they are 'working to rule' (or less).

The other significant contributor to engagement is the investment of *self* and *identity*, an embracing of the role, being *fully present in the activity*. The most revealing indicator by far is best described as *abundant unsolicited storytelling*, which is something that occurs regularly in interviews. It begins with willing, spontaneous history-giving about a given topic:

> AW: Yeah, so you're leaning towards what sort of jobs at the end?
>
> Sam: Ah, anything outdoors... I've just been down the Franklin River for the first time... I was, as a trainee guide I went down there... That was really good. Got to do a day's guiding down there. And umm I just sit up the back of the raft and do a lot of guiding and yell out the commands and everything. Yeah.
>
> AW: ... All right, okay. Now, what do you get out of that?
>
> Sam: Umm, being outdoors. Yeah and with the people, that's great... And also you get paid as well, so... It's a dream job for me.

Such storytelling often incorporates rich imaginings about the future:

> ... want to do trips down the river and bush walking and stuff... I haven't done a lot yet, but yeah, I've hopefully got a lot of work over this summer to do. (Sam)

Conversely, lack of engagement is minimal investment of self and identity; and is what Goffman (1969) would call having significant 'role-distance' from the task. It is revealed when individuals are present (in school, work, or job-seeking activity) in body but not in mind (other informal programs, daydreams, being 'wasted'). It is also indicated by lack of grounded connections between the topic and the individual's own life-stories. For example, some simply say, as their sole rationale for being at college: 'You need to go to college to get a job.'. They have bought the line, but it remains un-grounded in their own stories of identity, and in their day-to-day practices.

The notion of *practices of engagement* can be seen as relevant to all social relationships. Although this chapter is looking most directly at relationships with schools, workplaces, and job-search programs, these are not happening in a social vacuum. They are both affected by, and reflected in, other engagements with the social world. Some examples of this relate to formal and informal programs.

Engagement in 'formal' and 'informal' programs

Respondents' 'informal' or 'alternative' programs are shared 'unofficial' definitions of the situation, and group practices associated with these definitions. Details of these are prolific in the stories of most of the respondents. Informal programs are most common where people have a shared history.

Some alternative programs fit in well with school, work, and job-search routines. In many cases informal programs, such as lunchtime chats, free-time together, social space-fillers, are treated as subject to formal ones. *In most instances formal and informal programs not only accommodate each other, but each also becomes significant in the maintenance of the other.* For Todd, 'having a laugh' is an important part of the day in a routine service job. Kelly and Andrew both explain how the loss of their old classmates and of their valued (informal) social program *was a significant reason for not staying on* at college. These ideas are not new. Other research with young people has elaborated similar themes, for example, that friendship is central to the experience of school (Coleman 1971), just as 'having a laff' is an important part of work on the shop-floor (Willis 1979).

In other situations and with other actors, informal programs can have priority over formal ones. This is true of Sarah and Kylie's experience. Sarah explains that she often intends to go to class, but then friends will bring out: 'a little something to share... And then you can't go in to class. You just feel paranoid like: "everybody's looking at me".' She explains that going to maths, 'wasted' is 'a really bad idea'. Here, informal activities come to significantly undermine participation in the formal ones. Such daily battles are particularly an issue for those who are already less engaged in the formal programs.

Interestingly, in Sarah's story, through her different engagements in formal and informal programs, school has become both a source of alienation *and* of social connection.

'Just Doing It'

In the absence of others with whom informal programs are shared, or in situations where no informal program has developed, individuals simply 'do time' – they 'just do it'. Phoebe has explained how school [college] is boring her:

AW:	Are you going to stay there?
Phoebe:	Yeah
AW:	Why?
Phoebe:	*'Oh you need college to get a job'*
AW:	... and job – what are you going to do?

Phoebe: I've no idea – I'm like the only one in my class who
doesn't know what I want to do.
AW: [So, college] … do you like it?
Phoebe: Nah, I'm *just doing it*.

For those who are attached to college or work but disengaged, and those who find themselves without an informal program in which they can engage, *all* options involve *withdrawing* self and identity, attention and energy from the scene. Respondents do this either by stopping, or simply *disengaging* and 'doing time'. So the option is either to be *not there*, or *not there in spirit*. What actually happens seems to depend upon the level of control that individuals have over their own commitments.

It would be untrue, though, to suggest that people are either fully engaged or fully disengaged. Engagement varies in degrees, and these degrees change with time, in lives that are also made up of other priorities. Even 'good students', oscillate between informal programs, doing time, and engagement.

Doing time, as reported by respondents is not comfortable. It is boring. It also involves some cognitive contradictions that are fairly hard to live with. For example: I don't see the sense in school/I have to come here; I hate bludgers/I am not working; Here is what I want to be doing/I'm not able to do it. Even for the most pragmatic of respondents, doing time is usually accompanied by fairly high levels of frustration:

I don't like sitting around doing nothing day in and day out … just sit there all day looking at the TV and listening to music – get up every couple of hours and… make a cup of coffee – and have something to eat and stuff – just drives you mad. (Nigel)

Doing time includes (usually fairly passive) hopes that it will not always be like this:

I'll grow out of it. (Ben)

or,

One day I could wake up and everything will go right for me. (Nigel)

and *only sometimes* are there clear expressions of anxiety:

Simon is being interviewed with his cap pulled down over his eyes. Between chain-smoking, sniffing, and rocking on the edge of his chair he speaks in short, almost unintelligible bursts. (Fieldnotes, 1998).

For some respondents, doing time is a lifestyle. It also co-exists with increased use of stress-relieving medication. For some, this is the central feature of a survival agenda. Dope reduces the angst about the situation in which young people find themselves, and becomes an alternative program with social engagements and connections in its own right. Several respondents also explain that, as an informal program, marijuana openly competes with their more formal commitments: by commanding the same time-periods; by chemically inducing 'laziness'; and by dulling and over-riding other stories of identity, and projects. In these ways the ritual becomes both a *response to disengagement* in formal programs, *and a powerful amplifier of that disengagement*.

Doing time together can become the basis of scavenger hunts for other informal programs. Individual stories reveal that groups are creatively cobbling together programs, using all kinds of available resources, such as cars, events, animosities, histories, last-week's stories. All types of activities are included, from the titillating to the mundane (just hanging around shops), from the socially sanctioned, to the 'senseless' (lighting fires in bins, car antics on the school oval) to the illegal (midnight drag racing). Driving around (and around and around), weekends partying, petty vandalism, historical 'feuds' between towns, and even involvement in car theft are discussed in interviews as seeking meaningful activity. Informal programs like this mean something to engage in, to invest in, to do together, to talk about and plan, to tell stories about, to embellish, to re-tell together. Other research also describes this behaviour (Corrigan 1982). The issue is not so much about 'leisure', or 'leisure boredom', as it is often superficially portrayed in youth literature and policy documents, but about creatively finding meaning and social connectedness in day-to-day life.

When informal programs are regularly repeated, they begin to get their own touch of formality, rules and routines. What started as something to do becomes the basis of some respondents' stories of identity, or occupation (for example: being a midnight drag racing champion; becoming known as a party animal; being my mate's bodyguard).

Issues of meaning and relevance

Respondents *all* say one thing clearly – albeit in very different words – that they engage where it is *relevant*. Relevance demarcates what is worth doing, struggling with, or putting oneself out for. Relevance, in turn, rests upon what individuals know, understand, are familiar with, and feel safe with. It also depends upon their stories of what they themselves are doing. Respondents of different cultural orientations are finding different things to be meaningful and relevant. Correspondingly, issues of work, education, and job-seeking are themselves all located very differently in young people's lives and frames of reference.

Exploring respondents are those who (still) have clear, 'global' stories, but they are neither one group, nor homogenous. Work can be: about a specific vocation (Nicolette wants to be a counsellor); chosen for prospects of a good career (podiatry has good prospects and Alyssa does not mind playing with people's feet); about more significant contextual factors (Mel wants to have her own business in a rural area and this seems to be a good way to do it); or rather than a specific job, a guiding set of principles and area of interest (Peter wants to be doing research, and helping to do 'something useful' like reducing land-degradation).

Among those *exploring* there are gender differences. The young women were talking in terms of being less bound to one job, and also discovering that they may be less available to be as career-focussed as they thought that they would be. Wanting to have families played a key role in these changes in ideas. For many, as in other research (Wyn 2000; Harris 2002) a key shift at this point is realizing that they need to negotiate or manage these complexities on their own.

The common thing about this group of individuals, male and female, is that they all expect work to be fulfilling in its own right, as a career, and as a formal program in which they will *engage*. Consequently there is a lot of emphasis on what they are doing now, the *right choices*, and *wanting to get the early career stages right*. It is this issue which stresses them, and it is this for which they are seeking support. Education and entry-level jobs are often understood as *relevant*, in this light. So too are other strategic steps, such as getting cars, moving, and finding part-time jobs to fund their priorities.

By way of contrast, among those who are *settling*, getting straight into local work after year ten is the most relevant thing, and a meaningful goal in its own right. This is a cultural orientation where *all meaningful (relevant) things are contained within The Valley*. In a climate where the work ethic is so significant, going to work straight out of school is ultimately the *most meaningful* thing.

For *settling* young men, there are other dimensions of meaning. Work is about belonging, as it is only via their projects (*doing* things together in a culture of *few words*) that young men are connected to other men in their community. Teenage activity revolves around 'blokey' projects, and they are already embedded in this world.

The familiar, and what I/we 'can do' is a significant part of meaningful work. Mastery of a project is a significant anchor for identity. In interviews, *settling* men's spontaneous storytelling is about competence and 'can do'. Work is about identity, how men become men. In a cultural climate where 'can do' is honoured, technology is recognized for the threat that it is. Other studies have documented 'exaggerated masculinity' or male 'physicality' (White 1997) and the way this overlaps with what is required in tough physical work.

There are still other layers of meaning for *settling* respondents. Time and again people from The Valley reveal in their comments that work is not just meaningful because of its *content*, but because of its much richer symbolic value. For example, in the data-gathering stages of this project, several adult locals helped me to fill in a table locating where all year ten leavers in the last ten years had gone. Their responses conveyed a quiet, if not proud, sanctioning of good, honest, humble work. The justification: 'we will always need garbage collectors' is as much validation as is required. The young men echoed these judgements in their own stories.

Further conversations revealed that this could be read on several levels. Doing 'real work', or useful work, for this community has significant meaning in itself. Old Methodism and a working-class work ethic provide a historical platform from which to value only 'useful' work. As Brett says:

A few jobs aren't worth paper they're written on I don't reckon.

Likewise job-security is a significant meaning for the men in itself:

I chose this because we will always need mechanics. (Mark)

Mark's comments may well also reflect local history and cultural exposure to issues of redundancy and lack of security. *Security* is a priority for some young people over job-satisfaction, earning potential, or career opportunities. In a national climate of precarious employment, this focus makes sense.

Finally, these things speak volumes about traditional roles of men, as providers of security for their families. From their earliest essays in year seven and eight these young men showed that the job was not just *a* part of what they saw themselves doing, but it was *the core issue*. These things, together, in whatever combination, mean that work is not just meaningful, but it is *central to their nobility*. So, to be *settling* and to be unemployed involves disconnection from: a role supporting a family; public face; the shared life of blokes; valued activity; self concept and pride. In short, unemployment means dislocation from livelihood, from community, from self (as identity is defined by what I do) and from the things that are most meaningful. It leads to a very *relevant* struggle to get out of this situation. It also means that to stay on at school is not just inconvenient, not just irrelevant, or a strategic detour, but a daily violation. It stands between these respondents and all of the things they find most meaningful.

Wandering respondents are the ones who (even at interview three) have glamorized plans and very unclear stories about how they would achieve them. Ideas of good work are (still) characterized by lack of real-world connections. Accordingly, neither entry-level jobs, nor continuing education are being treated as very *relevant*. A lack of engagement in these formal projects is the result. Here unemployment and truancy feature. Young people are leaving school because it is seen as irrelevant to their needs. They become alienated in environments that are not seemingly related to the world to which they are seeking access. Rather, these respondents seem to be seeking access to a world more like the one they have seen on TV, which is both effortless and full of commodities and fun.

The respondents who were *retreating* did not, in early interviews or later conversations, say what they wanted to do. This has meant that very little of what is formally on offer can be framed as relevant. As three out of four have disappeared from the study at the time of the third interviews, it is hard to tell what they are thinking now. It is important to let both their absence and their silence do the talking.

Through their different frames of reference, individual respondents are finding themselves quite differently located in relation to the things that are meaningful or relevant to them. Of course, then, they are also responding with very different levels of engagement to the institutional settings in which they find themselves.

All respondents are, in some sense, negotiating with the process of this research in the way that they would any other formal 'youth processing' program. Those *exploring* tend to make use of the opportunities for self-development (wanting to keep transcripts, even making notes of things to talk about in interviews). Those *settling* are often amused and not really sure of the relevance, but are usually (except when in vocational crisis) good-natured and co-operative. Those *wandering* will engage fully while it captivates them (thankfully in all cases it still does). Those *retreating* show a crystal clear pattern with third interviews: agree to do it, make excuse/not show up, make another time, again no-show. These tactics avoid trouble but also avoid confrontation (though honest refusal). I suspect that these are well-learned survival skills.

In school, in work, and in job-seeking activities, patterns of meaning and engagement are cyclic. For example, Sonia's commitment to the idea of becoming a secretary has led to engagement in the Vocational Education and Training (VET) program at school, which then shapes her level of skills, her sense of identity as a secretary, and her new networks. This process of increasing commitment to an identity in both public and private spheres is what Becker (1963) and Goffman (1961) called a 'career'. For Sonia, alongside some other significant relationships, this forms a foundation for making a life involving a livelihood, meaning, and social connections.

Conversely, though, lack of meaning in formal process leads to lack of engagement, which leads to lack of meaning ... and so on. At the time of our final interview Kylie was finding it much safer to withdraw her energies from the social world. To do 'nothing' represented far less trouble. Her Dreaming world presents a much safer option:

> AW: So when you do your dreaming thing is that just pure dreaming?
>
> Kylie: Yeah that's just dreaming because you know that's not going to come true anyway.
>
> AW: Yeah – so you can do it and you don't get hurt?
>
> Kylie: Yeah! Most of my dreams are all happy anyway. Yeah – I never have sad endings on my dreams....

Among the *wandering* and *retreating* respondents this tends to show up in terms of a routinization of life and skills with much smaller networks, and smaller numbers of social commitments which challenge or stretch identity definitions. They will tend to spend days in the company of peer groups, families, or simply their own heads. While these privatized lives are safe and meaningful, they are also quite structurally vulnerable (for example, dependent on welfare) and isolated (dependent upon each other).

Something else common to school, work and job-seeking is that they all involve a measure of challenge and day-to-day struggle. For example, even the 'best' workers get hassled at work, and the best students say that they find school tiring. Respondents indicate that if projects are meaningful, they will tolerate hardship. If struggles are meaningful, energy will continue to be invested. Sometimes, in fact, the struggle is an integral part of the way that different projects are storied and valued (for example, 'hard study' and identity as student, 'real men' and 'hard work', 'party animal' and 'being wrecked the next day'). Note here the significant role of shared meanings and cultural differences in ways of making sense of an activity. The mythology (shared stories) around different struggles are what makes those struggles meaningful to different cultural groups.

However, the fragmentation we see in some of these young people's trajectories, that is, their strings of commitments, often short-lived, reflects the fallout from struggle that has not been made meaningful. This is not simply an issue of a social group's limited cultural understandings or practices. Not all struggle can and should be framed as noble and meaningful; some struggle is simply the result of inequalities of opportunity and broader social injustice. It would, for example, be a fallacy to suggest that these young people should just recognise that dull work is good for them and get on with it. As Johanna Wyn and Rob White (1997) have suggested, it becomes disingenuous to advocate work as a good option and ignore the conditions under which some young people must work. Likewise, to go about educating these young people about why it is good for them would be to perpetuate this injustice.

A growing body of literature suggests as industrial societies we are creating more ways of offering struggle which is less than noble to our young. This happens through the casualization of the labour market. One of the issues of today is the proliferation of short term contracts at the expense of training and career paths. Effectively we are creating 'part-time jobs that go no-where' (Wyn and White 1997:124). Labour forces have been restructured to the point where many are now not able to enter the labour force in their youth (Dwyer and Wyn 2001; White and Wyn 2008).

For young people who find it hard to get a foot-hold in the market, economic reform, competition policy, the deregulation of industrial relations and trade liberalization all have the power to profoundly affect them through further loss of social protection and income security (Bessant 1996). If government policies formally only recognize unemployment as being the result of inadequate training for the individual, then many individuals are set for a lot more struggle. In effect, the push to get educated and be job-ready is setting up individuals to fail in a society where there are simply not adequate jobs for these people.

Even when work is found, activity that starts as being relevant and meaningful can progressively become less meaningful. In the 1970s, Willis (1979) referred to the factory doors becoming a prison to working-class lads. In contemporary industrialized societies, early school-leavers can also find themselves at a real disadvantage in the longer term, locked out of the formal economy.

Of course, a significant issue for some respondents is the collapse of the rural sector (see chapters 2 and 3). Under current social conditions, opportunities, and the things that are meaningful for many respondents exist in diverging social worlds, with each increasingly removed from the other.

These things together spell out the diminishing of what many respondents would see as good futures, meaningful struggle, and these being replaced by struggles which many are finding less meaningful.

Coherence and incoherence in stories and commitments

These third interviews are very revealing, not just in terms of what different individuals are saying, but what they are doing, their patterns of practice, and *how* they find meaning in past, present, and future. Some are actively making their peace with what has happened between interviews. They are storying the things that worked (the wins) as 'how we/ I did it' or 'things to do again', and the things that went wrong (the losses), as 'what not to do next time'. History is being processed (to greater and lesser extents) into patterns and frameworks of 'what I know', 'what I can do', and 'what I am doing', and into cumulative wisdoms which will guide further action.

Meanwhile others are doing something different. When asked specific questions about how they got to where they are they will say: 'I don't know, it just happened.' As we talk about what has changed, we will venture into a land of relatively un-storied incidents, fragments, isolated happenings, and conflicting accounts. These represent individuals' vastly different ways of working with their own life-history. There are corresponding differences in the ways that respondents are dealing with their futures.

In the two years between re-interviews, many plans have been upset or disrupted (perhaps no apprenticeship, no job). Nearly everyone has had other life-issues that have imposed on plans and thinking about the future in the form of sickness or injury, loss of significant relationships, changes in family circumstance, changes in nature of friend-ships, or blocked options. For some, these register in a major way in our conversations, explained as new directions, whilst for others, they have not been drawn into coherent stories and may well remain as unconscious saboteurs of action.

At this point, conversations with *wandering* and *retreating* respondents drive something home. *Assumptions about futures and being able to plan them belong to the privileged. They belong to those who come from stable worlds, those who have a measure of control over their own lives, and those who know that they have.* Other research has pointed out how one of the effects of confused feedback is learned helplessness, or a significant loss of capacity for decision-making (Seligman 1975). In Kylie's story this manifests as the withdrawal of her will to make certain decisions. 'I don't plan,' she says, 'because it just doesn't turn out to be right.' The world where people plan, and things work out, is not the world in which she lives.

This is, as much as anything, about the journey of the individual through time. When understandings, learnings, decisions, and prac-tices are seen to fruition, built upon, or otherwise rewarded, there is some kind of emergent journey (or several concurrent journeys) taking place, going to somewhere or to several 'somewheres'. On the other hand, when understandings, learnings, decisions, and prac-tices are undermined all the time, the result is fragmented journeys, lack of engagements or temporary engagements with institutions and other forms of community life, and lack of coherence in commitments.

These things have profound implications. While some respondents are very actively involved and engaged in the busy process of building futures, reconciling the past and now, and reconciling now to the future, others are simply not able to engage in these practices.

Those who are engaging in the process of building futures, whether global or local, are *making sense of now* in the light of these futures. For Sonia, to go to work in town and live in The Valley means that she needs to have a car, which in turn means that she had better get a holiday job *now* rather than go and spend time with her friends down at the beach. Although not comfortable, her days at work contain *meaning* in terms of an implicit reward, her car. Likewise, Joel will work nights and weekends to build up his own nursery business, in order to have a job when and if he gets laid off from his other work. Though there may not be many spare hours, there is a quiet satisfaction in making this dream a reality.

When *the meaning of now* is interpreted only in terms of explicit and immediate reward, tolerance for daily struggle is also lowered. Ben says that he really wants a job – 'just anything really'. We talk about criteria for good work. He explains: 'If I didn't like it then I'd just quit and stop doing it.' Without strong lines of reference to the future, to engage in things that are boring or hard simply does not make sense:

AW: Year 11?
Ben: Yeah I started doing that and then they sent me a form that said I had to pay them $270 a term... didn't have enough... I don't know I just couldn't be bothered.

There are still other implications. When *the meaning of now* is interpreted only in terms of explicit and immediate reward, this means that 'buzz' (adrenaline rush, fun, scares) has a much higher profile in the structuring of day-to-day life. It also means that other valued projects which do not entail a high and sustained measure of 'buzz' will receive only sporadic commitment. Ben will decide to do something and then become his own worst enemy. He will start school and then not show for classes, restart school and then quit. He says that he absolutely detests walking but that he hasn't got his driver's licence yet:

AW: What goes wrong with that?
Ben: Every time I get $25 so I can get my birth certificate I spend it on something else. So I haven't got that yet.

In the absence of a story that makes the struggle meaningful, individuals stop doing the things that are unpleasant (when tired, when bored, when it is hard, when scared). This is particularly the case if history has taught them that the chances of being rewarded for effort are minimal. If they feel they have no choice, they are simply disengaging (there in body, but not in spirit). So we find individuals doing time, or paralyzed, or simply giving up on significant career steps because they were hard. When there is a hazy definition of the situation, fragmented stories of what they are doing, or simply no recognition of the relevance of what is happening, it is discomfort that has the deciding vote in what happens next. By way of contrast, those who have a definition of the situation and reconciled, grounded stories of their aims have a reason to keep doing it, or alternatively, a reason to call 'enough!' and go and do something else (reflection and evaluation, decisive action, pro-activity, deliberate choice). Fear or discomfort does not have the final word about everyday practice when there is meaning and purpose breathed into it. The struggle is framed as meaningful.

These things have *implications* for attaining a livelihood. For some, school and the job-search do not make much sense. These people (because of social practices which are a result of cultural location and history) are effectively excluded from engaging meaningfully or consistently in the formal programs on offer. The result is marginalization, either outside these programs or within them. Respondents demonstrate that, when this is the case, we are likely to find them engaging elsewhere (informal projects, daydreaming) and building their 'careers' and group stories in other places (in their social lives, in new family units).

In a competitive job-market, amidst structural changes that affect everyone, those who are already privileged have a relative advantage. Youth-processing institutions (for example, school, job-search) are built around the *practices of the privileged* – geared towards making futures, and based upon the *assumptions of the privileged* – about even *being able to make futures*. Not all respondents have grown up in that world. And so, we are finding that neither can all respondents, at this time, partake of this world. It is simply not the world of their lived experience.

Making other lives

Although many are engaged in school and work and job-seeking, one third of respondents are making lives often within, but despite, institutional arrangements. Their struggles are important to document, because they are in their own way embodying the struggles of their generation, of people retained in education systems, on dole cues, and within work situations that are less than meaningful.

In the context of the lack of entry-level jobs for young people, retention policies, and 'pathways to no-where', there has been some international debate among youth researchers about whether this is a 'generation on hold' (see Côté and Allahar 1994; Dwyer et al. 1998). This group of respondents from the Making a Life study presents a mixed picture. Some are clearly very engaged, right now, in the processes of making a future. They know of no other social order and are engaging fully in this one (see Wyn and White 2000). Others, who are drawing on local stories of 'how it should be', talk about the lived experience of being stuck and waiting. Some have engaged in as small a social world as possible and stopped talking. Many, though, are simply daily engaging in other projects. This last group needs a particular focus here, and this is their story.

Turner (1976) was perhaps a symbolic interactionist ahead of his time. He predicted that increasingly people would be less able to find 'anchorages' for their identities, or meaning systems to which they could devote themselves within institutional frameworks. This theme has been picked up by McDonald (1999) among working-class youth in Melbourne's west, and in the international literature exploring choice biographies. This is also a particularly salient issue for respondents in the current study.

In the midst of conditions that are less than ideal, the perspectives of young people often reflect optimism. Young people are not passive and are engaging with their conditions in new and diverse ways, responding 'as best they can' to their circumstances (Wyn and White 2000:167). They find other ways of making meaning and social connections. In the context of the unattractiveness of the formal programs on offer, the diversity of young people's arrangements is evidence of the will to live, the will to make life meaningful. The sting in the tail, though, is that often these programs do not fit well with formal programs and institutional frameworks (school, job-search) and further marginalization is the result. Sarah's story of creative practices and the institutional responses will exemplify these patterns clearly.

Creative practices

Sarah explained earlier that school is still a central institution, but she uses it to a different end. Emotional energy and identity are still being invested in 'careers' and in projects, but they are of an immediate social, not of an occupation or future, kind.

> Sarah: I think the Friday onwards is the important part of the week. But Friday at school um, is good, though. There's always excitement in the air.
>
> AW: Anticipating?
>
> Sarah: Yes, what's going to happen that night – and you have no idea when you, walk out the door.

This is a way of structuring the week. Shared meanings produce the social ritual and rhythms that make day-to-day life more coherent and meaningful:

> AW: So what does a weekend like this give you, what's the main satisfaction, or enjoyment or whatever?

Sarah: I think that every week, from Monday to Friday I live for that weekend, and plan that weekend, and once it's over, um, it just takes you back to Monday again and – start again. It gives you some ideas of what to do though, for the next weekend.

AW: So every weekend you build on what you learned last weekend or –

Sarah: Yeah trying to have a better time, and a better time…

Building the weekend has become core business for Sarah. Building a career of better weekends. A kind of self-sustaining resonance has developed. Planning leads to regular and socially shared victories (including 'buzz'), and these small wins provide direction and energy for further engagement and investment.

Some other issues emerge here. This is the kind of 'resonance' of effort and feedback which some other respondents (not Sarah, not her many peers) are reporting from within education and occupation systems themselves. Why not for Sarah? Is it because the system is failing her or because she had never invested herself in the first place? Probably both. Analogously, different ways of making a life look a little like the weekly serial/short story versus the epic voyage. Education systems fit better with the actors who are engaged in the epic voyage.

From interviews, it seems as if getting a job has never been core business for Sarah, unlike some of her *settling* peers who are also stuck at college. Sarah has presented as pragmatic and uninvested in this topic from the start (in year eight essay, year eight interview, year ten interview, and now, in two long interviews). Her stance is by no means antagonistic or political or aware of the socially systemic nature of her situation. For example, she is not saying: 'Stuff the system because it has made no room for me.' Rather, it seems that her world-view or consciousness just has not got room for work ethic and job. These ideas are simply not meaningful or *relevant*. Despite many lines of questioning, in interviews Sarah would just not talk about working as a lifestyle. Her primary social others, the women of her family, have been marginalized in occupational terms. As a cultural reference group, they have made lives that are meaningful to them without it. It seems that the tradition continues through Sarah. *Patterns of exclusion become self-replicating through generations.*

Before this analysis becomes too deterministic, let us hear again from the human (agentic) side of these negotiations. Two years later, I would meet with Sarah for coffee to catch up on developments, and specifically to check the validity of what I was writing with her words. We talked through this text (above, below) and she left with a copy to read more closely. We would regroup on the phone later in the week for her feedback. Then she explained: 'This is alright... It's just not all there though. Where is the bit which talks about the importance of family and friends?' 'Ach' I confessed, 'I may have missed that. What shall I tell the readers?' 'Tell them', she said:

> Tell them that working is not the aim of life. That being with friends and family is, for some of us. Tell them that being a full-time mum is as real and important as any other plans – probably more important. Work is not helpful when you want to be with your kids.

Meaning, livelihood, connectedness, multi-dimensional lives and work-life balance... Sarah's message resonates not only for others of her generation, but also for others across generations in industrialized countries. We agreed that her point is important and belongs here, as is, in this book.

I am grateful to Sarah for making this point. The economic rational world is not the only one at play here. In the context of wider cultural assumptions, even as a well-trained feminist I realize it is too easy to uncritically draw on paradigms that celebrate full-time work as a norm and as *the* measure of success. I am encouraged and challenged by the work of Karen Nairn and Jane Higgins (2007) whose intervention, as researchers, is in the way they tell such stories. Young people are written as subject to conditions but also as acting subjects, motivated not only by economic wellbeing but also by how they want to be in relation to others.

Now, in a climate of increasing work hours, time-poor families, dormitory suburbs, and the growing body of evidence of the impacts of these changes on public and individual wellbeing, these economic-rational models of success look questionable, and no more sustainable than any other. Perhaps it might be time to listen more closely when people tell alternative narratives of the future.

Institutional responses

It seems that for individuals who have their primary engagements in alternative programs, the lived experience of formal programs (education, job-search) is 'hassle'. Sarah explains that she is putting in a minimum of effort at college because her core purpose is elsewhere. The school apparently does not perceive this to be a legitimate option.

For its next move in the negotiations, it has passed details of her absences onto Centrelink (who pays the Common Youth Allowance). This institution responds to Sarah with a threat: she is going to lose her money. So this week she has been on the phone placating the appropriate officers.

Sarah's relationship with college is pure, calculated pragmatism. It is also significant to recognize that the Federal Government is involved in a very pragmatic relationship, via the extended schooling infrastructure, with Sarah and several thousand other young people. This is a kind of mutual 'using' of each other via the education system, a mutual 'holding pattern', to meet other agendas. For Sarah, it is important to be there for the social project. For the Government, unemployment figures are lower than they otherwise would be.

What looks superficially like a win/win situation is actually more sinister. The relationship is not just pragmatic, enacted *in spite of* the goals of the other. Each party is seeking short-term gain, but acting counter to sustainable patterns for themselves. The relationship careers towards a mutual self-sabotage. Just as the government jeopardizes its own education system because of a glut of students who simply do not see the relevance of being there, so Sarah jeopardizes her own chances of education and career. Amidst systems that are increasingly punitive and coercive, getting caught-out simply means that more creativity is required in the dodging next time.

Avoiding formal program requirements without publicly contesting formal definitions involves 'artful dodging'. Artful dodging is also present in relationships with unemployment programs and employers. It can be seen when individuals find ways to fill in job-search forms with minimal effort, when they take a break whenever possible at work, or find ways to weasel out of work contracts with college teachers. In this case each is instrumental in the frustration of the other, but more than this, they reflect *mutual disengagement.*

Just as many young people are failing to engage in school, other writers point to the ways in which education systems are in many cases failing to engage in the most central issues of contemporary young people's lives. Preoccupation with the Fordist industrial-era goals of simply providing a work-ready workforce (Wyn 2007) or with a questionable 'mainstream' of contented students (Dwyer 1996) ignores the needs of many.

At worst, in the cases of education and welfare these relationships are based on a lose/lose contract. While those respondents who are unemployed are creatively rorting the (however inappropriate) system, systems are expending more and more resources surveying and controlling those in their care (Kelly 2003). Teachers are spreading resources more thinly in chasing up reluctant students, while the said students are often quite cheerfully undermining their own future life-chances.

As other past research has demonstrated (Willis 1979; Connell et al. 1982), the creative exercise of agency does not always lead to an improvement of life-chances. Young people's creative practices of engagement, their immersion in alternative programs, and their practices of creatively making other lives can be understood as manifestations of the will to live, the will to socially engage, the will to story and to find meaning in day-to-day life. As such these programs can be heralded as evidence of young people's survival strategies and as meaningful projects in their own right. At the same time, however, they represent the ways in which agents can quite willingly and creatively be involved in the process of diminishing their own life-chances.

Often, marginalized young people have been presented in research and literature as angry or upset, as anti-authoritarian, as overtly resisting institutional controls (for example, see Willis 1979), or even as quietly wounded conscientious objectors (see Presdee 1990). These respondents, though, present several different pictures. Except those *retreating*, they show few signs of anger, they are not mobilized 'against', not an organized resistance, or a conscious counter-culture. Many of them are just individuals who are dispossessed and doing time or doing other things, *within* current institutional arrangements.

Around one half of the respondents who stayed in this study, though, by their own admission and/or by what we can observe, do not neatly 'fit' the structures that are there to process or to shepherd them. These are the ones who want to be *settling* (but for reasons well beyond their control have not been able to do that yet). They are the perennially *wandering* and the silently *retreating*. Although these are local cultural patterns, we need to be clear that the dilemmas they face are not simply a reflection on the qualities of the Myrtle Vale young people. Other research suggests that the comfortable 'mainstream' is a myth, and that there are many more young people who are marginalized by current arrangements than policy makers would like to think (see Dwyer 1996). What we can see from the Myrtle Vale research is how some much broader social patterns are played out in the lived experience of one small, localized group of individuals.

In particular, there is a good fit between post-compulsory education to *exploring* as a cultural orientation. Only certain types of stories, certain histories of trust, certain negotiation strategies (for example to plan and project), leave respondents equipped not simply to *get to* further education, but *to make use of it.* Other literature also questions the relationship between retention levels and students' active participation (Dwyer 1996), and also the need for learning to reflect real roles for young people in communities (Holdsworth 2004). Meanwhile other research suggests that according to employers, many school-leavers exit without 'the basic skills to make them employable' (Semmens 2000).

It is equally significant to note the links between class and accessibility of education. Although not all of those who are *exploring* are middle class, *all (except two) of the middle class respondents are 'exploring'.* Education is the breeding ground of the powerful, but, in the stories told in this research, it is clear that it is most accessible to those already most powerful. This study manifests some patterns already familiar from other writing (for example, Bourdieu 1973). *All of the other diversities that have been discussed in this chapter, and all of their associated perils, primarily belong to non-middle class kids.*

Lessons to learn from engaging with these stories

This chapter has explored ways of conceptualizing young people's transitions. 'Static' ways of mapping their movements make little sense of the diverse and ever-changing patterns in these respondents' trajectories, and the youth transitions literature shows that this is a common research problem. In order to understand what is taking place, ways of writing more dynamic, processual accounts are needed. This chapter has presented one such account.

Because objective, distant and statistical records of institutional attachments and/or student 'outcomes' say nothing about young people's lived experiences of these transitions, they have very limited potential to tell us about what young people are actually doing. Understanding what young people themselves are doing – and able to do – becomes particularly relevant in a social climate of increasingly precarious employment opportunities, increasingly circumscribed welfare provision, and increasingly coercive school retention policies. It is only through talking with these individuals that we can really get a sense of what they *are* doing.

The chapter shows how an interpretive approach actually makes much more sense of the patterns in respondents' lives, and can lead to a much richer way of mapping their movements. The approach, which focusses on their *practices of engagement,* is processual rather than static, and thematic rather than specific. It is essentially about relationships.

It is about the ongoing relationships between young people and the institutions that shepherd, train and employ them. Even more fundamentally, though, it is about the relationship between on the one hand, young people's stories of what they find meaningful and valued, and, on the other hand, the options that they find open to them.

In terms of empirical findings, the chapter shows how respondents are *engaging* very differently in school, work and job-search programs. It shows how their own informal agendas can either complement or cut right across their more formal commitments. It reveals some exponential or spiralling patterns in respondents' lives showing: firstly, how what is meaningful (that is, what is happening in respondents' stories) continually shapes their practices of engagement (in this case with school, work, and job-seeking); and secondly, how what is happening *vis-à-vis* these significant institutional attachments and day-to-day encounters impacts upon their stories about identity, meaning, and their desires to engage. Respondents' lived experiences are varied, and while some are finding themselves well supported in major life-projects, others' lived experiences of school, work and unemployment are much more about doing time, getting by, daydreaming, artful dodging, and avoiding hassle. In the ways that we tell such stories, it is important not to simply focus on individuals' failure to fit into a given system, but on a much greater mismatch of history and expectations. These are stories about individuals who have no way of engaging with institutions that never really engaged with them, or the things that were meaningful to them, in the first place.

Of course, how young people are able to engage in the social world at all depends upon their ability to access some significant resources. This will be the focus of Chapter 7.

7
Resources

Young people have access to different resources for the project of making a life. Everything discussed in earlier chapters is pointing towards this one central theme. Across the globe a large body of work clearly demonstrates that young people have different levels of access to some practical resources that help each to make a life, for example education, healthcare, work, and housing. Meanwhile, other research shows that growing up in isolated communities can further limit access to many of these important things (see Chapters 2 and 3). Within *this* rural study, respondents' own stories have highlighted significant differences in their exposure to, and familiarity with, geographical, social, and 'systemic' worlds (Chapter 4). In turn, these young people have had access to different cultural ways of negotiating the changes that face them (Chapter 5). So, individuals' current practices of engagement in their work, schooling, and wider communities are a direct result of being differently resourced for these encounters (Chapter 6). When respondents were re-interviewed in 1997 and 1999, the issue of differing access to resources was highlighted in new ways.

Before the third round of interviews, interested respondents had each been given a package of their own interview transcripts and essays from 1995 and 1997. In 1999, four years after their first interviews and essays had been gathered, most were interested in looking back. While some clearly re-engaged with these versions of their own stories as resources, others did not. The conversations and interviews that followed were both varied and fascinating. By this time respondents' trajectories were taking very different directions, and in later encounters we had a chance to reflect on and unpack the developments together. This process reinforced some earlier ideas, but it also highlighted changes.

Most significantly, these second and third interviews show something of the *extent* to which individuals are being differently equipped, or resourced, and also how different *starting points can multiply* or increase themselves *within individuals' lives over time*. This chapter will present a picture of some of the most clear and profound differences that emerge, particularly as articulated in these moments of reflection with respondents. For most of the chapter, my aim is to draw out and name the types of resources that feature within these young people's stories, and the implications they discuss for their projects of making a life. Later in the chapter I will place particular emphasis on the way that combinations of resources (or the lack of them) are working together, compounding individual and group situations, to make respondents' life-chances profoundly different to each other. It is important to unpack these things in detail precisely because of their subtlety, their pervasiveness, but also their power to shape lives and lived experience. The following chapter (Chapter 8) will look more closely at 'resource flows'; at the everyday ways in which resources are becoming available to individuals.

Recognizing different types of resources

Not all types of resources are self-evident. Social policies and programming for young people will often work within very practical parameters, focussing only on immediately obvious, concrete factors (for example, physical proximity to local services or job opportunities). However, a focus only on practical resources provides a 'thin' or limited story about what is happening. Material conditions are important, and underpin individual and community lives, but they present only a partial picture of the opportunities and barriers faced by young people.

Conversations with young people can help to broaden these understandings. By listening closely to young people's biographical stories over time, it is possible to map a whole range of far less tangible but equally (if not more) powerful resources in use, for example things like language, story, symbol, and meaning (see Wierenga 2001). This chapter will highlight why it is important to consider access to these more cultural resources in decision-making.

For several decades now, ongoing and compelling discussions about resources have been happening within the sociological tradition in the literature about class and social reproduction, inequalities and life-chances. As these works tend to focus upon more hidden structural and cultural forces, the recurring challenge is how to converse respectfully and authentically with young people about these complex topics. Although links between social processes and individual lives might look quite clear to analysts, these analyses may have little resonance with young people's own lived experience. Young people may have little access to the languages in which the wider patterns are being discussed, so direct questions about these topics may not help. However by listening closely to young people's biographical stories over time, and reflecting with them about the content of their own stories – asking the 'how' and 'why' questions – many began to identify different layers of resources on which they were drawing. Their input has potential to inform deeper understandings.

An example might make this clearer. Suzy has a history of wagging school, getting expelled and recreational and habitual drug use. In our third interview, over café lattés and lunch, we talked about the question about how, in the light of these patterns, she came to be doing well in school now, while her friends are still 'hanging around in the Mall and on methadone'. Significant reasons include the fact that she was able to move towns, to go to different colleges and schools, and that her parents were well enough equipped to afford supporting her to try several alternative schooling options. However, there are countless layers of other resources that she has been making use of – to get to where she is now. Listen to her explaining:

Suzy: ... um so he (past teacher) asked me what I was doing with myself now. He was very very very surprised to hear that I was in year 12 – for a start like the look of shock on his face was like (laughs) you know like he thought I'd be a bum or something!

AW: Well you could have gone either way really couldn't you?

Suzy: Yeah, well definitely I made the choice for myself to keep going and do it.

AW: You made the choice – what made you make the choice – like when did you feel that the choice?

Suzy: ... I made the choice half way through grade ten...

AW: So there was a decision point?

Suzy: Yeah I realized this is not the life for me – what am I ever going to do with myself if I don't go to school.

AW: You can remember consciously thinking that?

Suzy: Yeah. Like I base it on grade nine – 'cos like in grade nine I had a lot of friends who were like street-kids, or people hanging around town – like I know them all and they're still

> friends – I just don't hang around with them (laughs). I don't want to be part of that life – and – I took a look at them and that's what made me – I don't want to be like that – I don't want to have nothing better to do than sit in the Mall all day – pretty boring. Yeah …because of what they're doing they're never going to have the chance to change that really. I mean that they might but it's going to be bloody hard.

This conversation captures the dialectic relationship between, on the one hand, the lived experience of making choices, and on the other, people being resourced differently in order to negotiate the social world. Suzy made a choice, and there is no doubting the significance of that defining moment. As the result of a defining moment like this one, the world is storied differently, engaged with differently, and negotiated differently. No matter whether this story is understood as resourcing her changes of direction back then, or authored to make sense of action in retrospect, this is a point only of academic debate and almost irrelevant. Suzy's stories are the resources that make current directions meaningful and worth engaging in. As such, they are crucial to social processes, and to her project of making a life.

More to the point though, in her storytelling about this incident Suzy is in fact listing the resources that she draws upon in order to negotiate the world in the way that she does.

Firstly, she draws on preferences, understandings or cultural definitions: about the potential value of education ('what am I ever going to do with myself if I don't go to school'); about the meanings surrounding time ('I don't want to have nothing better to do than sit in the Mall all day'); and about the emphasis placed on individual agency, perseverance and hard work ('I made the choice myself to keep going and do it').

She is drawing on understandings about self and identity ('I don't want to be like that'), on a well rehearsed story of progress ('Like I base it on grade nine') with a 'turning point' ('I made the choice') and an empowering punch-line ('like the look of shock on his face was like… you know like he thought I'd be a bum or something!').

But there is still more going on here. Suzy is also drawing upon cultural practices that are familiar to her, or habits as resources: viewing self through the eyes of another ('he was very very very surprised to hear that I was in year 12'); self-analysis, self-awareness or reflexivity ('I realized that this is not the life for me'); self-talk or self-coaching practices ('what am I ever going to do with myself if I don't go to school'); exercising alternative subjectivities or ways of thinking, or analytical separation from the flows of activity that are going on around her ('like I know them all and they're still friends, I just don't hang around with them'); and contrasting self to others; 'them' and 'me' ('I took one look at them and that's what made me – I don't want to be like that').

Each of these types of resource will be fleshed out later in this chapter. The key point here though, is the value in 'thickening' stories about young people and their differently available resources. Each of the layers listed above can be recognized as significant and overlaying resources for the ways in which Suzy is able to negotiate the social world, to engage, and to make a life. Thick, grounded stories, and multiple levels of analysis are required to do justice to these layers of lived experience.

Time and again, through each respondent's stories, patterns in the use of different kinds of resources are being revealed. As above, these resources are *practical* (the real-world-easy-to-see-and-count type); they are *symbolic* (individuals actually 'speak their tools' for making sense of lived experience); and they are *embodied in practices* (for example, habits) (for detail, see Wierenga 2001).

Table 7.1 shows how these differ from each other. Practical resources are things which individuals tangibly and concretely make use of in day-to-day life (for example, money). Resources of meaning and symbol are specifically about the way in which individuals and groups

Table 7.1 Different types of resources-at-hand

Type of resource	Examples of resource
Practical resources	transport education healthcare shelter
Resources of meaning and symbol	storylines conceptual frameworks/schemes definitions of identity stocks of knowledge language preferences/orientations
Resources of habit and practice	habits of reflecting and storying doing abstraction engaging in others' stories

make sense of themselves and the world around them. Resources of habit and practice are also cultural resources – these are the things that individuals and groups 'do'.

These three layers (practical, symbolic and habit) are, in one sense, artificial distinctions, because in real life individuals' 'resources-in-use' are all woven inextricably together. We will return to the implications of this at the end of the chapter. But, just as teasing apart the threads in a piece of fabric leads to an awareness of the strength of the weave, teasing these layers apart can help observers to see each more clearly, and to recognize the complexity and strength of the 'weave' within recurring social patterns and within individual lives.

Resources-out-there vs. resources-at-hand

To be 'resourced' implies that resources are not just available, but that they are being accessed by the agent in question. In the earlier quote, Suzy is mentioning, in turn, *only* her 'resources-at-hand'. Resources-at-hand are the things which respondents are using to help them negotiate the social world. They manifest both in the content and in the form of social practice. Likewise they emerge in our contacts and interviews, explicit or implicit within the things that are said, and embodied in the things that are done.

'Resources-at-hand' are distinct from 'resources-out-there' or 'resources-on-offer', which may or may not be accessible to young people, even if those making policies and providing services think that they are, or should be (for example, see chapter 5 regarding different students' access to continuing education). The only significant unit of analysis for this chapter, therefore, is respondents' 'resources-in-use' or 'resources-at-hand'. Emphasis remains firmly upon the individual or social group, and what they are doing, and able to do, with what resources. If this approach is adopted, there are implications for research and policy, and for interventions with young people.

Practical resources

Practical resources are the visible and tangible supports for making a life. They include such things as food, shelter, safe and effective ways of getting around (transport), education, work, and healthcare. An extensive body of youth research has already covered these things.

Just as practical resources become breeding grounds for other resources, the converse is also true. The lives under study here demonstrate that there is a strong relationship between lack of provision for basic needs, and lack of access to other resources. This also echoes the stories of respondents in other longitudinal studies (Banks et al. 1992; MacDonald and Marsh 2001). In the Myrtle Vale re-interviews it soon becomes clear that the lack of the basics – a safe home, of transport, of healthcare, food, – over time, are encroaching on the more complex and creative projects of making a life – that is, on relationships, passions, educational qualifications, ability to find and sustain work, or other life projects.

Shelter is significant. William highlights the cycles and 'catch 22s' involved in not having a safe home. He lives at Arthur's Caravan Park: 'because it's cheap!'. Poverty leads to more poverty. A lack of permanent solutions forces William into a lifestyle of more costly options. He often runs a fan heater and pays to use basic amenities. Young people find it hard to get other aspects of life under control when home is a wild frontier:

> AW: (to William): So what is it like as a neighbourhood?
>
> Will: It's not good. You walk around the park and there's a heap of drunks there – and they're all carrying on being idiots – yellin' and screaming – playing music – really don't make no sense to nobody – just causing havoc.
>
> AW: Do you feel like you're unsafe?
>
> Will: I have been lately, feeling unsafe, 'cos I keep getting' broken into. People keep crawlin' though me window and seeing what they can 'ave.
>
> AW: How does that make you feel?
>
> Will: Bit worried when I leave the unit unattended.

If William leaves his caravan for long, his experience tells him that his belongings will be stolen. He explains that this precludes other options for active social participation, like visiting mates or seeking work. In effect, the poverty and crime in William's community also gets in the way of his own attempts to make a life. A broader literature on community and poverty, community and crime, or crime and social cohesion reveals detrimental effects on the life-chances of those living in unsafe communities, or communities where poverty is an issue (see Williamson 1997; MacDonald and Marsh 2001; White 2001).

Like an unsafe community, home that is full of stress or conflict can also hamper engagement with the world. Elizabeth explains that she used to stay in her room because of fighting in the lounge room.

Meanwhile, for Beth, living with her father's alcohol problems meant survival, rather than creativity, was her focus: 'Well that was it, wasn't it? I was trapped in a way.' Other resources and relationships are affected too. For Fiona, a domestic refugee from a newly blended family, the share-house that she moved into actually led to significant social stigma, and this still complicates her life four years later:

> Gosh I still cop crap about that – about when I used to live with four guys – about where I used to live – that really upset me because I was going out with one of them and not all of them…

Fiona's story, like the others, shows how other far more subtle but fundamental things (for example, in her case social reputation and community acceptance, even years later) are also at stake in the quest for a safe home.

Transport (safe ways of moving around) is an issue for lots of young people, but particularly for rural people. Put simply, the distance adds one more degree of difficulty to things that are already challenges. So while going to school year-after-year may be hard, getting on a bus at 7.30 every morning and getting home just before tea-time makes it harder.

Respondents explain that it is also logistically more difficult to engage with the social world when all the 'action' is further away. Other research with rural young people (Hillier et al. 1996) lists sexual exploitation as a direct result of transport issues (sex is a trade-off for getting a lift). While this study did not explicitly reveal the same, other more subtle forms of oppression and confinement are operating. Jasmine explains that when she stays over at friends' houses in the city, so that they can all go out together, she ends up doing things that she later regrets. The evening's activities are negotiated on other people's terms, and this means a significant loss of autonomy and control, and compromises that scare her. So rather than going out: 'I prefer to stay home – because at least then I know that I'm not going to get into any trouble.'

Food/Nutrition is also a significant issue. Myrtle Vale District High School staff identify that some students come to school without having had breakfast and that this is affecting energy, performance levels and concentration in class. Staff also explain that there is a strong relationship between this pattern and students' socio-economic background.

Economic stability is central to this picture. A lack of money means that other things also become beyond reach. As discussed in Chapter 2, this can be true within individual lives, within families, and within entire social settings.

Healthcare is easy to overlook if systems are working. However, among all of those interviewed, only working-class families reported problems with 'ADHD', alcoholism, epilepsy, and with the ability to cope as a parent because of debilitating physical illness. Although the middle-class families involved in the research may well have confronted some similar concerns, the fact that only *some* respondents raised them in interviews points to broader social issues. It points to the differential distribution of resources which assist with management of these health conditions, but also the structural conditions that foster the problems in the first place. Only for some, these become issues that would impinge upon working, schooling, and upon futures.

Practical resources: the implications

This list of relevant practical resources is potentially limitless (for example, local work options, qualifications). The point here, though, is that each resource multiplies within individual lives, in turn providing links to other practical resources. Two other significant implications arise from *all* respondents' stories. Firstly, access to practical resources means access to more choices. Secondly, it means protection, by offering more chances.

Firstly, regarding more choices, access to extra practical resources manifests in the ways that individuals and their families have more options for confronting challenges, or more ways of making hard things work. Continuing education becomes difficult for rural people, but Emma can live in the city. The young people who go to university are either those whose families have the resources to move for the duration, or who have infrastructures in place to send their children elsewhere to live.

Access to practical resources means that individuals have more choices in the ways that they engage with the world. Examples shared earlier (in Chapter 4) include the flow-on-effects of geographical travel and exposure. These effects manifest within individuals' lives and stories later as increased scope in available geographical, social (networks) and institutional worlds of resources which they draw upon. Access to these practical resources has meant expanded opportunities for creativity.

Differences in access to options also manifest in conversations and in follow-up-interviews. Although one group is locally resourced, and the other is more globally resourced, among those *exploring* and *settling*, most choices are flanked by multiple good options and are a platform for creativity. Pete's interview starts in the following way:

> Um, I was just finished year 12 and on holidays and I'm not knowing what to do next year... I've been thinking all through college to go to Uni, but just the last month or so I've been thinking to go away for a year. Just travel around Australia or something and then go to Uni.

and Dale's:

> I like it [heavy warehouse work]. Uh – one day – if I didn't work in another job, and done this (gestures at home grown part-time business) full-time I'd make a lot more money than I do... When I started it was just a hobby.

For others (particularly those *wandering* and *retreating*), options are more limited:

> Oh the Social Security just rang up one day and said that they had work and that was it – I sort of didn't have a choice in the matter. (William)

Secondly, access to practical resources means more chances. Access to practical resources (for example, safe homes, ways of getting around, work options) means that individuals have more chances to 'stuff up' with relative impunity. Many individuals are able to engage in experimentation, exploration, play with options, some (like Suzy) even severing links with work or school. However, in terms of reconnections with these institutions, only some can find their way back. For others, hastily made decisions or 'cluster movements' mark the beginning of more narrowly defined careers and dramatically reduced institutional support. An earlier deviation can become the basis of an alternative or 'deviant' career.

Here is one example. Ben and Simon have trouble attending classes in year 11, and they stop going. Their families are neither geographically nor economically well situated to shop for a suitable school to accommodate them. Once they quit school, issues of geographical 'stuckness' and local peer culture work together to keep each of them well locked into their previous choices:

> Only went to a couple of classes – spent the rest of the time just mucking around with me friends. Then I quit – I haven't been doing

much really... a lot of them spending time in the bush smoking dope – that's what I was doing. (Ben)

At the same time, their own networks are able to offer little by way of work, or other legal means of support. These things shape not just who gets named as naughty, but to whom the label sticks (see Becker 1963), who gets told not to come back to school, and who can go elsewhere and start again. Other studies have shown how access to resources impacts on criminalization processes. At a community level, complex patterns of locational disadvantage, social cohesion and exclusion dovetail to create climates for criminal activity (Williamson 1997; MacDonald and Marsh 2001; White 2001).

To 'choose to change' is a manoeuvre that may be reserved for the more privileged. In this context, Suzy's (earlier) story reads like the tale of a cat with nine lives. Suzy's uncle owns a clothing boutique, and her mother owns a café, and each is a setting in which she can find work. These options become effective buffer-zones between Suzy and potential crisis. When someone's parents are co-owners of the system, by birthright they get more chances to get it wrong, to change their minds, or to change course in mid-flight. This is important. Internationally, research is showing that complicated 'transitions' (in and out of home, in and out of work, in and out of education) are increasingly becoming a reality for young people in industrialized countries (Côté 2000; Dwyer and Wyn 2001). Having links to significant practical resources, in this case, safe homes, other schools, work options, potentially makes these juggles and transitions far less hostile.

On the basis of these stories, young people's access to practical resources could be said to serve a two-fold function, both in providing greater options for creativity in their negotiations and engagements, and also in creating a layer of protection around said negotiations and engagements. In a time where citizens are increasingly placed as 'consumers' (Wyn and White 1997) and lifestyle 'choice' is heralded as a way of life (see White and Wyn 1998), this is a critical issue.

Access to practical resources is actually shielding many of the young people from external risks. This becomes very significant if we accept that we are part of a global society where risk and uncertainty are also growing issues (Beck and Beck-Gernsheim 2002). In a 'risk society', access to economic resources and related practical resources acts as buffer-zones, and risks are shifted onto others. Likewise, in a national economy that 'requires' a certain level of unemployment in order to have a ready army of wage-labourers, Suzy is now in school *and* working, while Ben and Simon are (usually) unemployed.

Other kinds of resources

Practical, tangible, and physical resources like those outlined above are hugely significant in shaping young people's lives, their learning, their wellbeing and social participation. However, repeat interviews reveal that other kinds of resources, of meaning and identity, of habit and practice (refer back to earlier scheme), are also powerful carriers of social birthright (Wierenga 2001). These resources also multiply over time and have the power to shape lives. These patterns have significant implications for learning, for active social participation, and for wellbeing. A more detailed analysis is written elsewhere (Wierenga 2001) but the patterns are outlined below.

Resources of meaning and symbol

In interviews, *individuals speak their tools* for making sense of the world. Diverse sets of meanings – about identity and reality – form resource-bases for negotiating and engaging with the social world. Early symbolic integrationists and phenomenologists provided some useful ways to describe these ideas. The character of things is mediated by symbols (Mead 1955:125). Individuals represent and interact with the world through symbols (Berger and Luckmann 1967; Strauss 1977). Over time the way individuals understand and respond to the world becomes part of their identities, and their 'moral' careers in the world (Goffman 1961). Interview data is full of examples.

Some of the most pronounced include resources of identity (me, us and them).

Resources of identity: 'me'

In interviews, individuals are drawing on definitions of, and stories about identities in two ways: for mobilization and for resistance. Firstly, using phrases like 'what I do', 'what I don't do', 'what I like', 'what I hate', 'I'm always...' and 'I never...', individuals are framing and outlining different conceptions of 'self' and their varied, recognizable social faces of 'me'. Grounded within histories, these have implications for futures, providing recipes, proscriptions, prescriptions, and sets of permissions, for different negotiations and engagements. While the significance of such stories emerged with early interviews (refer back to Chapter 4), it presented even more clearly in repeat interviews, by which time respondents' increasingly different engagements were feeding back into more concrete and defined definitions of themselves. For example, from earlier hoping to be a secretary, Sandra is now half-way qualified to be a secretary; Fiona has shifted from rebel to activist, Simon, from 'Homeboy' to potential music DJ, and Sam, from outdoors person to potential adventure tour guide.

By now, five years of hindsight reveal the power of being able to tell clear stories of 'past, present, future, and me', in terms of accessing other resources. In contrast, individuals who earlier told unclear stories, have been ill-equipped to powerfully negotiate changes (see Chapter 5), and are having trouble engaging meaningfully with ongoing school and work-focussed institutions (see Chapter 6), which in turn impacts on their possibilities for other forms of social participation.

Stories about identity are also being used by respondents as a form of resistance. Sonia's stories about being 'different' or 'other' to her friends have become an integral part of her career as a conscientious student:

> ...and one of my friends said before 'you know you've changed heaps – you never used to be like that – to state your own opinion'. I used to follow but now I'm not a follower any more, I do what I want.

Identity definitions are about claiming and owning certain ways of engaging in the world. These stories about 'me' can form a symbolic shield:

> I can't really see the point in people coming here and not going to class – what's the point in coming really – it's stupid.

Such stories do not only deflect the sting of difference, but employ or make use of it: defining against, and claiming the difference as right, legitimate, or preferable. The description of 'the other' has become a necessary component of this self-definition:

> It's like with um one friend she's always had somebody with her, like she won't do anything on her own, like she's always got to have someone with her. She wanted to get a job ...and she said: 'Do you want to come, do you want to come?' and I said: 'No I don't want to work there 'cos I've got this other thing lined up.' and, she didn't go. She didn't go 'cos she didn't have anyone to go with. She didn't

> go 'cos she's a follower – like she's always just stuck with other people.

Time also features in these stories. Individuals who have been most powerful, most directed, in their own negotiations also have clear stories about the difference between past and now, now and future.

> One thing that's changed lot since probably grade, maybe grade ten is I've really learned to put my foot down like somebody would say to me: 'Let's go do this', and I'd say: 'OK' … *but now* if I don't want to do something I'll just say I don't want to do something like they won't force me and it's like: 'No I don't want to do it just drop it, OK?' (Sonia)

Like practical resources (for example, cars, computers) such definitions and resources of meaning can open possibilities or close them down. It all depends upon who 'I' am, who 'they' are, what 'then' means and what 'now' means. These things depend upon the different culturally available options.

Stories about identity should not be overlooked in any exploration of young people's most significant, and differently available resources. Definitions of identity can function just like practical resources. Firstly, they multiply within individuals' lives. Secondly, as recipes, possibilities, or a set of permissions for creative negotiations and engagements with the world, and thirdly, they are being used as a protective or fortifying interface for negotiations with others in everyday life.

There is also a significant relationship between this type of resource – symbolic resources (in this case, related to identity) and the practical resources mentioned earlier. In defining self in certain ways, individuals literally define themselves into or out of practical possibilities (for example going on to education, or 'I don't go to doctors'). This is as powerful a force as any practical barrier to access.

Resources of identity: 'we'

Stories about 'me' are enmeshed with stories about my people, be they family, peers, mentors, or community. For most respondents in this study, the frequency of spontaneous we-references suggests that membership of inter-generational groups (clans) is far more central to identity and story than peer-group membership. We-references can become almost invisible as they are easy to take for granted. They only become really noticeable in the lack (see Chapter 8).

Understandings about 'we' locate individuals in social space and time – not just within their present company, but (for the luckier ones) among those who have gone before and those who will come after them. 'Predecessors' and 'successors' are very significant in making sense of life-course and status-passage (Strauss 1977:10). In interviews, respondents are creating understandings about the themes that are important to them (such as self-reliance, a close community) by invoking a company of those present, predecessors and successors:

> One thing most of *the Jamisons* [my family] like to do is go out bush and get [fire]wood … (Noah)

While the embodied experience of existing here and now is one focus of everyday life, for some respondents, dreaming, planning, and thinking ahead are also significant. Anticipated future company are engaged as recipient, audience or witnesses:

> Just things that, like I've always planned to – as kids we've always gone to Fiddleback for Christmas and I've always wanted to do that with my family as well… All the stuff I've grown up with, I want to give my kids the same. (Mmmm hmmm.) Like the way my, like with my Dad, he likes going fishing or, just taking the kids out in the boat or going down the beach… Like we've always had great fun down there, and that's one thing I want to do as well. (Sonia)

For others, future plans involve, instead, a quest to balance the ledger of history:

> I don't want to be one of those families where you know, one of the parents isn't there … I want [my kids] to have a nice normal family life like I've never had (laughs). I really want to do it. (Fiona)

These stories, and the company within them, become a core part of what individuals are about.

Respondents' available understandings of 'we' are functioning like other resources. They multiply over time – identities can be sources of mobilization as much as products of it. That is, the way people understand themselves shapes action, which shapes the way that they understand themselves. 'We' is also central to respondents' ability to be creative. A large proportion of respondents' repertoires about 'I' are made up from components of 'we'. If there are limited 'we's that young people can draw upon, there are also very few I's, and correspondingly, very few options and permissions. These give rise to 'thin' stories about possibilities for 'me'. At their best, 'we' forums do not simply mean options for creativity, but also protection for the young within the company of the pack. Shared practices and traditions provide not only rich sources of material for individuals as they plan futures, but also places of return, of security, when life changes or the world seems a little crazy.

Identities in context: subjectivities

For some decades writers about young people have recognized the role of identity in the ways that young people are able to negotiate the world. Languages about these topics are often psychological, reflecting psychology's historical domination of 'youth' writing (see Jones and Wallace 1992; Wyn and White 1997). More recently, through the sociologies that have focussed on knowledge and power, a focus has turned to realities, experience, consciousness, and how things become known to and embodied by individuals. This is the study of subjectivities.

Respondents have diverse resources-at-hand for making sense of the social world in which they live. In terms of contemporary sociological thought, the notion of *discourse* (Foucault 1980) or different socially available storylines might seem a most obvious conceptual tool. However the fine-grained data in these young people's stories also has called for a more eclectic toolbox. Other sociological traditions provide more useful, and publicly accessible (if overlapping) ways of making sense of this data. The conceptual tools I have found most useful come from social anthropology, phenomenological and other interpretive traditions, through 'schemata' or 'frames', 'stocks of knowledge', 'themes', 'convictions', 'language', 'orientations' and 'preferences'. These lists and descriptions are covered more fully elsewhere (see Wierenga 2001).

Resources of symbol and meaning: the implications

Each of the things mentioned above – different frames, schemata, stocks of knowledge, themes, convictions, language, orientations and preferences – are resources which differently equip these young people to negotiate and engage with the social world. Each is a collection of the symbolic tools with which individuals make such differentiated choices. As Willis (1979) suggested, it is only through the combination of the operation of creativity, will *and culture,* that some social differences could ever be so successfully perpetuated in young people's lives and between generations.

Further, these 'symbolic' resources have similar implications to more 'practical' resources. When accessible and accessed, they become tools of creativity. They also provide protection by equipping individuals to make sense of, and find their way within the (often crazy) world that surrounds them.

Following Garfinkel (1967), contemporary authors have been writing about the issue of 'reflexivity' and social change. 'Reflexivity' is agency reflecting upon itself, and also upon its conditions of existence. It entails the capacity for autonomy and creativity (Giddens 1994b). Giddens and other authors (Beck 1992; Beck et al. 1994; Lash 1994; Beck and Beck-Gernsheim 2002) suggest that late modernity creates conditions of 'increased reflexivity', where individuals need to be increasingly mobile or open to change, and increasingly reflexive – that is 'reflexively mobilized'. Within a setting like this, 'symbolic resources' become far more important. They determine the extent to which individuals can be reflexive and reflexively mobilized. In effect, different access to information means inequality of 'reflexivity chances' (Lash 1994). This means there are different opportunities for the individual to reflect upon themselves and/or their conditions, and to act creatively in a changing world.

Within this conceptual framework and within these understandings of social change, symbolic resources like the ones discussed in this chapter become increasingly important.

Resources of habit and practice

The most pervasive, powerful, but subtle differences between repeat-interviews are still to come. When analysing the interviews for my PhD thesis I found that significant chunks of transcript could best be differentiated by using 'verb' categories like: 'storytelling' or not; 'doing abstraction', or 'doing a concrete'; doing reflection; doing critical thought (Wierenga 2001). This material again reinforces the idea that social differences (class and gender) are not best understood as categories of people, but as differences in practice, 'in what they do with their relationships and their resources' (Connell et al. 1982:33).

Implications of habit and practice

The practices listed above are prominent examples only (for more examples, see Wierenga 2001). Particularly those practices pertaining to local life have received insufficient explanation because of my own 'outsider' limiting frames and resources for understanding them. The point, though, is that *habits and practices are cultural legacies that shape possibilities.*

Resources of any kind mean power in negotiations. As the examples above have shown, this is also pertinent to understanding resources of habit and practice. Like *all resources* discussed in this chapter, resources of habit and practice firstly: multiplying themselves (over time, as above) within group and individual lives, in practice; secondly, offer possibilities of creativity (about ways of engaging, negotiating); and thirdly, offer a layer of protection (accessing resources external to the situation; some degree of analytical separation from what happens around them; accessing tools for 'crap-detection'). Put simply, some habits and practices leave individuals able to be far more pro-active and flexible in the process of making a life.

Interwoven layers of resource

People's ability to activate resources is a central part of agency (White and Wyn 1998). The findings discussed above suggest that agency involves being able to access and to activate resources at many levels – particularly practical, symbolic and habitual.

Respondents' stories have already demonstrated how access to particular resources (like language, themes, or habits of storying) becomes multiplied within their lives over time. These patterns are made more complex as layers of habits and available symbols are overlaid – they multiply with and compound each other in practice. So, for example, respondents' habits of storying the possibilities for themselves are greatly enriched by a large repertoire of articulated passions or themes. Habits of critical analysis of others' stories – or culturally shared storylines – are made all the more powerful by rich vocabularies (such as frames, schema, language) of symbols with which to do that.

The relationships of all of these factors within the history of a social group – shared practices, habits, and symbols – Bourdieu calls 'habitus': 'history turned into nature' (1977:78), and: '... a system of lasting, transposable dispositions which, integrating past experiences, functions any moment as a matrix of perceptions, appreciations and actions...' (Bourdieu 1977:82–3). He sees habitus as both 'structured structures' and 'structuring structures' (1977:72), and as being central to understanding the processes of cultural reproduction of inequalities.

All of this also points to the interwoven-ness, rather than the opposition, of issues of agency and structure. Social structures, rather than obscuring individual and group action, are intimately involved in the production of that action, and are productions of same (Giddens 1979).

At a more grounded level, though, we could say that people who can access certain understandings and ways of doing things are also able to access certain practical opportunities, and that engaging in these in turn will offer access to certain other understandings and practices (and so on).

It is important here to look at how tangible (practical) resources relate to the less tangible (cultural and symbolic) resources. This is not the place to enter classic sociological debates: 'subjectivism' versus 'objectivism' (Bourdieu 1977); 'cultural autonomy' versus 'economic determinism' (see Williams 1981b). Note, though, that for the respondents in this study, there is a clear relationship between physical conditions and cultural practice, between being able to access practical resources, and patterns of accessing resources of symbol and habit. Over the time of this study, the causal relationships seem to be going both ways.

Williams (1981b:189) points to 'the degree of closeness... between the conditions of most practices and a deeply organized form of social relation'. At a grounded level, this is exemplified as respondents' social practices are a reflection of where they have come from, and they also play a large part in where they will be able to go.

Being engaged in the world always involves creativity. Within the context of social change, and as we have seen in The Valley, at this time all are being stretched (at least a little) beyond what they know, but some will be able to be far more creative with the constraints and opportunities that face them. Those who are being most oppressed by their situations need to be the most creative with challenges – and are often facing them with far smaller resource bases and with very limited repertoires of possibility. Giddens explains this pattern thus:

> The more the demand to 'make one's own life' becomes acute, the more material poverty becomes a double discrimination. Not only is there a lack of access to material rewards, the capacities for autonomy enjoyed by others may become crushed. (Giddens 1994a:188)

Here, we return to the 'weave' of the different resources. The effects of this 'weave' compound within communities, within families, within trajectories. Cumulatively, available resources manifest as different choices and chances, tools for creativity and layers of protection. This leads to spiralling patterns, or exponential patterns within individual lives: greater access = > use = > greater access. Put bluntly, the 'haves' usually continue to get more, and 'have nots' mostly still have not. This is the social reproduction of life-chances. Other research with young people (Banks et al. 1992) shows how the 'haves' in fact 'have' on many fronts (political participation, stable relationships, high quality of life, education, high status of jobs) and others do not. Several different analogies suit this picture: available resources are woven together like an elegant fabric, a safety net, or like gridded-up bars (being trapped or excluded).

There are implications here for young people's wellbeing. Eckersley (2005) highlights that quality of life decreases when there is a growing discrepancy between the haves and the have nots. In terms of mental health, it is not so much lack of access, but the gulf between realities and what is and desired that matters. In a rude twist of history, too, as the local and wider world changes around communities like Myrtle Vale, there are also some 'haves' who increasingly 'have not'.

Understanding these issues of 'resources-at-hand' is central to under-standing social participation and youth agency. Each of these things manifests in the individual trajectories of respondents, in the seem-ingly insignificant comments in interviews, in their negotiations to date, and in their meaningful engagement or lack of meaningful engagement in the situations in which they find themselves.

Beyond resources, to resource flows

This chapter has looked more closely at the nature and significance of the different 'resources-at-hand' young people are working with as they make a life. Respondents' stories showed how the creative work of idio-syncratically 'making a life' and making sense of their own lives (even to aspire, to story, to negotiate and to engage) is constrained and shaped by the availability of this practical, symbolic and cultural raw material. Practical, symbolic and other cultural resources weave together, as under-standings and practical infrastructure, as goals and the means to attain-ing them, as dreams and the chance to make them into realities.

Young people and their resources have been a little de-contextualized from their relationships in this analysis. The truth is, though, that these different resources only ever flow within the context of social relationships. This is where the next chapter will focus.

8
Resource Flows

The previous chapter showed how the resources which young people access are of very different types. However, respondents' stories suggest that their resources become available to them in very similar ways. That is, different resources have similar patterns of 'flow' within their lives. These 'flows' are the focus of this chapter. They are implicated in the ongoing patterns within individuals' lives and stories, and also within the dramatic changes.

Even though young people may not have very sophisticated accounts of economies and their place in macro-social systems, it is not possible to understand their activities, or even the possibilities without first hearing their stories about the resources, the sources, and the resource flows that shape their negotiations. These insider accounts are actually significant reports about social structure and process that decision makers cannot afford to ignore.

How these young people are getting access to resources

One day, when I was telling Kurt's Mum about my research, she shared this story with pride: 'We weren't at all sure that Kurt was going to be alright – he was smart with an attitude problem.' (I had discovered the 'sharp end' of his tongue when I asked him for an interview in 1995). Kurt had 'nothing lined up' when he left grade ten. One Saturday, a few weeks after he left school, a friend of Dad's arrives and mentions an apprenticeship that another mate is looking to fill. 'Kurt!': Mum says. 'That's what I was thinking.' When fronted with the idea, Kurt has other plans to do a bit of casual carpet-laying with a mate. Dad's friend and Mum explain the value of this compared to the other job. Kurt is both keen and reluctant: 'I'll go Monday.' Mum says: 'Go now, you'll miss it.' Dad's friend picks up the car keys: 'Come with me and we'll go now.' Kurt got the job.

Kurt's relationships link him to resources, and not simply the resource of the job. There are several other layers of resourcing going on here. A 'trusted other' brings an idea. The idea is judged as one worth engaging with because certain meanings (about the 'relevance' of this apprenticeship for Kurt) are effectively communicated. The same other (coach) brings Kurt an (implicit or explicit) definition of himself: 'You could do this.' Coach gets him there by providing a lift or practical infrastructure. Coach also offers Kurt safety – company into the unknown world. Coach brings modes of practice: 'we'll go now' and propels him, time-wise (there is no time for fear to grow), as Mum later says:

> Gee they need that push though – even if I said we'll do it and gone to get my car keys, by the time I got back he would have changed his mind. (Fieldnotes, 1999)

In this story, Kurt is able to access new resources. The 'resource flows' set out a pattern which is replicated in other stories. Firstly, what happened is social, relational, and contextual, not simply about Kurt and his own choices or mindset or what he knows. Secondly, the flow of resources happens in the context of, specifically, at least one 'trust relationship'. Without the coach, even if Kurt needed a job and knew about the job, he simply would not have gone. Thirdly, there are enough layers of new resources here, a kind of critical mass, to make the difference. Fourth, the resources become 'useful' because they provide him with new input and with ways ahead. Fifth and finally, once Kurt has been there with his 'trusted other', he can go there by himself again. He does. When Mum told me the story, Kurt was a fourth year apprenticed fitter and turner.

Sonia's story of how she came to be a trainee secretary has some similar elements: She likes and trusts her Aunt; Aunt offers Sonia new definitions of herself, concrete opportunity, safety, exposure, and practice:

> She's worked there, I guess that's basically why I really want to. Because she always, you know, she's always said to me: You should do that sort of thing, because I think it's you.

When respondents answer questions about what has happened and how it happened, their stories are unique. However, the stories hold some common plot-lines and reveal some similar social processes.

Patterns in the stories

These patterns reflect not just how young people get jobs, but how respondents are accessing resources for their own negotiations, resources to make a life. The patterns apply to developments in their lives around learning and work, health and wellbeing, and social participation or expressions of citizenship more generally.

Interview data is full of stories of *practical resources* becoming available through trusted others. Mark gets a loan to buy his car from Dad, and can engage with friends locally but also closer to town. Dale got his home-business and earliest tools through working alongside his Pop. Mel can only maintain a gruelling fitness schedule and compete in elite sports because her parents will faithfully drive her and cheer her on. Chapter 5 provides a case study of post-year-ten practical options becoming available through trusted others.

Likewise, *resources of symbol and meaning* are also becoming available through trusted others. It is within the context of relationship, of 'inter-subjectivity' or shared understandings (Berger and Luckmann 1967), that new things become meaningful and relevant. Within his relationship with Dad, uncles, and brothers, Noah learns the intricacies of Holden engines. Within her relationship with her sports-coach, Mel learns to think about herself as a potential sports-coach. Within the safety of her relationship and new home with John, Beth learns a language with which she can speak about her abusive past, and also her possible futures.

One prevailing figure in many of these stories is the 'mentor' or coach. These mentors translate or re-translate reality, bringing new stories, languages and meanings. Significant characteristics of the relationships include trust, mutual respect, and that they emerge organically through two-way-flows of communication. The most effective mentors are those who know richly the respondents' own universe of meaning. That is, they are fluent in the young person's stories, conceptual schemes, themes, theories, passions and convictions, in their languages of words and other symbols. The relationships, therefore, involve mutual opportunities for translating the world, and pointing out why new things could be possible or 'relevant' (Wierenga 2002).

One-to-one conversation is a significant forum for making meaning. The telling and re-telling of stories adds robust-ness; 'thickening' individuals' 'thin' stories about themselves or the world in which they live. (See also Michael White's work on 'narrative therapy': White and Epston 1990; Epston and White 1992; White 2000, re the role of the other in thickening individuals' 'thin' stories). Storying is significant because it is about the individual's ongoing relationships with themselves (see Chapter 4), with the world (see Chapter 6), and it also provides a way to access resources from other times and places (see Chapter 7).

Not co-incidentally, respondents who, in interviews, do not share any stories of passionate engagement with the world, are also the ones who do not share any stories about coaches or mentors.

Another very powerful figure in some respondents' stories is 'the prophet'. (There is some overlap with the mentor but the 'prophet' can be a trusted distant figure.) Strauss (1977) introduces the 'prophet' as a trusted other who both points to new directions and re-interprets the path (for example a religious or political leader, teacher, artist). The dynamic here is not just about the availability of new symbols, but about the radical re-arrangement of symbols already familiar and in-use, and the dramatic transformations of understandings and stories that can follow this move. The 'prophet' appears within respondents' stories occasionally, as teacher, as adult friend, as TV program, musician or novelist.

Resources of habit and practice are also only becoming available through trusted others. This flow of resources can be as much 'osmotic' as deliberate. As Elizabeth explains:

> I've grown up with [Dad]. He hasn't really taught us, but you just watch him and do the same things he does.

Habits are caught as much as taught. Identification is of paramount importance – 'people like me', 'we', and 'us' become generalized forms of the 'trusted other'. Otherwise, social practices are simply things that 'other people' are doing, (for example, *other* people go to university) and they have little or no impact.

Different lives, different stories, different resources, same flows

Although the resources that respondents are using to make a life are very different, they have similar ways of flowing around. Drawn from every perceived story about 'resource flows' in the interviews, here are the common patterns of how new resources are becoming available to respondents:

1. Resource flows are social processes, dynamic and contextually enmeshed. Of particular interest are the relational dynamics of both *being resourced* and *engaging with resources*;

2. A *trust relationship* is always involved. This can be with persons, groups, institutions or systems;
3. At any given moment, judgements about whether there is *enough* shift in resources to make a difference for the individual concerned are impossible to make from the outside. This depends upon how respondents engage with new resources or loss of resources, and upon other concurrent flows of resources and how these are understood;
4. If new resources are going to be useful, there needs to be access to the *'means'* as well as the *'ends'*;
5. *'Been there, can go there again'*. More precisely, been there with trusted other, can go there again.

Among this respondent group, these seem to be the simple principles behind why social patterns endure within stories, lives and families. But they are also the processes by which changes in respondents' lives are happening. More evidence for these claims will be explored later, but first, some definitions are needed.

Trust relationships

'Trust relationships' hypothetically involve a spectrum, at most, of putting life in someone else's hands; at least of bottom line safety, ensuring that the encounter will ultimately be more about gain rather than damage. The trust relationships in question here are mostly mid-to-low end on this spectrum. They are about having *enough* history (or vicarious history) of safe encounters with the 'other' to warrant engaging this time (for example, going to school today, or having a conversation with parents). The higher the stakes, the bigger the stock of trust will need to be.

Nor does mistrust necessarily infer the expectation of being annihilated by the other. The same kind of spectrum applies. Often, trust relationships are simply not present or substantial *enough* to facilitate the particular transactions in question (for example, Suzy going to school, Kurt alone visiting the fitter-and-turner who wants an apprentice).

'Been there, can go there again'

Once individuals have been somewhere, they can think to go there again. Geography is both a good example and metaphor for this pattern. In Chapter 4, *some* respondents are familiar with parts of the social world outside The Valley because they have lived or been there with their families. When respondents story their futures, it is only *these* young people who can plan their ways back to these same places (specific) or to outside The Valley (general).

Places that individuals have *been exposed* to *and engaged* with before can be visited again. Respondents are functioning with their symbolic resources and habits in much the same way. Ideas, definitions, themes, theories, language, and practices introduced by trusted others and engaged with by the respondent, are resources available to be visited again. *Exposure plus engagement* in any kind of resources is leading to an *increased repertoire of possibilities for present and future negotiations.*

A play on words could be illuminating: Resources are re-sources: their use involves re-visiting, re-membering, re-applying or re-turning to the things that trusted sources or allies have already made available. Again, here is a word borrowed from writers about 'narrative therapy'. 'Re-membering' (Michael White 2000) is about invoking the company of those who were teachers of meaningful ideas.

An extension of 'been there' is 'we've been there' (a kind of vicarious storying). When someone, a trusted other, part of 'we', or 'one of us' is already 'there', respondents will often think of joining them:

> I'd like to go to Queensland. I haven't been there, and I'd love to go there because I body board, that's my hobby... well if I like it I'd probably move up there, I've got family everywhere. (Debbie)

> P'robly go to New South Wales or something like that. Got relatives there so, easy. (Brett)

Young people who have not been before will think of going there because:

> *...[it's] not like I'd be lost up there* [laughs] ... My Nan and Pop live in Queensland... So I could go up and live with them and look after them and that, pretty good, or I could live with Dad or I could live with my aunties there... (Debbie)

I've got aunties and uncles, I've got about half a dozen uncles up there somewhere. (Brett)

Practical resources, ideas, or habits of trusted others are also being borrowed and tried on for size:

AW: So who got you inspired with guns?
Mark: Um, don't know, don't even know why I started working 'em. Um… think it was the fella I used to sit next to in grade six. Used to like guns, just always look at books.

'We've been there' also works as a bridge to other projects or commitments:

AW: Have you been doing the football since you were a little tacker?
Todd: Since about 1988.
AW: Oh. And what, what got you into it?
Todd: Oh. I went to football with me brothers one day. And then I just, and then I just liked it.

The extension of 'I have been there' to 'we have been there' (and survived) is one of the things that now gets some of Myrtle Vale's young people up to college:

Elizabeth: I hate going up to grade ten like, 'cause this year flew by so if next year flies by, I'm gonna be in college. Yep, scary.
AW: You feel not ready for college?
Elizabeth: Noo, well, my sister seems to have, like she's um met really nice friends and that. So that bit's all right, but it's just the part of having to go up to town…

Those who have been there often become translators of information about the things to come:

If I have to do extra hours or tutoring or whatever, I'll do it, just as long as I get up to level three… like [friend who finished college] said, they help you out up there. They'll help me, so that's good. (Max)

And they make it safer for others to follow. Engagement with places, peoples, situations and social others is transferable within groups, within 'us'. Likewise, so is mistrust.

Habits of trust and mistrust

Trust reflects a history of safe encounters or vicarious safe encounters. In contrast to this, Suzy has learned after 17 years that it is simply too costly to engage with her father:

> … I didn't used to think I could go without it – but I definitely can – I'm not missing much that's the way I see it.

This stems from a history of betrayal of trust:

> And I'm growing to hate him more and more 'cos he's done that to me – like he's – he made the choice – he didn't have to choose at all – drove me out.

and from repeatedly being hurt in the encounters:

> Recently I have tried to have contact with him – rang him up every month or so like when I was at work I'd ring up. But he doesn't do the same. And I saw him the other day in Town – went over to talk to him, he was sitting in his car and he had nothing to say to me – besides like: 'How are you'. You know. And like I was so offended.

There is an ongoing wrestle between what 'is' and what 'should be':

> … but you know a few months ago I – just thought I'll wipe him out of my life, I can do without it. 'Cos I thought before, you know, I need a father 'cos, you know, but I've realized that I don't, it's not sort of going to make a difference. I love me Dad though, I'm a real Daddy's girl, my brother's a Mummy's boy and I'm a Daddy's girl but I can't have that. So.

and the decision to finally disengage also involves loss:

> AW: Is it kind of like you still love your father but it's just not worth the effort?
> Suzy: Yeah – yeah… I don't think I can – I don't want to go through all of that emotional crap any more – like I've stopped letting it mess with my head sort of thing – like I don't need it.

Suzy is being far more articulate about this process than most. She is also talking about a very significant other. In the case of less significant others, or relationships where the stakes are not so high, respondents' choices not to engage can be far less aware or agonized. Choices seem to be evolving in day-to-day practice according to habits and to paths of 'least resistance'.

Habits of trust or mistrust can be very specific (as above), or can become more generalized:

> Kylie: But I don't trust anybody.
> AW: Do you trust you?
> Kylie: No.

Practices reflect both individual history and group history. Lived experience is reified and passed on as stock-of-knowledge (Berger and Luckmann 1967). Clearly, this includes historically based understandings about who is trustworthy (or not) and why. This is evident when parents do or do not trust me (the stranger who is asking to interview their kid) upon first contact. Implicit messages include: 'Poor dear, how can we help you with your project'; versus: 'What do you want?' or: 'You hurt my kid and I'll rip your bloody arms off.' Reactions are clearly delineated along the lines of class and global / local culture. As 'The Stranger' asking questions, I represent different things to different cultural groups (that is, the student with an interesting project or the potential city bureaucrat who might hurt us).

Among respondents, habits of trust are being extended differently to *individuals*, but also to other *groups* and to *institutions and systems* according to group histories. These are not usually made explicit or named, but are part of cultural orientations, part of people's ways of being and functioning in the world. The Eldridges are of self-sufficient working-class stock. After much distress, their solution to their children's unemployment is to re-mortgage the house, start a business and employ the kids. Individual and group habits reflect both basic assumptions and repeatedly learned lessons about allies and alliances.

The different sources of resource flows

As explored briefly in Chapter 4, when respondents tell stories about their lives, the listener can be offered a tour of their universe of meaning. When young people talk, it is possible to learn about the flows of resources through their lives.

In interviews, respondents inadvertently list their resources (like Suzy did early in the last chapter). Likewise, resource *flows* are often spontaneously flagged by statements about what person x did, always says, or does. The types of resource flow are many: '*taught* me', '*showed* me', '*took* me', '*explained* to me', '*told* me', even '*yelled at* me'. But they are all about 'been there, can go there again', physically, symbolically or in practice.

Often spontaneously, even more than when asked, respondents will name or cite the sources of their practical tools, their understandings, and their practices, as they speak. In this way, it becomes possible to map resource flows with them. The most frequently cited sources are families, friends, teachers, community members, and on occasion, mass media. It is worth briefly exploring the role of each in resource flows.

Families: for history and context

One of the most significant characteristics of families is that they have the potential to provide focussed inter-generational forums for young people to make their lives. Many respondents are drawing richly upon the resources that these trust relationships bring. Families are implicated in the ways in which young people are physically being resourced and also in their practices ('cultural capital'). But, the most interesting, yet untold, stories are about flows of the symbolic, and things of 'meaning'.

I am witness to intense negotiations between Pete and his parents about whether to go to university next year or take a break from study. The errors and collective wisdoms of previous generations become involved in the drama being played out in Pete's dining room. As Pete sits down to work out what to do, Mum has this to say:

> Mum (to Pete and me): I had suggestions saying you should do this, but that's your choice and that's how I always think it should be. You can suggest but you can't make – it's not fair. (Yeah.) And in the long term, I don't want him to be 45 years old and saying: 'It was my mother's fault. She made me do that.'

It seems that this is an issue that resonates within family history:

> Pete: [I'm] thinking that I'll go to Uni.
> Mum: Mmm. I'm certainly not going to push that, I mean I'm, we have this thing in our house that John [Dad] always says that. His mother went out and got him a job, you know he was at college and he'd been there for a week and his mother came home and said: 'Oh, I've got an apprenticeship for you'

and he said: 'I didn't even want to do it' so he always has
this thing about: 'Ooh, I'm never going to do that to my
kids.'
Pete: Bloody mother. (All laugh.)

That 'we have this thing in our house' highlights a thematic or
recurring issue – the family have been here before. In fact, as Pete
does his thinking out loud and Mum adds her wisdom, a whole host
of other witnesses and their contributions are invoked into the
conversation:

Mum: ... But he still blames his mum for it, after all these years, he
           still sees that as her fault. And um –
AW: Gee, it stays with you, doesn't it?
Mum: It does.

The learnings and resources that Pete can draw upon at this point
are not just his own, not just his Mum's, here in the room with
him, but his Dad's and Grandmother's as well. In this story, learning
is a family experience, and involves the cumulative and abstracted
wisdom gleaned over the last 45 years. Before Pete makes his decision,
guidance comes from many sources. After the fact, his own actions
will be 'thickly' storied by many voices, in languages of shared
understandings.

In family relationships where conversation is fluent, where ideas and
projects are shared, where stories are told and retold, rehearsed, embel-
lished and 'thickened' in the context of the insights of others, learning
is a group exercise and it is abundant. However, not all respondents are
able to draw on these kinds of relationships:

The only time my mum talks to me is when she's crabby with my
brother. (Kylie)

For young people 'going solo', who do not have inter-generational
forums in which to safely discuss their decisions, finding direction and
learning from lived experience can be much harder. When families are
estranged, or when families do not talk, their children have trouble
accessing some of their potentially most valuable resources:

And none of my uncles and aunts are talking to my mother at the
moment because she's stubborn, and I get caught in the middle

> because I talk to all of them and she thinks that I'm betraying
> her. (Kylie)

Young people are making sense of their own stories in the context of
the bigger stories shared (or not) by their people.

Relationships are repositories of stories of identity (Neimeyer 2000).
They are also repositories of other significant information. It therefore comes as no shock that respondents who talk about bad memory,
(some even can not remember me or this research from year to year),
come from the most fractured social situations:

> I can't even remember last year. (Kylie)

Among respondents there is a correlation between badly fractured families and those who talk about loss of memory:

> ... when we were split up, we still moved round a bit and so I can't,
> 'cause I've got a really bad memory as well, I can hardly remember
> any of my friends... (Elizabeth)

There are significant links between memories (or memory) and continuity in significant relationships.

Elizabeth talks to the significance, of family, of ongoing relationships
to knowing who she is and where she has come from. In constrast to
her first interview, by her second interview she is flying. 'What has
changed?' I ask her. She explains that her family has re-united, giving
her a chance to spend time with her mum. She has been able to hear
her stories – her own early childhood stories and the stories of her
people: 'I have a grandma and cousins in the USA!'. In this way
Elizabeth can get a feel for who she is, and just as importantly, for the
historical and relational space into which her own life fits: 'It kind of
helps put more roots in'.

She points clearly to the sheer power of not knowing these stories in
terms of silencing her, and of the consequence in anxiety, confusion,
and isolation.

'Watching my sister'

Interviews reveal gendered patterns in resource flows, and this shows
up most clearly within families. Among the respondents, young
women in particular are learning from *the stories of the women around*

them. Interviews show that they (more than their brothers) are gathering resources from vicarious experiences:

> AW: Where do you think you get your understandings of how things are going to happen?
>
> Tamara: Watching other people. 'Cos I seen the mistakes that [my sister]'s done.... It's kind of like: 'I'm not going to be like that.' It's kind of like that and it's kind of like I'm not going to be like my Mother too 'cos my Mother said, she was going to be a teacher. But then she met Dad and, got married and got pregnant and so she didn't follow it on and like, Oh God I do not want to do that. '... 'Cos she said the other day: 'Boy I wish I'd carried on with teaching'. I'm like: 'You should have done!' ... And that kind of puts perspectives on everything as well.

Among respondents, to do this is very 'woman'. To self-analyse, and to analyse the stories of others around them, is a strongly gendered pattern in this group. The three young men who also do this are drawing heavily on close female relationships and conversations with their mothers:

> Pete: So I took it pretty easily half way through the year, didn't I Mum?
>
> Mum: Yeah. A bit, yeah. We've had a bit of a talk about what needed to be done, didn't we?
>
> Pete: We talked a couple of weeks ago.

Respondents' grade seven and eight essays about role-models also show gendered patterns, in the ways in which young women and young men make use of the stories around them. While young women are drawing upon those immediately present (friend, sister) and *their* learnings, young men are usually aspiring to emulate more distant figures (Jean-Claude van Damme, basketballers). Over time, it seems that young men and their people are also less verbally focussed in their time together, and more into doing things. Among this group of young people, far more than fathers and sons, mothers are instructing their daughters: 'Don't do what I did...' and their daughters are listening to them.

Mothers as the lyricists of life

If life is music... then mothers are the lyricists of life. More consistently than anybody else, mothers are the ones putting words to discernible patterns in the world around them, and mentoring their children as they also put words to life. Most young women and some young men say that Mum really helps them to make sense of things:

> [T]here was a whole book that she got on parents helping kids' careers and all this. And she got some stuff for me as well when she was in there... Yeah, she knows that I don't want to make mistakes so she is trying to help me at the moment. Which is really good 'cause, oh I freak out, the idea of choosing a career... (Max)

> Like, um, I sit at home and, cause like my Mum, like I said to her: 'Oh, I'm not going to be able to be a vet.' 'Yes, you've got it in you to be a vet, course you can do it.' So that, that really made me decide a fair bit too. On what I wanted to do, 'cause um, not like she pressured me or anything, it's just she gave me a bit of confidence so I could make a decision sort of. (Sandra)

These patterns raise some significant questions, particularly for the families of women who find themselves silenced. What happens to inter-generational wisdoms in their families? Will the *retreating* young women be the lyricists for their children? Is their silence an echo of their own mothers' silence?

Families – resourcing their children to different ends

In 1995 I interviewed six respondents' parents (one or both). Since then, conversations have happened around town, around interviews, when getting permission for interviews, and even during interviews with their children. Through these conversations, different families reveal a little of how and why they are sharing their resources with their children.

Parental agendas, what they want for their children, make a really big difference to what resources are being shared. Success, 'the good', and desirable outcomes are framed quite differently in different homes. Practices reflect quite different understandings and cultural models of conscientious parenting, and different cultural orientations.

- 'Giving them wings' and 'keeping them close'

It seems that parents' expectations and practices are as globally or locally based as their own children's stories. The parents of *exploring* respondents have had deliberate policies for expanding their children's horizons. Helen (Mum) explains:

> We had a choice between sending the kids to a private school or taking holidays with them. Now they've been to New Zealand, Thailand and Malaysia. We all love exploring... It also gives the kids more freedom. Layla went to Melbourne and back with her friends when she was 18. *It gives them wings and teaches them not to be frightened.*

Not surprisingly, their son, Pete now also approaches the issue of leaving as a journey of discovery. 'You never know. I could end up anywhere!' These parents are also fully expecting that their children will go places that they have not been, and have experiences that they have not had. As Helen (tearfully) says: '*Well you don't give them wings to keep them close.*'. Another mother says:

> I expect that they may go. There will always be a degree of closeness – I expect that we'll always be close emotionally. (Julie)

By way of contrast, for Jenny (mum to a *settling* family), desirable outcomes are measured in terms of family proximity:

> He's unemployed and the place he lives in is a dump. But he still comes home – we're really lucky that he still comes home... we're doing OK. (Phone conversation, 1999)

To go outside The Valley lacks meaning for some families, as Noah's Mum explained when he went to the city to college:

> I'm not really sure why he's gone up there – I think because all 'is friends did. (Fieldnotes', 1999)

or Dad:

> Well, while there's still no jobs down here he might as well be getting an education. (Phone conversation, 2000)

Education is named as a 'holding pattern' until Noah can get back to the core business of working down here. Noah's mum believes that her children will stay near to home, like she did. Both parents are still looking for a practical opening for him 'down home'.

- 'Negotiation skills' or 'sorting it'

The processes look quite different in working-class and middle-class homes. Observations, conversations and interviews leave an impression that the former are far more likely to 'be told' and the latter are likely to be 'negotiated with'.

Exploring parents say that they are endeavouring to build kids' character, and to do this it seems that they are actually resourcing them with intangible but transferable means which ensure that a wide range of options will be open to them:

> Guide them earlier on. Give them background values when they're younger. Also a range of experiences to broaden their outlook. Let them have experiences so they can make good choices. (Howard)

Echoing a wider literature (and also echoing the previous chapter) this is Bourdieu's (1984) 'cultural capital' in action. Practices of problem-solving is one example. In Pete's story (above), he and parents are deep in negotiations about what he is going to do next year – take a year off and travel, or go straight to Uni. The issues are presented to him like a puzzle – so how are you going to solve this one, Peter?

Ways of showing concern, rather than levels of concern, differ between these parents. *Settling* parents acknowledge: 'Our job as parents is to give them a better life and a better education than what we had.' (Bron and Shayne). However, reflecting upon abstract means is not a luxury that all can access. The concrete facts, the current conditions absorb energy:

> We're just living from day to day. It's all you can do now. (Bron and Shayne).

'Sorting it' often involves physically embodied interventions. Negotiation by proxy is one example of 'sorting it' (see Chapter 5 or Kurt's story above). Here is another mother's way of 'sorting it' when the issue is the protection of her child:

> And I turned round to her and I said: 'Nobody intervenes with this family and tells you not to see me!'. I said: 'You will come here

– when you want to – and *if he says no – I'm going to have him taken out and taught a bit of a lesson.'* (Bron)

Good parenting, by any of these parents' definitions includes protecting the young. This was just one example of more radical 'embodied' protection.

* Words and ideas or 'doing things'

Language and the way it is used in different families has profound effects. On the basis of practices of language use, mostly gained at home, young people live in different realities. Language marks the co-ordinates and fills life with meaningful objects (Berger and Luckmann 1967:21). It delineates exactly what is perceived, framing lived experience (Strauss 1977). Language use in some environments allows young people to express their insights and mental life (Willis 1979) and to practice accounts of their own identity.

Some parents are seeing conversation as a central part of their parental role. Not surprisingly they talk about it easily:

> We talk about the future together a lot. At home we try to balance out any negatives by talking things over – about things that are not right – about options and so on. (Julie)

> Being a part of a family means we share experiences – we wait to hear the stories over lunch – and the whole family – we all experience it. (Helen)

Meanwhile, working-class parents were likely to look at me strangely when I asked what they were aiming at for their young, or what parenting is about (as if to say: 'is it not obvious?'). For many years the lingering questions were: 'What are you doing?', 'Why?', and 'How?'.

Language gives access, and stories give access, to different ways of understanding the world. Learning can be vicarious and it can be cumulative. Basil Bernstein (1977) discussed these ideas in terms of 'elaborated' and 'restricted' codes. However, the point to grasp here is that these families were doing something *different* to middle-class parents, which was *not simply a poor relation of the same practices*. Asking my questions was not providing answers.

A social rule sometimes becomes evident only when it is breached (see Garfinkel 1967). So it was with 'good parenting'. Near the end of the research one mother made some sense of it all:

> I'll tell you Ani, half of the parents around here don't *do anything* for their kids – they just live in their own little world – and the kids learn to do nothing – see this poor guy here – he's 18 and he'd never even been on a bus by himself. A lot of parents just don't *do things* with their kids and you need to. (Conversation with parent from fieldnotes, April 1999)

This parent is not referring to 'talking to your kids' or 'teaching your kids' but to '*do things*' with your kids. This is not about conversations, abstract ideas, theories, or transferable skills, but it involves an embodied and concretized form of enduring faithfulness.

These parents' codes of practice are probably equally as elaborate as their verbal counterparts, but have a different fit with researcher expectations, and with the wider social conditions. The value of *doing things* with young people cannot be underestimated in terms of individual lives and possibilities. To *do things* with a young person leaves them with significant legacies to which they can return:

- Things that '*I can do*' (history, story, expertise/ competency self-respect);
- Things that '*I could do*' (future, story, exposure to both grounded possibilities with *real-world social, geographical, and experiential connections.*

Indeed, interviews leave absolutely no doubt that for all respondents (but especially for those *settling*), to '*do things*' is where they get their ideas for their own stories. The value of 'do things' cannot be underestimated in the culture of this town, where to 'do things' is both the central social rule, and the way to self-respect. This raises some questions about the interplay of local culture with wider social processes under conditions of rapid social change.

Families and their own resources

Some rural working-class parents are going to extra-ordinary lengths to resource their children under the current social conditions. This is not to say that middle-class parents do not resource their kids, and pay for it, because they do. The difference is that insulating their children's futures from harsh social conditions, and providing infrastructure for building futures despite those conditions, really seems to be costing some working-class parents enormously.

Amongst rural *settling* families, resourcing the young is often expressed as extreme faithfulness in infrastructure provision – *finding* the job, *being* the transport, *doing* the liaison. Basically it means being a personified interface to get working lives established.

> I'll never leave a kid on their own and say – right you're 17, you make your own way.' (Angus)

This faithfulness comes at a cost. Todd works in a casual retail job, 30 minutes away by car. Dad drives him there and back every time. Todd gets called in at erratic times on odd days, often to work late and with very little notice: 'It doesn't do to say no when they call you.' 'Why?' 'They stop calling you.'. Because of this he cannot plan his life. (I had a small taste of this when we had to re-organize our interview three times because work had called him in). Dad is on call constantly too; in the way that Todd cannot plan his life, Dad cannot either. The new economy's flexible workforce comes at a cost, and that cost is borne by Todd's family, and others like him.

Closely related to all of this is the current crisis of the *settling* families, for whom the very concrete, very grounded, very specific and very applied wisdoms and learnings of many generations are being devalued by social change. When the rural, working-class cultural patterns of providing infrastructure for their children do not work any more, this leaves whole families at a loss:

> I think I got it wrong with the older one. Used to be that getting a job was the answer and now I don't even know if we did the right thing... He was making a nuisance of himself at school, so I said: 'If you can get a job you don't have to finish.' And he did. And then what was I supposed to do. There's only part-time work, casual work now with the apples and that. So he's working half the time and living on nothing the other half. (Phone conversation with 'Jenny', 1999)

The rudeness of the current situation becomes apparent. The rules have been changed, so to do what is meaningful and responsible, to keep the kids close and get them jobs, may well be to limit their chances. To have them leave would be to have them shut off from embodied assistance (unlike the often disembodied, or more abstract and transferable resources flowing though middle-class parents). To send them out is to send them somewhere that parents cannot be with them, cannot *do things* with them, and cannot guide or protect them. What we are witnessing is a severe disruption of cultural patterns. The social changes happening in rural communities like Myrtle Vale are doing violence to these traditional resource flows, rituals and ways of life.

Social change leaves most parents a little out of their depth, but some are being stretched even further. Parents are being called upon to go places where they have not been before. Some are finding the resources to get there. Bron, a working-class parent, realizes that to get back into the workforce, Judith is going to need all of the schooling she can get. So the family all go to the TAFE (Technical college) orientation day, with her. She says (laughing heartily):

> Bron: I just sat down and crossed me arms – all went over the top of me.
> Judith: ...Mum didn't understand what they were trying to say.
> Bron: So I was just a pretty face in the crowd (laughing).

For Bron this has involved a quite uncomfortable and disarming decision to go right outside her own comfort zone. But she knew that it was important to be there.

There is a lot of action in the interface between families and institutions / systems, and other good research has tracked this over past decades (for example, see Jones and Wallace 1992; Jones 2002). Connell et al. (1982) spearheaded a body of literature which specifically explored the patterns in relationships between families and schools. And, as in this literature, the Making a Life research shows that where there are histories of respect, familiarity or trust with institutions, respondents and their families are far more comfortably able to engage in negotiations, drawing upon their history and their resources as required.

On the other hand, where there are histories of mistrust, other strategies are involved. As they face their own kids' unemployment, the Eldridges are re-mortgaging their house to plant an orchard where they can work. Schools, Centrelink (Social Welfare Office), the tax office (et al.) have all blended together to become a 'hostile other'. They know, from lived experience, that they can expect little practical help, and they find little sense or hope and, above all, *little dignity* in their interface with 'the system'.

Amongst all of these families, the bottom-line of parenting is preparing their children for futures (infrastructure, promise of infrastructure, advocacy). To parents of other cultural orientations, this means different things, though, with varying implications.

I think what you gotta do is keep giving them direction. (Jenny)

Parenting is about preparing them for later life. Trying to get them to handle money properly, teaching them to mix, teaching them manners... (Howard)

However, not all families involved in this research seem to be quite kid-focussed or even 50–50 kid-focussed. In some situations, parents' own issues or crises clearly have the main stage:

I can't have Simon at home – it's just too stressful. We fight all the time and with my [health problem] I just can't handle it. (Parent, 1997)

This can be a specific crisis for a specific time, but, for others, negotiating around a parents' crisis is a way of life. One example of this is Beth and Brett's family. Family practices revolve much more around managing Dad's issues than equipping kids in any way. Dad flies into a rage at the thought of each of them leaving home. Beth explains later that she effectively needed her partner as a 'bodyguard' for the manoeuvre, and also afterwards: 'while he got used to the idea'. She also explains that keeping the kids at home is as much about access to their money as anything. Dad is an alcoholic. Rather than ideas of fostering independence, his own thirst/immediate needs / survival is paramount in their negotiations. In a society that is not always good at resourcing the sick to get well, these young people are not only unsupported, but they carry the full weight of their father.

Less dramatic but also evident are other families who seem to have abdicated as care takers. This includes families who simply do not, or cannot, prioritize equipping their children. Conversations suggest that they have given up on the wider situation:

AW: Do you reckon your kids will get jobs?
Mum: Nah, not down ere.
AW: Is it ok if they don't?

> Mum: Yeah I'd say so. 'Specially if there's no jobs about. If there's
>   no jobs, there's not much choice.

or that they have given up on their offspring:

> 'E's lazy. 'E likes the money but he doesn't want to earn it. 'E's never
> done anything. (Bron)

Kylie's mum offered a mini-history as we headed upstairs to do her interview:

> See if you can get some sense out of her – I haven't been able to get
> any yet.

If they are not talking much or doing things together, parents' and child's stories, and their definition of the situation, can be independent and at odds. This leaves the child with fewer resources to draw on in terms of building their own futures – fewer ideas, fewer life-lessons and fewer exposures:

> Kylie: I need a new Mum, would you adopt me? (both laugh)
> AW: I remember you asked me that two years ago too. What do
>   I do that your Mum doesn't?
> Kylie: I don't know, you talk to me.

The value of parents is not lost on the luckier respondents. Mel puts it well:

> So, I have family support, so I think that's fairly important, so if you
> want to do something you've got to have support... See, I have lots
> of friends, like their parents don't support them at all and they're
> just like, *it's like a battle to do everything.*

The significance of family support in creating a life cannot be understated. Supportive families are providing their young with tools for creativity and, as best they are able, different layers of protection around young people's own negotiations with the world.

The sense I get when I engage with almost every respondent's family is of people who are doing the very best that they can by their children, with the resources that they have in hand. The point is that *different families have access to different resources. Parents can only share with their children the resources they have been able to access themselves.* In a society riddled with inequalities, of course these resources will continue to be quite different for different families.

Peers

Peers are sources of practical resources and of new opportunities, as young people continually go places and do things together. They are often implicated in each other's habits, captured in the now extensive bodies of research on youth subcultures and identities. Equally interesting, though, are peers' roles in sharing symbols and ideas, and doing 'reality-checks'. Respondents (particularly young women) report constantly 'reality-checking' against each other. Friends can be invaluable reflectors and co-creators of identity:

> Yeah. Like me and Sarah, we've been together and everything since grade seven. Umm, yeah, we know heaps about each other. We tell each other everything. We share everything. (Kylie)

The role of peers becomes especially significant when family is not available. Several respondents are drawing heavily on peers for their insights and projects. In interviews they voice their appreciation of these life-lines:

> Actually, she's very important. Like, if I didn't have a friend like her, I don't know what I would have done. (Kylie)

Although relationships with peers are often characterized by trust and faithfulness, they lack the benefits of inter-generational insights, breadth of life-experience or wisdom. Many of the ideas shared do not mesh with broader realities. Simon wants to become a famous DJ. This is his only dream. His best friend has told him that if he really wants to become one, he will: 'That's all you need to do – really want it and really believe it.' When I ask, Simon will elaborate no other plans because, encouraged by his friends, he is adamant that this one is going to happen.

Peer groups may be functioning very creatively, but sometimes from narrow resource-bases. Sarah and friends analyse everything: 'the way boys don't' (Sarah) but the tools are drawn largely from each other and from mass media input. Although together they have quite sophisticated habits of storying and analysis, they have access to limited symbolic tools with which to do this (for example, stories of romance and betrayal and concepts like 'being true to yourself') and little language for the broader social context in which they are seeking their private destinies. As such, they have limited repertoires of storylines available for making sense of their own lives.

Young people can provide each other with the most faithful and consistent relationships. But they can only share with each other what they can access from the social world around them. And those who can only draw from peers will have access to a limited range of ideas and a limited range of habits and practical resources. Kylie's group of close friends party at the weekend, and they are her only human confidantes and companions. Since she has discovered that partying is something she would like to avoid, she now spends her spare time 'doing absolutely nothing'. Party vs. nothing: She has no other options on offer.

School

Whether implicitly or explicitly, respondents are often citing their old school as a source of ideas, habits, and practical resources:

> [My] teacher was in the shop and he said: 'They're looking for a trainee at Woodman's', so I went over, and he said come back at nine in the morning – [I got an] interview... started work the day after that. (Brett)

The school, more than any other source (except some families), has been instrumental in opening respondents' possibilities beyond the local. When I interviewed six staff members in 1995, senior and junior teachers alike pointed to this as their mandate:

> This is the central point of the school. It's classed as a disadvantaged area. We receive funding to broaden kids' horizons. (Teacher, 1995)

> Our cultural enrichment budget goes to expanding their world – getting them out there, we want to widen relationships, values, the way they look at the world. Here outlooks are restricted – knowledge of current affairs, even among adults is really poor. (Teacher, 1995)

A broad range of 'horizon-expanding' activities have been happening throughout the curriculum (and beyond). From before-school-hours 'life-skills' programs of cooking and eating breakfast, to the yearly 'City scavenger hunt' for all senior students, to weekly Saturday night pilgrimages to the basketball game in Hobart, the emphasis has been upon taking students to new places (physically, symbolically or in practice) so that they may go there again themselves.

Staff point to the conditions within which many of the students grow up: to poverty in families; the 'slow social development' of many; to students who were 'bright eyed and full of hope' when they started high school but who became 'despondent' by the time they understood their options; to a culture where education has not been seen as useful; and to parents who themselves were scared of the school (perhaps because of their own childhood experiences).

Radical new directions were adopted by the school in the early 1990s 'after a particularly bad patch'. Changes were for 'teacher survival', and 'harm minimization' for all involved as much as they were about 'maximizing opportunities'. The resulting changes meant transforming programs within the school from ones where many students could not succeed, to ones where all could (and very publicly – due to the community-building ethos of Lightwood Valley News). Making school relevant to local people meant substantial alterations to the curriculum, including life-skills subjects, the school farm, and boat-building. Other priorities have included constant creation of bridges between community and school (at the time of early interviews there were 150 parent and community volunteers involved in the school), and between Myrtle Vale and the outside world (as above). The school's task has been understood as not simply academic, but also social. This radical change has created interesting struggles over priorities.

As a 'liminal' community, of not-quite-insiders, not-quite-outsiders of Myrtle Vale, the teachers at this school have huge potential to shape local young people's lives. A teacher confesses: 'I see the school as the one shining light for many of these kids.' (Teacher 1995). For these teachers, the source of their greatest power is also the biggest limitation they face. They are mostly 'outsiders' who bring new ideas in. They know that what they are doing is both important and often countercultural:

> I try to extend kids to a fraction more than what they're capable of. But if it's not subtle they refuse to do it. It's better not to try. A little success leads to more, and to willingness to have a go. (Teacher, 1995)

Consistent policies and a radical curriculum would mean nothing without trust relationships. They still do mean nothing to some young people and their families. Some students remain inaccessible, just as teacher world-views and class projects are inaccessible to these young people. But deliberate and consistent policies *combined with trust relationships* can make a large impact in a small community. A core of teachers have settled locally, the teaching appointments of some, to The Valley, now spanning decades.

Individual teachers have had powerful impacts on many respondents' lives (I have analysis codes dedicated to respondents' 'mentor-teacher' or 'faithful teacher' stories). Low student numbers, small class sizes, and relative intimacy with students have allowed specific teachers to be powerful mentors and prophets to many, and as such, shapers of student culture. Six (mostly long-serving and mostly senior) teachers are repeatedly singled out by respondents. These reports come from not only academic students, but also young people experiencing academic and life-problems:

> I can honestly say that I miss all of the Myrtle Vale teachers. 'Cos I loved that school so much. The teachers down there are too good to be teachers – they shouldn't be teachers they should be my friends. (Kylie)

> Yeah Mr (*) was always having me into his room for talks and that – whenever he got me into trouble he'd always know that there was something wrong so I'd end up in his office having a big talk to him or out in the corridor – he'd just always talk to you and stuff. (Ex-student 'Leigh', from fieldnotes, 1999)

It is impossible to say how many of the positive changes that have occurred since this research started are a direct result of extremely committed, ongoing and intentional relationships with these (not quite) outsiders. During early interviews, several school-leavers spoke quite cynically about their futures, and scathingly about the school. More recently, since 1997 or 1999, although students may have been critical of individual teachers or subjects, it was very hard to find a school-leaver who would criticize the school. Changes are most evident among school-leavers, who were *still children* when the policy directions shifted, and were even younger when key staff appeared. These stories also suggest that criteria for 'mentor-effectiveness' and group cultural shifts involve not just issues of mutual respect, but also time invested (over *years*).

Levels of trust in schooling still vary, and so does the impact of the school on different young people. For many, the established and strong bonds of trust do not easily transfer into new areas (for example, looking for work outside the district or 'going on' to year 11 and 12). Changes *are* happening in young people's engagement in the outside world (see Chapter 5) but much more slowly.

Meanwhile, much is being expected of teachers. Going places (physically, symbolically, in practice) with students means stretching finite people, finite time and finite resources. In a climate of constant attacks on education funding, the changes discussed above are remarkable. Respondents' stories highlight the importance of ongoing resources for this kind of public infrastructure. Diminishing funds for public education pose a direct threat to local, committed, and very effective communities, like this small school.

Communities

Young people's communities shape who they become. Young people have access to different communities, including communities of interest, networks, family friends, sports teams, and internet-based networks. Some are drawing resources from global communities, others, more locally. But there are also those who are embedded (globally or locally) and those who are adrift.

Fragmented networks are often a symptom of parents' crises. Marriage breakdowns, poverty and cheap housing mean that some respondents' families are mobile and socially disembedded. In this way the most mobile young people can also become some of the least resourced. *Wandering* families lose potential to be known, and for real, and acting, extended kin to resource their young.

Conversely, within the Myrtle Vale community itself some are embedded and stigmatized. These are children from families who are at odds with community sentiment. In a small town, shared sentiment and practice can be extremely punitive, leaving those *retreating* unable to draw resources from even the figures consistently around them.

Communities can only share with young people the things that they can access themselves. As shown in Chapters 2 and 3, the impacts of social change (globalization of world markets, technological change, government and private sector rationalizations) have savaged many of the things that Myrtle Vale had to offer its young people (for example, jobs, futures, services). Meanwhile respondents' stories are clearly highlighting the importance of resourcing and protecting local communities, for their own sake.

Mass media

Mass media are functioning quite differently to other sources. Media flows are almost always implicated by respondents' uncertainty about 'where I got that idea'. Rebekah is responding incredulously to a transcript of her previous interview:

> I must have got that from a Dolly magazine or something. I don't know why I would have said that...

Exchanges between mass media and young people must be less memorable-event-based processes than flows between individual actors. Rather, there is a kind of saturation by a slow drip of ideas, which although subtle, is very powerful. These sources can leave a trail of material that has little integration into young people's everyday lives:

> Ben: Yeah, I wouldn't mind going to umm America. Travel in America.
> AW: Why America?
> Ben: I don't know. I've always just liked it.

More than ever before, via mass media, young people in rural communities are drawing ideas from other worlds. Among this respondent group, this has varied implications. In some respondents' stories they have clearly been useful for expanding horizons and providing new ideas. Pete tells a story of awakening to issues of racism in America and Australia after watching a particular TV program. After doing sociology in year 11, Rebekah is using reportage of current affairs to sharpen her own perceptions. During her year nine interview, Elizabeth engages in some elegant moral 'hypotheticals', resourced by themes from 'Sabrina the teenage witch':

> 'Cause like you wish you were a witch so sense that you could change your clothes and make yourself really popular and stuff like that, but then you think about it, the stuff she does is quite bad 'cause you can't really change people's opinions or that without discussing it with them first.

Interviews show, though, that respondents are making use of media input very differently. In one of his grade eight essays, Ben relays some of the messages that he is receiving. (For ease of reading this time, spelling has been corrected, punctuation added):

I plan to have a good wife, children, a big house, swimming pool, BMW, one 4WD, a Falcon and a Torana and a good income and *if I want these bad, I will get them.*

Some respondents are claiming highly commercialized images as their own stories:

AW: What do you see yourself actually doing?
Phoebe: Something in entertainment, behind the scenes.
AW: Does it pay though?
Phoebe: I don't know – be the next Steven Spielberg.
AW: Aah that pays – but how do you get there?
Phoebe: Prob'ly got to go to uni as usual.
AW: You really don't want to go to uni?
Phoebe: Oh – my cousin's going to uni – she hates it. (She changes the subject.)

Phoebe is in year 11, but is not involved in any theatre or production work. Storylines from TV are most heavily made use of by those who have access to few real-world stories that give their lives meaning. These stories stand out because of their lack of passionate connections to everyday projects in the real world. They correspond with fragmented networks, and with absent 'significant others'. The problem is, as Bruner (1987:21) suggests, that unless individuals' stories 'mesh' with those of their communities, both 'tellers and listeners will surely be alienated...'.

A related issue is that input from media sources is primarily symbolic and in the realm of ideas. This is quite unlike other sources where, within trust relationships (for example, with family, friends, school, community), information may well be backed by opportunity, where shared practice makes things possible, where means or chances of real-world-assistance often accompany goals.

Figure 8.1 shows the sources that different respondents cite in their stories, and are drawing upon. It will look familiar (from Chapter 4, revisited in Chapter 5). An extra layer of analysis has been added; the vertical axis focusses on flows of ideas, or goals, while the horizontal axis focuses upon flows of real-world assistance, physical resources and practices, that is, the social means of attainment. For respondents who are *exploring*, global goals and global means are available through the combination of trusted sources (listed). For those *settling*, local goals accompany local means. For those *retreating*, trusted sources are

<table>
<tr><td rowspan="2">Goals:
(flows
of ideas)</td><td>global</td><td>Exploring

family, school, peers, local community, non-local communities of interest, TV, mags, books</td><td>Wandering

TV, peers, isolated family members, isolated teachers</td></tr>
<tr><td>local</td><td>Settling

family, peers, local community</td><td>Retreating

peers or isolated family members</td></tr>
<tr><td></td><td></td><td>many</td><td>few</td></tr>
</table>

Means of attainment:
(flows of real-world assistance)

Figure 8.1   Means, goals, sources, and different resource flows

providing access to little of either, *whilst for those 'wandering', global goals accompany very limited real means*. Media input, in particular entails a disjuncture of ends and means, between the ideas, and the practical resources and habits with which to follow through. Laura (see Chapter 4) never did become a model. After fleeing to the city, she fled back to Myrtle Vale. She lives in The Valley alone with her baby.

This study suggests that *mass media, as sources, are powerful supplements, but poor substitutes*, for other more immediate, mutual, and embodied flows of resources. The unique contribution of the mass media is the *decontextualized idea*. Because TV introduces repertoires of ideas from outside respondents' relational and accessible world, some respondents are able to use this powerfully to expand their horizons (as above: Elizabeth, Rebekah, Pete). Where other sources and resources are abundant, TV becomes just one more useful source.

However, the mass media are different to other sources by being *disembodied*. An idea is accessed by the respondent, but there is no relational 'other' on the hook, and so the source remains unaccountable for any practical follow-through or any real-world assistance. Also, backed by corporate interests, most media conglomerates are not driven by any particular relationship with, or concern for, these young people. Ironically the best-resourced sources are often also the ones who will help respondents least.

Implications

The stories within these pages highlight that although young people make individual lives, it is the patterns of relationships that make all things accessible. This chapter has highlighted the role of families, friends, teachers and wider communities (including the media) in making resources accessible to young people. This is a partial picture, as young people are also active participants in the patterns, and will re-claim the focus in the next chapter.

Throughout this chapter, respondents' stories have shown that although there are different types of resources, these are becoming available to individuals in very similar ways – specifically through social relationships of trust (with individuals, groups, and / or institutions). History (both individual and group) plays a huge role in the shape of such relationships. Families are particularly significant others in these resource flows, and how they equip their children makes all the difference in terms of how their children are able to access other sources (for example, school, peer, community, media input), and make use of other resources. However, it is also clear that families themselves are differently resourced, based upon their own trust relationships, which are themselves the result of history.

The individuals in this study have unique lives and stories, but they are also very clearly patterned. Respondents' stories show that resource flows are gendered; the things that women share with each other and access from each other are usually quite different to the resources that Myrtle Vale's young men can access. More profoundly, though, the different resource flows explored in these chapters (especially within families) are the embodiment of class, that is, the different things that people do with resources and relationships.

None of this – the documenting of patterns – is to deny the possibility of change within individual lives or group circumstances, and it is to these important social dynamics that we turn our attention in the next chapter.

9
Familiar Patterns and Transformations

When working in youth practice and policy it is important to understand day-to-day activity in the context of a larger picture. However, thinking too much about the big picture, the inter-connectedness of social problems, and the structural nature of the causes, can lead to a reluctance to get out of bed in the morning, or at least to the onset of professional paralysis. Exclusion, inclusion, class, gender, opportunities, constraints, inequalities in life chances... The patterns are too familiar and can feel absolutely entrenched. One of the recurring questions for those of us who work with young people and communities is about whether change is possible.

Sixteen years after starting work with this community, and 12 years after stopping my work to start listening, I can bear witness to evidence that change happens. The accounts from Myrtle Vale may not be universal, but they resonate with stories from elsewhere, and hold some clues for further action. Within the day-to-day encounters, familiar patterns are constructed, replicated but also transformed, and herein lies hope.

This chapter pulls out a magnifying glass on some of those encounters in young people's lives, both positive and negative. Longitudinal qualitative research provides an unusual opportunity to look at continuity and change over time, and to explore in greater depth the role of young people in the resource flows that surround them. These social processes are unfolding not only *on* and *for* young lives, but *with*, *by* and *through* them. In policy and practice the young person's own role in the creation of change is often missed, mis-calculated, or added on as an afterthought. Yet the data explored in this chapter shows why the active role of young people in their relationship with the institutions that manage their lives, and to subsequent interventions, needs to be a central concern. This is about working with human subjectivity and human agency, rather than in ignorance of these dynamics. If these findings can be generalized, this is also an important part of understanding what works for young people.

Young people in resource flows

The previous chapter looked at the important roles of families, friends, schools, communities and mass media. In terms of understanding dynamics, the central figure was almost always missing from the equation: the young person themselves.

To put this in theoretical terms, other writers about youth have (I believe, rightly) suggested that Bourdieu's (1984) notion of 'cultural capital' 'exaggerates a good insight' (Connell et al. 1982:188). In that model, individuals seem to become only vessels of things passed on by others: They are seen as *tabula rasa*, and their role is effectively obliterated. Young people *are part of resource flows*, through their engagement with social others, and with the resources that those others bring. But their *encounters are also shaped by the resources and strategies that they bring*. They bring not only group culture, but also idiosyncratic understandings and practices. Negotiations reflect the ways in which social life is being differently understood and storied by each individual, on the balance of cultural and biographical history. These young people also become sources of resources for others.

Continuities over time

Biographical research presents an unusual opportunity to explore the dynamics of change and continuity. This theme has been explored in depth by other researchers conducting qualitative longitudinal research with young people (for example Thomson et al. 2004).

Here, in the Myrtle Vale research, there are some things that stay the same from story to story, interview to interview, parent to child. During her third interview, six years after the beginning of the research, Sonia is looking at her pile of essays and transcripts for the first time (I had failed to get it to her earlier). At the same time she is unknowingly telling a story that she also told in her second interview:

> [My parents are] going to wait till we get a bit older and move out – they reckon they're going to build a one-bedroom house so we can't stay there (laughs). Said: 'Doesn't matter we got tents! Pitch them

on the back lawn.' (She pauses and stares at her transcript.) Oh I actually, just I just told you this (laughs.) I just read that then!

We both laugh in recognition, and we are surprised that, even two and four years later, not just the stories, but even the conversations within them, are the same. This is an excellent example of what happens constantly in interviews. These young people's lives are thematic, and they usually have continuity of access to the same significant resources and relationships, to similar practical, symbolic and habitual material that they had available last time.

Beyond the things that stay disarmingly the 'same', of more interest are the 'continuities' and the patterns that seem to reproduce themselves in different forms over time.

As shown in earlier chapters, the continuities in young people's lives are part of bigger patterns. Each is accessing their resources through his/her networks, but *their networks, in turn, have different networks*. Another way of putting this is that *each is accessing resources through particular trusted others* (individuals, groups, institutions and systems), who are in turn *also being differently resourced by their trusted others*.

The above has clear implications for each person in terms of understanding *agency, as well as life-chances* and equity issues. This is particularly so if we recognize that trusted others can be *not only individuals, but also groups, institutions and systems*. These things make up social structure. Differentiated patterns of resources, opportunities and real-world possibilities are the result. Another outcome is seen in the formation of islands of culture (subcultures), with *access to different tools*, different ways of doing things and understanding the world, and different knowledges and ignorances. In terms of patterns in respondents' trajectories, these differences have shown up as different cultural orientations (*exploring, settling, wandering,* and *retreating*). Circumstance and cultural practices are complementing, amplifying and compounding each other within lives and between generations.

These things also make sense of what happens under conditions of social change. Those with more limited networks, those with fewer diversified resources, and those who are drawing upon the most localized of sources, are the ones who are being hardest hit by rationalizations in government services, by changes in labour and industry, and by the shrinking of this little town. It is not just that young people's own networks are small and localized, but that their *networks' networks' resources are being depleted*.

These processes look familiar beyond Myrtle Vale, and patterns similar to these are recognized in contemporary qualitative longitudinal studies from around the world (for example see MacDonald et al. 2005).

In the moments

The continuities in the Myrtle Vale young people's lives are made up of millions of moments, of tiny incidents where particular resources flow, or not. I have explored these dynamics in much closer detail elsewhere (Wierenga 2001), and the patterns are illustrated throughout this book. Other youth researchers have explored the significance of moments in time (for example, Thomson et al. 2002).

Strange things happen when respondents' engagement is met with a 'win'. A win leads to further engagement, which *sometimes* leads to a win... In the same way that disengagement compounds itself, engagement is breeding new engagements. Added to this, each type of resource will operate like a currency in its own right, unlocking other resources (see Chapter 7). Further, stories also show how often these patterns are amplified or magnified many-fold by serendipitous events.

'Serendipity' is about unpredictable and fortuitous connections, coincidences and other little gifts of circumstance. Every story about real-world passions or vocations is made up of such strings of events and encounters. Alyssa is going to Adelaide to study podiatry. Work-experience convinced her that this is the kind of career she seeks. She chose the work-experience placement after a conversation with her family doctor. The podiatrist with whom Alyssa did work-experience (now a mentor) went to Switzerland last year. It is now Alyssa's dream to travel to Switzerland one day...

Through their social engagements, unexpected happenings and chance meetings are multiplying respondents' opportunities many-fold. Each engagement potentially leads respondents into contact with new people who may become trusted others, who introduce them to new ideas resources, which lead them into contact with new people... Importantly, these runaway sequences are easy to map and understand in hindsight, but impossible to predict.

This is also one of the mechanisms by which inequalities of opportunity persist. Differences in respondents' life-chances happen when some are involved in circumstances through which the same or similar flows keep happening, while, for others, flows are reduced. Meanwhile, still others are involved in exponential or outward spiralling patterns which loop successively to new resources, to new projects and to new trusted others (individuals, groups, institutions and systems). The 'haves' are always getting more and the 'have nots' continue to have not. Lack of social engagement leaves little room for serendipity.

Even in the most consistent of stories, there are changes over time. As careers (in the broadest sense) unfold, language, ideas, and technical understandings become more sophisticated, and stories about selves are woven more intricately into projects. But stories are also changing with circumstances, and discredited ideas get 'cooled out' with increased life-experience and maturity. These patterns are familiar, to some extent, in all interviews. Other biographies provide opportunities to explore the dynamics behind the more dramatic changes.

Changes

Generally this book will have created a picture of continuities in circumstance, of relative predictability in trajectories, of young people's lives that nestle comfortably into familiar patterns. On the whole that is what the data reveal. Over time, though, some individual respondents' trajectories have also proven to be less than predictable:

- Noah (earlier cast as the archetypal *settling* respondent) continued schooling to year 12. He says that if there is nothing local available, he might seek a job in Hobart;
- Alex, a well-resourced *exploring* young man, left school in the middle of year 11 and did not know what he was going to do next;
- Suzy, in her second interview, is involved in Hobart's drug scene, expelled from school, alienated from family, and very fragmented in storytelling. Earlier she had been *exploring* but, this time, is she *wandering*? By her third interview, she has changed mode again. She can coherently explain what this crazy few years has taught her, and where she is going now as she prepares for university;
- Beth, who in her first interview was very much *retreating* (she would only say 'I dunno', and shrug apologetically), can now tell a simple, hopeful story of where she has been, and where she and her young family might go next.

Against a backdrop of research which can look deterministic, these stories show that onlookers could *never* say young people who were *wandering* or *retreating*, were all doomed from the start, that those *settling* would all linger (either happily employed or unemployed and embittered) in The Valley, or that all *exploring* individuals would go on smoothly, successfully, and well-supported, to live happily-ever-after in middle-class suburbia. Thankfully, observers would also be wrong if we assumed all respondents would stay neatly in a typology box.

Engaging with the changes in lives, and with surprises in the data is a useful practice. For it is through interrogating the surprises (the data, not the respondent) *with respondents*, retrospectively, that the most interesting findings emerge. Questions like: 'What happened to you?', 'How on earth did you get here?'; or 'Can you tell me how this happened?' lead to joint explorations where they tell stories and/or theorize, as we both name the changes that we see. Together, we are mining older stories for new meanings. At this point, several respondents are able to speak directly to the issues of empowering/disempowering changes in their lives, and to say what has happened for them. Their stories are well worth re-telling.

In interviews, we focus on the changes that respondents see as meaningful. That is, if *they* identify changes, we focus there. If *I* identify changes, and these have little resonance with their own stories, we move on. The changes that they choose to talk about are both great and small (for example, succeeding at a project, being involved in a car accident, becoming a champion, losing a dream, gaining a career, losing a pet, gaining a Mum, losing a Dad), but they invariably link back to themes of empowerment and disempowerment. That is, the stories link back to common themes of individuals gaining or losing the resources with which they can make a life.

Turning points

Turning points in young people's lives and stories represent a moment, or a series of moments, when there is a shift in resources – at a critical mass (Wierenga 2001). The shift may be about gain and/or loss of significant resources. The moment may be a single event (for example, a car accident, getting a job), or may be many little moments (new friends, repeated failure). While, for the observer, these events can be hard to pick, to the individual concerned one significant shift of resources can change everything. This is particularly so if it involves stories about identity.

Alex's back injury means more than an inability to play the sport he loves. With the injury goes a dream, a passion, a career in sports and in sports medicine. These were central to his stories about identity. His dropping out of college with no plans might make no sense to an outsider, but from his perspective, there is simply no reason to continue. A profound loss of meaning is a crisis:

> I can't think straight, all I am is angry.

While at one level, the termination of her relationship with her father is tragic, Suzy has a lot of other things going for her. She is bright, energetic, has a wide circle of friends and extended family. Why then all this 'crazy' or 'risky' (sic) teenage behaviour: wagging school, drugging, frenetic changes of story? It is only as we look back to her first interview that we notice how closely intertwined her stories about identity and world-view, politics and mission statement are in her relationship with her father. By her third interview she is settled again, but has abandoned 'all that hippy crap', and many of the politics and beliefs that she shared with her father. The loss of this significant relationship also means, for a time, the crippling loss of stories about her own identity.

Losing and finding the plot

'Losing the plot', a colloquial phrase, is actually a very apt description of a significant social process, which I have explored elsewhere (Wierenga 2002). Crisis entails the loss of the plot, or the storyline, and story is about ongoing relationship to self and to the world. Further, story is the conduit through which so many other resources (from past and present) flow. *Losing the plot means a stem in the flow of all kinds of resources.*

The interrelationship between different practical, symbolic and habitual resources was starkly shown in the interviews *Those in crisis, those who lose their story, also concurrently lose their way and lose their voice.* When individuals lose their way and their voice, they are in a far worse position to access new resources:

> I just got so bogged down – totally – and once you get bogged down you can't do anything – like you can't get back out of it – because it's too hard.

This was also true with the resource flows between us. I was far less useful to the voiceless, just as they were far less available to me. Young people in crisis were always the hardest to negotiate with on my part, and it was visibly hardest for them too. This again raises questions about the *retreating* young women who stopped talking to me. What was happening to their stories?

The best insights about change, crisis and resource flows happen when respondents emerge from their crisis and have a story to tell. In lieu of a grade ten interview, Richard had yelled: 'I've got nothing to say to you!' Two years later he explained: 'Sorry about that, I didn't know what I was going to do.'

In the same way that losing the plot is about loss of story, 'finding the plot' is literally about finding a significant storyline. Our conversations reveal concurrent shifts of new resources, young people finding their stories, finding their way (practical resources, ways of doing it), and finding their voice:

> Mum helps a lot now though, 'cause I can talk to her about everything. I go home and I tell her everything that's happened. But I never used to [be able to] do that. *I've come more open, I reckon.* (Elizabeth)

During re-interviews, I was stunned at the changes in Beth ('I dunno'– see Chapter 4). Beth has a new mentor (partner) in her life, who spends a lot of time interpreting the world to her, and listening to her. On her second visit, with some excitement, she haltingly told me the barest outline of her story. Several times during the story, she called on her partner to translate for her, nodding furiously as he did. At 18 years of age, Beth tentatively was learning a language with which she could understand and communicate 'past, present, future, and me'. As she did this, she began to make sense of her past. As she made sense of, and found meaning in her past, she could think about what makes sense for her future: 'I'd like to work in a shop, in our own business, and bring up two kids. I reckon I might be good at that.' As I left, Beth invited me to come back in a year, so she could continue telling her story.

Something which cannot be emphasized enough is the significance of trusted others in facilitating these changes.

Opening up and closing down

Looking back over the course of this study, on the two-by-two typology which has appeared throughout this book, it is possible to see dramatic contrast between left and right sides, between those who tell clearer stories opening up in hope, and those whose relatively unclear stories, closed down by fear. This pattern reflects the powerful interplay of circumstance and subjectivity.

Respondents' openness to new resource flows depends upon group and biographical history. Recurring hurts, disappointments and violence (symbolic or physical) are leading to withdrawal from, and restriction of, resource flows. Violence shows up as individuals close down in various ways, including a lack of willingness to engage in social relationships and in others' stories:

> I don't know. I think maybe I don't believe in love any more because every time you love somebody they always go away. So I think I've just given up on that too. (Kylie)

As shown earlier, resource flows can close down in relation to specific mistrusted sources, but also as a more generalized way of being in the world. Some respondents (like Elizabeth) retrospectively explain closing down over seasons of crisis. However, other personal and cultural histories have individuals living in a state of crisis, and more resolutely removed from new resource flows:

> Well I'm not a very hopeful... I don't hope for nothing. I can say I hope... [but it never happens]. So you just stop hoping for stuff after that. (Kylie)

There are strong links between hope and the inclination of respondents to engage. Over many years of fieldwork there are those who have just seemed to have closed down, a little or a lot, from interview to interview. They do this in relation to social others and in relation to the stories they tell or will not tell any more (for example *retreating* young women). Far from being irrational or lazy, these strategies can involve the will to survive, and are absolutely necessary for self-protection. Sustained close-downs, though, become part of compounding social processes. With age and lost opportunities (as schools finish with them, as they leave the known world, as familiar others leave them), close-downs are leading to inward spiralling patterns of not being able to draw upon new relationships or upon new resources.

Subjectivities: respondents' engagements with their own stories

Beyond trust in others, respondents' habits of storying, of inquiry, of attempts to explore, integrate and/or understand, each person also shows trust in their own observations, judgements and feelings. Through their stories, resources are flowing freely (or not) from other times and places into now. Sustained experiences of being trashed (by others and by life) are leading to an unwillingness, not only to engage deeply with others, but also to engage with themselves:

> Kylie: Oh 'cos these days I just don't take my feelings seriously. I don't know why but I just don't. I can say that I hate this person but I know that I don't – and I can say that I like this person but I know that I hate them.
>
> AW: So does it become like all a bit of a game?
>
> Kylie: Yeah – you get sick of saying stuff to people when they don't listen to you.

In her statement, Kylie is drawing close links between the kind of respect repeatedly shown by others and the level of respect that she can show to herself. Equally significantly, she draws links between the way that life validates her storying, and the way she bothers to story life. Young people who do not trust many others in a given situation, but are trusting their own judgements, have something very substantial to fall back on. On the other hand, individuals who do not trust themselves, their own judgements and perceptions, are losing ground fast. The fact that Kylie can articulate these things *at all* suggests that she is far from losing the fight. To even hold these stories together is to put considerable faith in her own judgement, and her stories give her some useful material with which to work.

These things become an issue particularly when communities are not telling stories which young people can believe. In Kylie's situation we can see tandem struggles for subjectivity and self-respect as ongoing, even played out during the interview. Interviews with other respondents suggest the same struggle.

Invisible travelling companions

Some respondents are showing great resourcefulness (resource-fullness or possession) within their struggles for self-respect and subjectivity. Always, when there is self-respect with no visible means of support, their stories will reveal a 'significant other' from the past who taught them that they were valuable:

> ... her name's Judy. She was 64 last time I saw her. She um, she was like my grandma, but I didn't have a grandma... and like she was just always there. (Kylie)

Michael White (1995) theorizes the dynamics of 're-membering', meaning people's capacity to draw back into stories particular individuals who, in the past, validated and gave hopeful messages. Such others become valuable travelling partners with respondents, even if only via their memory. Like the past encounters that undermine individuals' hope and confidence, these companions shape individuals' day-to-day negotiations, but are not often visible to the onlooker.

Why changes happen sometimes

Changes are about shifts in resource flows, but these shifts need to be of a critical mass:

> Elizabeth: Everything's kind of changed this last year.
>
> AW: I reckon. And what made the shift from I can't do this, to I can do this? Can you remember the sort of sequences?
>
> Elizabeth: Um, just things people said. Like my friends, especially (school-friend), would say: 'Yes you can, like you're smarter that me, you can do it.' and I'm like: 'No I can't' and so I'd try it anyway, to see if I could, could do it. And Mr B [teacher] he didn't come out and say, like you can do it, he just said: 'There's some people in this class' and he'd look around and he'd look at me, and he'd go 'who can do better' and like: 'Oh, he's looking at me.' And so that kind of like boosted me up, I reckon. When Mum talked, she said like: 'You can do it.' ... And so I think that kind of boosts me as well... Yeah. I shocked myself...

For Elizabeth, a combination of new resources bring about significant change. Friend and teacher re-define, Mum thickens the stories and adds context, and school marks provide a reality-check. But it is not just things people say that make the difference. Elizabeth's friend is there in her new class with her. Her teacher makes clear the way ahead. Both goals and means are available.

The trigger for change is not just the external factors, but the sense that Elizabeth makes of them. Like continuities, changes are often made up of the little things that add up to mean a lot. Change is contingent upon *enough* resource shift. 'Enough' is contingent upon the way that the individual concerned engages with any new losses or potential gains, and who is around in person or in memory, to make sense of these losses and gains with them.

Anything can happen but it usually doesn't

Many of the continuities in young people's lives are made of such moments, moments when, if individuals had been resourced enough, they may well have been able to make significant changes, or engage in different kinds of negotiations. Stories of change (for example, Beth, who moved out of a violent home and learned to tell her story) are evidence that this can happen.

The change in Elizabeth's story (above) is a kind of polyphonic (multi-voiced) or surround-sound re-definition of her. The more isolated a new resource flow, the more tenuous it is. This is why *it is important to work with young people in their <u>social</u> context, not just in their heads.* However, through her own reflective practice, her activities of remembering, crafting and speaking a new story, she is also a central player in this activity. This is why *it is important to work collaboratively with young people, not simply rearrange their social circumstance.*

Isolated, counter-contextual or counter-cultural resource flows can make new fragile links. Newly introduced resources can be rendered useless, unless consolidated by other resources (practical, symbolic, or resources of practice). Through some consistent community mentoring, Brett became a sailing champion. Later though, his new links to the sailing world were severed when he simply could not get a lift up to the city to sail. Likewise, the nearly possible option of year 11 schooling becomes quite impossible when peers are absent, classes are meaningless, and bus-rides are long and lonely.

Apparently, despite all odds, some tenuous links are being thickened with time, made robust through other complementary flows and through the individual's own practices of engagement. Noah continuing school is a good example of this. Between the school-class's 'cluster-movement' to college, the shared bus trip, the fact that this year many peers stayed on, the relevant, safe, and *do*-able automotive subject (coupled with his passion for working on cars), and the made-safe exposure to city employers through work-experience programs, there must have been just *enough* safe and relevant connections to see him through year 12. His story flies in the face of many others who simply have not continued.

It would be impossible to talk about changing young lives, without engaging in conversation with those concerned. Although the various elements of context are critical, the engine room is subjectivity. For the same reason, it would not be possible to catalogue external causes of such change using objective research methods or independent variables. In social context where there is increased emphasis on 'evidence based practice', insights gained from fine-grained qualitative studies provide some much-needed perspective. The interpretive tradition pursues a line of enquiry based on the idea that, although 'things' have 'causes', people have 'reasons' (Minichiello et al. 1995). Noah's reasons, in our third interview, encompass all of the principles of resource flows explored in Chapter 8 (but in his usual understated way). He would still prefer a job in The Valley but school is: 'Okay – it got better', his friends were there, the automotive course was 'good' and regarding work experience: 'I reckon I could go back there.'

Conclusion

The contribution these young people's stories offer is not just the way in which they show how social patterns of inequality are daily negotiated and replicated, but also in illustrating the processes by which lives are being changed. They highlight the powerful interplay of circumstance and subjectivity, of external conditions and of story, in shaping biography. For those of us who are interested in the circumstances of marginalized groups, improving young people's life-chances, and social change towards a more fair and equitable society, their stories of change can also be read as stories of hope. Research which develops understandings of how patterns continue, and how changes are happening in young people's lives process is absolutely necessary for informed action. In the context of this challenge, Chapters 10 and 11 will explore the implications of this research.

10
Implications and Interventions

Listening to young people's stories is significant, not only for them, and not only for the role that it can play in expanding academic understandings, but also because of the insights these understandings can offer about grounded social process, useful interventions, and informed practice in the real world. The substance of such conversations is about capacity to act, purpose, and human dignity in a changing world.

In this book we have travelled full circle, through young people's narratives to exploring the role of resources, which are distributed so unevenly, to the role of trust relationships, and back to the central activity of meaning-making. So, at the end of this research, we are faced with a fundamental trinity: the resources, the relationships and the stories, with each working in relationship to the other. This chapter begins to ground these findings to explore real-world implications when working with individuals and communities.

Although this research is about the lives of 32 youngsters in Tasmania, Australia, the questions being asked resonate strongly in other places. For example, questions of social change, and of how young people are creatively making lives in less than ideal circumstances, are being intensively explored in the Europe, the Americas, Africa, Asia and the Pacific. The challenges of growing up in rural places are as current for Canada and the UK as they are for Australia. Young people's ongoing negotiations with education, and the systems that process them, are a growing area of interest. Longitudinal studies have continued to emerge as an area of interest looking at biography, identity and subjectivity. Questions of the practicalities of research with young people are being asked by scholars around the world. Extensive fronts of activity are emerging about learning, about the social and structural conditions of young people's wellbeing, and about the dynamics behind social participation and citizenship.

A lot of powerful research has developed during the 12-year life-span of the Making a Life project. With one eye on the Myrtle Vale young people, and the other on different projects, I have had a sense of entire research communities either independently or collaboratively honing in to focus on areas that really matter. For example, resonating with this project's key findings, the dynamics of trust, resource and narrative are now being explored in depth by colleagues within and outside the youth research community. Theorizing is cumulative but it is also concurrent and parallel, and in a digital age knowledge is generated much faster than we can read each other's work. During the life of this project, an entire literature on social capital has built upon the earlier work of theorists like Putnam (1995) to explore the areas of trust and resource flows. Meanwhile another body of literature has grown around narrative. In the mid-1990s when I cobbled together a local theory about storying, the theory and references were sparse but inspiring (Bruner 1987; Massey 1994). A slow trickle of studies on narrative have now become a flood. As I complete this book, other writers have powerfully opened up the conceptual area of story and human dignity in a context of change (for example see Frank 2001; Poulos 2006).

Findings from a small numbers local study cannot be generalized to fit whole populations. However, conceptual discoveries are useful in other places, and it is in conversation with others' work from different settings that the implications of this research find a global home. These conversations cannot be exhaustive in one small chapter, and a literature review which might do justice to researcher colleagues' work would probably fill three books, but at the very least I can start by opening the findings of my own work up for dialogue.

Below I will do a whistle-stop tour of the areas where the Making a Life project seems to have particular relevance – the 'take-home messages' and challenges from this research project. These relate to young people's social participation, learning, and wellbeing. Then onwards, to a quick look at methodologies of hope and implications for policy and practice.

Take-home messages and challenges

Social participation and active citizenship

Something interesting happens when people's narratives are recognized and prioritized: it becomes impossible to talk about policy and practice without the input and voices of the people concerned. Their understandings, priorities, hurts and hopes become key subject matter, and the individuals or population groups being discussed become important participants in the conversation.

A Myrtle Vale townperson explained recently that a large food-processing factory has had to move north in The Valley because it could not find reliable workers in the south. Criticisms are leveled at young people within The Valley, just as they are at the wider population. When young people remain unemployed, and when job vacancies remain unfilled, local explanations mirror popular culture: 'They don't want a job', '… lazy', '… useless'. These are very 'thin' stories about what is happening in this situation. This research suggests that there might be a lot more going on than meets the eye. Assumed opportunities may not be accessible in other ways.

The challenge is to develop better understandings of people's resources-at-hand, and to hear and tell thick stories about these. Understanding these things moves the focus from the assumed pathologies or problems of certain groups and individuals, and looks instead at what people are using and able to access, to resource flows and how these can best happen. It puts listening on the agenda well before the posing of solutions. It positions the insider as actor, and it positions the practitioner or policy maker as learner. The result of these moves is that the imperative question shifts from 'what is wrong with you?' to *'how can we best resource you?'*

Understanding an individual's, or group's, social practice means understanding what resources (practical, symbolic and/or cultural) they are actually working with. This means taking stock of 'resources-at-hand' *with* them. What are the implications of these? How are they resourcing practice? Other direct implications for method must follow; listening, time-investments and trust relationships are essential. These things are important for understanding the key issues of young people's social participation in a time of big change, significant marginalization, and social exclusion.

Respondents' stories have been filled with personal topics (stories about friends, extended family, memories and dreams) which at face-value have little to do with resource issues. But, as individuals communicated about these things, they also shared accurate, very grounded details about the processes by which they could access social, symbolic, and cultural goods. A long list of trusted others (individuals, groups and/or institutions) could be read effectively as a catalogue of resources available. Few 'trusted others' means few available resources. Respondents' stories demonstrated how social structure is made of these relationships, with individuals differently able to draw upon the resources of not only their immediate networks, but also their network's networks.

The Making a Life findings reinforce what other Australian and international researchers have been saying for some time: that in research, policy and practice with young people, to focus simply in the individual and their development is to miss the point (Jones and Wallace 1992; Wyn and White 1997). Rather than a sole focus on young people's development towards independence, it is important to also recognize inter-dependence as an important social and family dynamic (Jones 2002; Lahelma and Gordon 2008).

Trust relationships themselves are functioning as resource bases, foundational to the life-chances of individuals. This idea has already been well covered in the literature on 'social capital' (Etzioni 1993; Cox 1995; Fukuyama 1995; Putnam 1995). More recently, in social policy, the concept of social capital seems to have been caught up in political rhetoric, and has lost its grounding. The idea has been used to serve various political agendas, where, at one end of the spectrum, it becomes a lament for the past, and, at the other end, it becomes the rationale for demanding that communities and families learn to look after each other, and solve their own problems.

The Making a Life research indicates that central ideas of resources and trust, and the relationships between them, need to be re-grounded and put to work. As we have seen in this study, young people, communities and families can only share from the resources that they can access themselves. In a time of rapid social change and amidst political climates of economic rationalism, resources are depleted in some sections of the community. Respondents' stories continually highlighted the significance of the ways that societies resource their families and communities. As the stories in this book show, when individuals' networks, and their networks' own networks' resources have been stretched, exhausted or are being removed, the results can be particularly devastating.

Learning

Contributing to a wider body of educational research, this project has allowed us to hear these young people's voices and to consider their resistances, for example, to continuing school beyond The Valley. These things have real-world implications for them in terms of life-chances. In order to work well with young people, it is important to think about how they come to know their worlds: their knowledge horizons and how they are bordered, the things that are relevant, the things that are meaningful. In a very real sense, some do not understand what is being offered to them in education. In another very real sense, we will not understand either, unless we listen to them. For example, some respondents (particularly *settling* working-class males) have very concrete ways of making sense of the world around them, whilst the world beyond their lived experience increasingly requires functioning at levels of abstraction. Education, then, would have to involve starting where they are at, and creating links between known worlds and worlds that they might actually need to know about. This sits in line with the informal education tradition (Dewey 1933). Although local teachers have managed to facilitate this kind of learning in stunning ways (boat-building to learn maths, school farm to learn science), young rural people like these get lost when they enter larger systems in bigger places. The challenge is about finding ways to stocktake resources-at-hand with them, and engage learning with priorities and life-story.

This, in turn, will depend on the shared narratives, or discourses, around the value of learning and the role of education. In Australia, like many other countries, our own systems are still fixated on the school-to-work transition. Chapter 6 revealed half the respondents saying they were having trouble applying education to life. If we take what they say seriously, tackling this issue does not mean 'dumbing down' or lowering expectations about what is learned, but emphasis on learning for real roles in communities, and learning for life in the twenty-first century. As Johanna Wyn (2007) and others have pointed out, some education systems were actually designed for a different era, providing workers for industrial society, where contemporary societies immerse young people in a whole range of other challenges.

I believe that there is also great significance in continuing to research these issues well, and in documenting the stories of those whose voices may not often be heard at a policy level. Through people's response to this research, already I have discovered that, within our seemingly impenetrable systems, there are policy makers who can hear these stories and do want to respond.

Wellbeing

Writers have identified the need to look beyond a narrow focus on health, or ill health (Wyn 2008) to focus on the social and structural conditions that enhance wellbeing.

In particular, respondents have highlighted the importance of *stable* community resources and long-term nurtured networks. At particular times of change and crisis, we saw all respondents drawing only upon their allies, and the relationships that they *already* trusted. Findings of this study suggest that in practice we can give young people all the information and opportunities in the world, but without trust relationships based upon individual and group history, they may be unable to make use of these resources at all.

This empirical finding has implications for the ways we might think about services for young people, and particularly for those who are 'marginal', 'hard to reach' or 'at risk'. Just prior to losing power in 2007, in 2006 the Australian Federal Government committed 1.9 billion dollars over five years towards addressing the nation's mental health problems. This followed a decade when government policies had systematically eroded the resources, trust relationships and dignity of families and communities. In emphasizing the pivotal role of trust and hope and everyday connections in the way young people access resources, the Making a Life research has highlighted, yet again, that economic rationalism is anything but rational.

Trust relationships are not soft and ephemeral fluff, nor luxuries of nice living. They take work, and we only realize their importance after a long, pragmatic wrestle with the hard realities of what works.

In terms of effective service delivery, one clear implication is the need for human bridges. Other writers have highlighted the way in which targeted services often miss the mark (for example, Smith 2003). Social changes are creating increasing, rather than decreasing roles for generalist, skilled, youth and community workers who have time to engage, link, and be advocates (Sercombe et al. 2002). Other projects have documented that it is only through workers with time, who relate creatively to whole people, without agendas, who can begin transformative work with the most marginal (Wierenga et al. 2003). In spaces which are open and non-judgemental learning can happen informally, a sense of belonging can grow, and skills and values can be caught as much as taught. (Hall et al. 1999). Ironically, as accountabilities tighten around measurable outcomes in program delivery across important areas like health, housing, juvenile justice, education, and work placement organizations, it is the perceived luxuries of gathering spaces, group-life, relationships, listening, creativity, and time which are shed. If this research and other related work can be trusted, these are the very things that make the practical elements of service delivery work.

Webs of relationships are actually the spaces in which resources become accessible, the bonds of trust are formed, and stories are told which make sense of what is available. The Making a Life research shows us that these intangibles are the elements which support young lives. These findings are not new, and practitioners in the youth sector have been saying this for decades. However, longitudinal, qualitative research affords the privilege to collect some unusual evidence.

One important design challenge is how to attend to trust relationships in a changing world, with global capital as a backdrop and geographical mobility as a lived reality.

Implications for policy and practice

As well as issuing challenges, thankfully, grounded research taps into possibilities. Respondents' stories highlight the challenges that they face and their own ways of creatively responding, but also some 'methodologies of hope' for those who live and work alongside them (Wierenga 2001; 2002).

Respondents' stories draw our attention to the ordinary, simple transactions which often do not make a big difference to young people and their lives, but which sometimes do. We see dramatic changes when an abused and frightened young woman is befriended by someone who helps her to tell stories about her past and dream possibilities for her future. We see turning points when a family friend introduces a boy with few resources to his sailing networks, and for a time, the boy becomes a world traveler in his mind and a sailing champion in real life. We see the world begin to open up for a group of school-leavers who, coached by their teachers from childhood, enter the outside world and face college together. And in the background we catch glimpses of a community which was nearly decimated in the early 1990s, steadfastly investing in, and undergoing its own transformation.

Food, roof, housing, health, education, legal rights, emotional and spiritual needs... when addressed discretely, the list of needs to address can be overwhelming. The Making a Life research suggests one way of thinking holistically and systematically, by attending to flows of resources. The study has highlighted the need to work concurrently at a variety of levels: young people's access to resources, their connections to community, communities access to resources, and the policy conditions that affect these things. In terms of useful social practice, the stories from Myrtle Vale might alert us to the relevance of working in a variety of ways across these fronts:

- In working with individual young people, the task is to hear and thicken stories, and build and facilitate networks of trust, where new repertoires of resources (practical, symbolic and habit) can flow;

- In working with communities, the task is about building networks of trust and facilitating flows of resources, within communities and with the outside world;
- In the political arena, the focus is on building, maintaining and protecting the resources that belong to families and communities. Other writing suggests this is not just relevant to rural communities, but disadvantaged or marginalized communities, and increasingly to all communities, geographical or otherwise, as these are the webs of relationship that underpin wellbeing, learning and participation, and make social life possible.

If we are interested in young people and their issues of life-chances and of equitable access to resources, research like this provides a call to action at each of these levels. As others (Apple 2002) have noted, interventions at the level of culture can be as powerful and as practical as interventions at the material level.

Working with young people

A genuine surprise for me during this research has been the pivotal role of narrative for young people to be able to access anything, even their own memories. This has implications for the way that they access any resource on offer, whether it be information, education, health, housing or other needs. This attention to human agency and subjectivity is, I suspect, the missing element in many failed attempts to connect the 'disconnected' with resource flows. The first task is to recognize and acknowledge a being with which to connect.

In the car (parked) after Kylie's third interview, when we are talking about how she has changed, she insists: 'You tell me.' (This is the same young woman who says: 'My mother never talks to me', and whose mother says: 'See if you can get any sense out of her, I can't'). When asked again, she takes a playful strangle-hold around my neck and shakes: 'I need this Ani! I need you to tell me... how I've changed!'.

This playful exchange, I believe, is also deadly serious. The story is alarming and hopeful. It is alarming firstly because it shows a young woman earnestly trying to hold her stories together, but very poorly resourced for this task by those around her. Her only trusted sources are a handful of close peers (and it is a good thing that they are around). Secondly, it is alarming because I am a researcher, and I now only appear once every year or two. She barely knows me, and if we take what she says at face-value, I am her best adult offer for this mentoring process. It is alarming, thirdly because Kylie is not the only respondent who seems to be grasping desperately at the (quite transient) interview process to give her a reality-check and reflection of herself. For example, during his third interview Simon does not talk much but he keeps rocking and sniffing, and saying: 'play the tape again. Can'y play the tape again'.

But Kylie's story is also hopeful. In our encounters, she is resourcefully, strategically, and playfully going after what she says she needs. At another level, she just authored part of a fairly clear mandate or job-description for anyone who seeks to be useful to young people in her situation (keep appearing over time, become co-story-er, reality-check, listen, thicken). That is a useful insight.

Other studies have tracked the impact of social change and increased uncertainty on young people (Sercombe et al. 2002; Eckersley et al. 2006b). The task of locating self, locating story, locating meaningful roles, or locating one's way is practical, but it is also existential and spiritual.

The young people in this study provided detailed advice on some ways ahead. They affirmed the need for looking-glass spaces where they could see, hear and track evidence of their own presence in a confusing world. They affirmed inter-generational links, significant adults spending time, and re-appearing over time. They affirmed the spaces for their storying, for claiming subjectivity, agency, a sense of dignity and capacity to act. They affirmed the detailed conversations which map resource flows and interpret what was relevant with them. These things go well beyond service delivery; they are about investing time in relationships.

Working with communities

This work explored the challenges faced by communities in a context of rapid social change. This is about globalization, world markets, technologies, and sustainable livelihoods, but it is about more than that. As in Myrtle Vale, international work (Fagan 2001) suggests that the central challenges for rural communities today – globally – go well beyond economic survival and are about loss of purpose and the need to find new stories that make sense of existence in a changing world.

My research with the young people 'making a life' in Myrtle Vale highlighted the importance of the flows of resources (economic, social and cultural) into the rural town and into local business, schools, families and then into young people's lives. Secondly, the work highlighted the importance of trust relationships (with families, teachers) to enable young people to access any of these resources, but also between these people and other places to create the flows. Finally, the research highlighted the powerful role of narratives – about past and future – in restoring people's hope and their capacity to act.

There are echoes of each of these patterns in the town's own recovery. For example, as documented on the ABC's *Landline* (ABC 2004), the return of economic viability to this town reflects new flows of resources; from outside, in this case through big business and enabling government, but also from inside, with civic groups and local organizations mobilizing concurrently. Meanwhile, the school has a (documented but not yet researched) role in restorative practices in the community, and in intentionally cultivating a local culture of trust. In terms of community and narrative, examples include the recent collective publication of a new book about local history, *Heroes of Lightwood* and the emergence of the 'Greencoats', a group of older activists who have assumed the role of community bards, proudly claiming history and re-telling it in the light of new imaginings.

A whole body of work has grown around community regeneration. The Making a Life study joins this work in illustrating how action needs to be taken to increase resource flows into, out of and between marginal communities. As much as this story of restorative social change is about the work of local heroes, creativity, bridging and bonding, social capital and trust, it also has some very hard edged policy implications. The study makes it clear that groups, communities, schools, families and services are only able to share with young people those things that they can access themselves. As John Wiseman (2006:95) notes:

> [W]hile local community strengthening strategies can lead to real improvements in community networks, infrastructure and capacity they are no substitute for the inclusive and redistributive taxation, income security, service delivery and labour market policies needed to create the conditions for sustainable reductions in poverty, inequality and social exclusion.

Working with populations

This work has highlighted the importance of resources, and the material conditions of existence. It has explored the workings of inequalities, particularly across the axes of class and gender. At the same time it has demonstrated the importance of culture and meaning, and the narratives people tell which make sense of their material conditions. These both re-create familiar patterns, and create the conditions for change.

As well as happening at individual and community level, these dynamics also happen at the level of populations and public. Areas where a lot of work is already being done include the different discourses, or socially shared storylines, surrounding the topics of learning and work, health and wellbeing, participation and exclusion. Many people across continents are seeking ways to embed more appropriate understandings in policy and practice.

Other foci are still emerging. The Making a Life research has highlighted the dynamics of hope and fear, of opening up and closing down, and the important role of personal and shared narratives in changes to lives and communities. Under conditions of rapid social change and uncertainty, this is a dynamic which warrants more attention, in relation to young people's wellbeing, and mental, spiritual, social and physical health (Eckersley et al. 2006a). Hope and fear, as we have seen, are central dynamics in young people's engagement in learning. Also, in a climate where young people are more connected than ever before by technology, but also increasingly separated by fear (Wierenga 2006), questions of dominant narratives around citizenship (why, what, who) become more important than ever.

In this context, I think often about the role of commercial mass media as bards, or keepers of the shared narratives. As others have pointed out, there are important roles in interrupting dominant narratives (Apple 2002), for fostering critical analysis, creating dialogical and inter-generational spaces where young people and communities can explore and invest in alternative storylines, and explore what really matters (Eckersley et al. 2006a; Eckersley et al. 2007).

Concluding comments

I started this book looking for a mandate for action, as someone who works with, lives with, and cares about young people. I stopped doing youthwork because the old narratives I could access did not fit the current realities. As with the young people, it seems that for practitioners there is nothing so powerful as a story about why we do the things we do, to help us engage.

This research has identified some key areas for attention. Particularly listening and learning, and attending to the dynamics of resource flows, narrative and trust. Perhaps the biggest challenge is how to embed these elements beyond one-off efforts, within systems that are usually doing something else. In relaying this story, it is heartening to recognize that there are already entire armies of folks in research, policy and practice working on each of these fronts. The themes are very local, but in a context of rapid social change they are also shared across continents. Perhaps all that one person can do is to be creative in their own patch and draw their learnings into the ongoing conversation.

This book is a new work of narrative – of storying past, present and future possibility. It is an exercise in reflective practice. For me it has been a powerful antidote to voicelessness, stuckness, and a sense of being overwhelmed by the tasks which face youthworkers, teachers, and those who live and work with young people. It has identified many agendas and possibilities for future action, as well as some of the resources at hand, and it has begun to map some of the sources of these. In all, the context will never be ideal, but there is plenty to be getting on with, and the company is good.

11
Research and Theory as Grounded Social Practice

When I started out as a sociology PhD candidate, a great deal of effort went into understanding and maintaining some binary conceptual categories. These include: What is theory? What is research? What are the distinctions between doing youthwork with young people and doing research fieldwork with young people? I knew then that it was important to break from *doing* things with young people and their communities in order to claim some space to *think* about what I was seeing, and to put a language around it that made more sense. However, a significant part of doing a project of this type – of 'growing up' as a sociologist and researcher – has been a growing awareness of the integrity of the whole, and the interrelatedness of all of these levels of engagement. To be effective, work with young people at a state and community level needs to be based upon coherent sets of assumptions and theoretical frameworks, about such topics as young people's well-being, learning and citizenship. These things in turn depend upon understandings about what is happening to our communities in the face of social change, to rural places, the phenomenon of 'youth', and the kinds of transitions that they are negotiating in contemporary societies. If it is going to be well targeted, both policy and community-based practice also need to be based upon grounded research. Research is greatly enriched in a dialogue with sociological theory, and our theoretical frameworks and assumptions constantly need to be grounded and challenged by the stories of real people. Each of these kinds of involvement actually requires and informs the others.

Conceptual models that have been useful for thinking about the research process have been about 'praxis', or thinking and action (Freire 1973), and the 'hermeneutic spiral', or doing and then better understanding (Heidegger 1962). For me, the lived experience, and the most useful image, is one of *spiralling* inwards and outwards: between research and practice; between engagement in the world of people's issues and engagement in the world of ideas of the discipline; between inspired thought and creative action; between the conceptual frameworks offered by the discipline and the things that only real individuals can teach.

This chapter presents an exploration of the spiral, and it is based around discoveries from the *doing* of this research. Firstly, I present a brief overview of research findings and contributions. Secondly, the discoveries made are a direct reflection of the kinds of research methods used, and so I will explore discoveries relating to the research process itself. Thirdly, I will argue that good research is about establishing a creative dialogue between the world of ideas available to us (the theory) and real people's lives and stories. I will explore some of the issues of involving young people in this kind of dialogue. Fourthly, conversations with respondents present challenges, but also provide information about 'methodologies of hope'. Finally, the chapter concludes with some learnings, reflections and unanswered questions about the social process of doing good research.

Finding a way out/finding a way in

Amidst conditions of rapid social change, there is strong international interest in how young people are creatively making lives within the situations in which they find themselves. This has been one such study. I followed the trajectories and stories of 32 young people from one rural Australian town, at first closely through formal interviews over six years, and then continued conversations with most respondents for over ten years, well into adulthood. I defined making a life in terms of establishing livelihood, meaning, social connectedness. The empirical focus of the study was upon trajectory and meaning, that is, what individuals were doing, where they were going, and the sense that they were able to make of it all.

This research has looked at how young people are differently making a life in the midst of social conditions that are not optimal. Earlier, through the youth research literature, I highlighted some issues that are common to young people growing up in many contemporary societies, but exacerbated by rurality. These included the effects of globalization in market economies and changes in local economies, their impact on patterns of labour and industry, and also the collapse of the youth job-market. In climates of economic rationalism we can see that rural communities are, at this time, left in a quite diminished position to resource their young in terms of livelihoods, and in terms of other social connections and stories about the future in which they can believe. Because of social inequalities such as class, gender and race, some are being affected by these social changes far more than others. Throughout the book, I have explored how these things shape the lives and lived experience of the young people from one small town.

In order to make any sense of young people's complex lives, listening to their stories is essential. The conceptual frameworks that we use when talking *about* them often bear little relation to their lived experiences, and can be fairly thin descriptions (in an ethnographic sense). On the basis of their stories, I have shared some thick descriptions about the process of making a life: about their transitions; about youth agency and social structure; about young people's own strategies, negotiations and engagements; about the social processes that see young people's life-chances structured so differently from each other; about the resources available to young people as they make a life; and about how they are differently accessing these resources.

A model of four different cultural orientations, or four different modes of 'storying', has been central to this study. It emerged from our early conversations and formed an interpretive framework for the whole research project. I used a visual representation of four types to describe and explain the effects of local history and culture on the different ways that young people were making a life. The inherent patterns were profoundly classed and gendered (refer back to Chapter 4). This same model became a way to explore a multitude of issues (listed above) in a processual way.

To sum up the findings of the book in only one paragraph would look something like this: the young people are making their lives differently from each other because they can access very different resources. The resources they access are of different types: practical resources; resources of symbol and meaning; resources of habit and practice. All different types of resources become available to individuals in the same way – always through relationships of trust – be that with other individuals, with groups, or with institutions. These relationships are a result of biographical and group history, so the individuals in the study are situated very differently in terms of the things that they can access in the process of making a life. Patterns of resource flows within these trust relationships strongly reflect local history, gender, and particularly class. In grounded terms, young people are able to make quite different lives because of the things that they can access through their networks, and through their networks' own networks. It is these things that make up social structure. Individual agency, then, also needs to be understood in terms of these stories, these relationships and these resource flows.

In this research, the young people's narratives and their practices of *storying* became a central feature. Throughout the preceding chapters, interwoven with emerging themes of *resources* and *trust relationships*, the notion of *storying* has shown itself to be significant to contemporary questions about young people's wellbeing, their learning and their active social participation.

If the learnings from this case study are transferable, they might also have layers of implications for understanding other communities' relationships with their young. For example, in this research, answers to questions of young people's engagement in *learning and work* clearly depends upon what is defined as 'relevant to me' in young people's own narratives about their lives. Answers to questions about their *active social participation* are wedded to questions of agency or capacity to *do*, their stories of who they are, the company they travel with, and their histories of trust. Likewise, answers to questions about *citizenship* are framed by individually and socially shared narratives of who 'we' are as well as who 'they' are and what 'they' mean. Young people's *wellbeing* depends upon finding ways of negotiating uncertainty, on narratives of hope or fear, on trust relationships with self and others, and capacity to access all kinds of resources through these. The 'take-home' messages of all this for policy and practice have been addressed more fully in Chapter 10.

In addition to the contributions of this research discussed so far, the findings of this study were closely related to the methods used. Many of the understandings developed were a direct result of the research processes, and this raised issues of how to do good research with young people. I will elaborate here on some of the issues involved in doing this research, and on some lessons learned in the process.

Research procedures/social process

Doing good qualitative research is not about procedures; it is about social relationships. During this project I learned that issues of social process, for example negotiations and alliances, meaning and engagement, trust and resource flows, are not just central to research findings but also to the research process itself. Discoveries are about listening and watching; insight is about asking and taking the time to understand. Continued access to people's lives, in order to do any of these things, is always about trust. Trust comes from communicating well and being trustworthy. Access to respondents, their stories, and to rich data are intrinsically bound up in the nature of relationships formed in the field. These relationships are forged through sensitivity in negotiations and face-to-face encounters. Equally significantly, though, they are about trying to understand well, being respectful of respondents' voices, striving to do some sort of justice to complex issues, and caring about how individuals and their stories are being represented.

To be an interviewer is hard work, but to be interviewed is to be vulnerable. In some cases I am asking a young person to do a thing that they have learned, for 15 years, not to do – put themselves out there, to be exposed. At the outset, we needed to negotiate together ways that they could do this without endangering their sense of wellbeing.

Some approaches that worked well with uneasy respondents were also ones that re-distributed power within the relationship. These included interviewing in pairs (far more culturally appropriate for at least four of the girls, who would do their thinking out loud and corporately), and also interviewing in the institution's time. Non-academic students were interviewed at school during maths period, or when not on a break at work (with teacher/boss cooperation of course). This seemed to change the power dynamics – even with all parties being aware of what was happening. It re-positioned the interviewer (me) as ally beside them (respondent) as they reclaimed some power over their time, outside the routines of the institution. Todd would not go back to work. When I suggested it he just grinned and kept talking (and he is a man of few words). When I suggested that Ellen go back in, she decided that there was another story that she had to tell me. It really helped that the work-supervisors and teachers approached were sympathetic to my research aims.

Some respondents needed to spend time doing things together with me, rather than sitting down and looking at each other. The latter is one distinct cultural way of operating that does not work well with many people. Particularly with males, there is a lot to be said for side-by-side 'walking-talking' or 'working-talking' rather than 'eyeball-to-eyeball-talking'. For other respondents, questioning me, and getting a clearer picture of my interests and agendas, was important:

How would I go about getting your job? (Sarah)

For another respondent, role-play was in order:

I'll do your job, and you can be me! (Kylie)

Each of these things is about establishing trust. In the field, it seems that the researcher's job is to fit in with/facilitate whatever respondents need to do to feel comfortable in telling their story. Accordingly we conducted interviews at home, at work, at sophisticated coffee shops sipping lattes, at school or college, in malls, driving, on the phone, or lugging rocks or stacking wood together, in parks with the dog, and alone, or with siblings, parents, or friends present.

Goffman (1969) used a 'dramaturgical' approach to describe the ways in which individuals manage identities and encounters: 'backstage' for the things that remain hidden; 'frontstage' for the public performance. It was sometimes inevitable, and often quite useful, to let respondents see my own humanity and the chaos of the research process – to have some backstage activity spill into the encounter. This diffused power issues, created humour and even fostered respondents' ownership of the whole project (for example Sonia explained to the tape recorder about the things it had missed when Ani messed up the recording).

Within interviews, tape recorders became useful as explicit power-sharing devices: 'The off-switch is *here,* in case you want to say something that you don't want on the record.' At other times, the (elsewhere expounded) 'switch off' effect (Measor 1985) meant that respondents (and particularly their parents) would share inside stories when the official interview was over. Sometimes, where reading transcripts was going to be an issue (for example, poor literacy, ADHD), we listened to the respondent's tapes instead. In other situations, tapes set up a kind of playful reflexivity during interviews; one respondent (not middle class, not *exploring*) enjoyed listening to what she had just said and commenting on it further.

Even for confident respondents, to be interviewed is a strange experience (see Measor 1985). So much depends upon establishing safety *early* for this fairly unusual exchange. This entailed negotiating differently with different respondents.

The issue of informed consent was very much about negotiated realities. Good communication is important. For example. 'Yes' easily becomes 'No' if a question about being interviewed is framed disrespectfully or timed wrongly. Whether individuals do want to/do not want to be interviewed is a very fine line, especially at first. The meaning of the 'ask' is being constructed as we negotiate.

Especially in early days, access depends upon relating well with parents and institutions as much as it does with the respondents themselves. This creates tensions around protocols: how to do the right thing by parents while simultaneously getting the negotiations right with their children? If going by formal rules, parental permission is primary, but that is particularly bad process with teenagers. Time-delays between the initial conversations with potential respondents and their first interview can provide space for fear to build, and this is not helpful either.

The same applies with negotiations through schools and managers at work. The last thing a researcher needs is to be seen by the young respondent to be colluding with parents/school/work in order to corner them.

It has been important to negotiate differently with different families. What are their expectations, their needs for information, or reassurances required first? Can I get parents' consent over the phone immediately after the young person agrees, and can we deal with the form later? Once parents knew me and the project, and understood that I really wanted to hear their children, there were few problems gaining access at that level (Connell et al. 1982 relate a similar experience).

Some negotiations, though, were harder in early encounters. Issues of social structure and wider power relations had an impact upon relationships with families *even before we met*. In the early phase of my university honours project (1995), I conducted some trial interviews in Taroona (middle-class suburb). Parents were supportive, even sympathetic, so long as exam times were avoided. They framed their involvement as 'helping you out with your uni project' [Poor Dear]: 'What are you doing your thesis on?'. Early encounters with working-class Myrtle Vale parents revealed something quite different. Paraphrased, initial responses were more like: 'Please don't hurt my kid.' It is wise to expect fear or hostility from those parents who are not familiar with social research or university. The researcher poses a threat and the onus is upon her to prove otherwise. That is gruelling, but fair.

When Noah kept losing his consent-form, there was something else going on. Consent-forms must be signed by parents, but in some cases they cannot read. It is important to be aware of that possibility, and to sensitively negotiate through it.

It is in the early stages of research relationships that rapport, trust and mutual respect take shape, or not. Watching vocabulary was also important, and framing questions in ways that were meaningful for respondents. Young people who are really powerless do not respond well when asked to do 'interviews' about 'choices' and 'futures'.

In other studies researchers have found that: 'poor rural girls have little sense of a future, or of possibilities outside their present life' (Yates 1996). Seeking respondents' world-views sometimes entails keeping the conversation topics very grounded, framed by the things that they are used to talking about (like 'tell me about your new job'/ 'tell me about Myrtle Vale'). This is not disingenuous or unfocussed, as all the significant research themes somehow become linked within their stories. We just have to find a safe way in.

'Rapport' could be defined in terms of resource flows between respondents and interviewers. Good rapport entails making full use of respondents' frames of reference, *their* language, *their* schemes and themes. This means listening well, so that the process becomes more collaborative; rather than simply doing research *on* young people, it also incorporates elements of exploring *with* them on areas of mutual interest. When the research process is about shared discovery, it is rewarding for all parties.

This project is not truly collaborative in terms of the tradition of Participatory Action Research (Wadsworth 2006). To describe it as collaborative would be to down-play the extent to which I set the agenda as researcher. On the other hand, to over-emphasize power differences is to sell the young respondents short. As discussed elsewhere in this chapter, power is diffuse, multi-centered, and operates in complex ways between us. I strongly believe that, without the collaboration (not simply co-operation) of most the respondents most of the time, this study of young people's lives would not be what it is. It was at the points where respondents actually engaged as researchers of their own lives that some of the sharpest insights emerged. At its best points, this research became collaborative, while at its most violent points it fell well short of this ideal (more on this later in the chapter). Considering these dynamics, perhaps the *ideal* of collaboration is a useful reminder of good process.

This is not simply an ethical/ideological stand but also a pragmatic one. A meaningful interview for the respondent also means more rich data for the researcher. Respondents' engagement in, and commitment to, the research process makes a qualitative difference to the type of information shared.

A good qualitative interview releases the storyteller to do their work. The order in which questions and themes are introduced either facilitates this process or gets in the way. In early re-interviews, it got in the way. I had mistakenly been asking distant, demographic questions first, and logically working up to things of trust and substance. It was, in fact, a much better process to let respondents' *own* passions frame the interview from the start. (This is harder with those who share few real-world passions, but more on this later). The first few questions actually establish frames of reference for the rest of the interview, as well as *lasting roles* and *power dynamics* (interrogator/subject or collaborative explorers). Consequently the best interviews began with very open questions like: 'So what is it that you really want to do?'; or 'What happened?'. The differences in topics covered also became a source of good data. Meanwhile, both the themes behind the interview, and the more closed demographic questions, were easily addressed by their stories, and in the dialogue that followed.

A community-based study leads to insights about young people's negotiations and practices of engagement *in context* (young people's networks and their networks' networks). Interviews with other sources (parents, school staff, community members) and observations meant triangulation of data, but also a multi-voiced account, which enabled a thicker description of social life in Myrtle Vale. Stories were often conflicting, reflecting different life-worlds in all their complications. Cultural orientations – *exploring, settling, wandering* and *retreating* – became useful frames for working with these different voices.

Other researchers (Connell et al. 1982; Measor 1985) suggest that the richness of the data from any interview is a function of the quality of relationships and the *time invested beforehand*. Within this study, doing longitudinal research has been essential to the kinds of insights gained. Time invested in relationships within the field grows exponentially in returns. The earliest and most stressful investments are met with small rewards. As trust grows both ways (see Wax 1971), fieldwork becomes much less uncomfortable. Alongside depth of rapport with respondents, and thickness of their stories, time (over years) and trust-worthiness return an abundance of new encounters and new stories. By 1999, I had been visiting Myrtle Vale, on and off, for seven years. In my researcher journal I noted: 'I think I only really arrived in the last 12 months. No, I'm not a local or an insider, but something has just shifted.'

That was the year the school asked me for help with a submission for funding, those who had been involved in the research wanted to hear what I had found out, and other parents started spontaneously telling stories of 'how the kids are doing'. A young man hailed me at the service station in Myrtle Vale, leaned on the car and playfully hassled: 'you never interviewed me!' (Fieldnotes, May 1999). Other young people in the school were regularly asking: 'When's *my* turn?'.

The previous chapter showed how trust (of people, places and projects) can be vicariously earned within groups. It seems that this applies to researchers as well – 'trust by osmosis'. Credibility grew once some key, trusted locals were obviously engaging with, and trusting, me and the project. (I had also experienced this phenomenon after a similar number of years of doing youthwork in another community.)

This whole longitudinal effort began as an honours project that simply, opportunistically, kept going. Interestingly, in an interview (ABC 1999a), Michael Apted explained that his legendary '7-Up' documentary series (Apted 2006) started in the same way: 'the original program was only going to be one film'. Respondents in the Myrtle Vale study were not expecting follow-up interviews the first time, nor the second, and each needed to be re-negotiated. The freshness of each interview became a distinct advantage. No one was under obligation from earlier commitments, no one lived their lives with the awareness of being continually watched by an interviewer, and re-negotiating each interview was always about establishing understandings and building trust. Also, I wonder who would have originally committed to such a long project – and whose stories would have been excluded from the start. One calculated guess is that nearly all respondents would have been middle class and/or female, *exploring* and *wandering*.

As it was, some respondents welcomed me back, one said she had forgotten what the project was about and who I was, others had vague recollections, and still other respondents negotiated their ways in and out of the research as they felt able. This was stressful at the time. How do you conduct valid panel-research when the panel keep doing erratic things? However, these fieldwork dynamics also led to some of the clearest insights (crisis as loss of story, crisis as generalized mistrust, often including mistrust of own stories, crisis and loss of voice). Over the years the project only lost four respondents, but gained communication with two who had not wanted to talk much earlier. Respondents' comings and goings provide rich data about practices, particularly if respondents can explain them later.

Returning again and again, before (early high school) during (the moment of leaving school) and after, meant firstly corroboration of stories, hearing multiple accounts of the same thing (good for thick description), and being able to follow some continuities and changes in stories and trajectories. It meant hearing multiple accounts about shared, as well as individual, lived experience. These young people are not simply respondents, but expert *insider-informants* on group and cultural processes. Returning also meant having access to older, forgotten stories and understandings, which could be re-visited with respondents. All of these are things that would have been missed in one-off interviews.

Thoroughly knowing respondents' earlier stories was an advantage. I had hoped to study respondents' old interview transcripts immediately before their next interview. Sheer busy-ness in the field meant that it did not always happen.

Reading transcripts together was also very useful. These became tools for validation, clearing misconceptions, digging deeper, documenting change, and reflecting. Storying is a collaborative process; stories are enriched in dialogue. Researcher reflections on respondents' stories, my re-framing of what they have said or thought, the bringing back of first-order constructs each can trigger new, even richer descriptions from respondents.

Returning again and again also meant being able to better understand local dynamics and targeting new questions well. Depth in the data collected is the result of an iterative or recursive interviewing process (Minichiello et al. 1995). On transcripts, I wrote codes insisting: 'must ask them about this next time'.

As well as revealing further instances of familiar patterns, the recursive interviewing style meant going back and interrogating the gaps and surprises in the data. It meant not burying and hiding anomalies (because they threaten to mess up neat theories), but digging them out for further inspection. It meant elaborating the conditions under which different things occur. When Mark got his secure job immediately after finishing grade ten, that did not seem to fit the model at all. In the lead-up to leaving school, he had no clear story of what he was going to do and it seemed he was not being pro-active. When I returned to the field, I asked: 'What happened?' 'How did it happen?'. 'Negotiation by proxy' was the resulting discovery (see Chapter 5) – a new idea that was then corroborated by others' stories. (Families' networks regularly secure local young men their manual jobs – and *they* bear the onus and feel the moral responsibility for that process.)

Longitudinal research has advantages for understanding social process. It offers (jerky) 'film' rather than a 'snapshot'. The panel provides a useful way of observing contrasts in context, in young people's negotiations and engagements, and their accounts of lived experience. Over time this method reveals patterns in these things (different resources, but similar patterns of flow and the role of trust relationships). Earlier hunches can be checked and verified or re-visited.

At the same time, though, social life is dynamic and complex. Multiple interviews from the same individuals often mean conflicting stories of the same topic. As noted by others who have conducted longitudinal studies, the effect can be to destabilize a sense of finality or truth for the researcher (McLeod 2000; Thomson and Holland 2003).

As they look back at their transcripts, respondents, too, have different ways of interpreting discrepancies. Some talk in terms of personal change. Meanwhile Ellen in her second interview says: 'You know, we told you so much stuff, and half of it wasn't even true!'. In relation to their own longitudinal studies, Rachael Thomson and Janet Holland highlight the value of not seeking certainty regarding respondent identities, and they emphasize the importance of recognizing identity as process rather than a completed state. 'Successive interviews gave us a better understanding of the individual, if not the "truth" of that person.' (Thomson and Holland 2003:237).

Practices and context have made a useful focus in this study, and this has allowed for acknowledgement of fluid identities, amidst recurring social patterns. Beyond the search for real 'facts, events, feelings or meanings' (Silverman 2000), respondents' stories can be read as 'cultural texts' differently constructed by individuals to create understandings, using available cultural resources.

There were gendered patterns in the types of data available to work with. It is harder to get inside what young men are doing, in particular their negotiation strategies. In interviews, young men are apt to provide shorter answers. They are usually willing to donate far less time in interviews to self-analysis, and to the analysis of their own negotiation strategies. In most cases this kind of practice does not seem to come easily, nor is it engaging. (The clear exceptions to both of these points are three young men who spend a lot of time consolidating their stories with their mothers). Other research has found the same, suggesting that our conversation-style interviews may be a more woman-friendly medium (Measor 1985). Another significant factor was my gender: as a woman researcher I had a certain rapport with the young women. Other gender items will probably remain secret men's business.

Trust relationships are not only of fundamental importance in the field, but also well beyond it, into data analysis and writing. There are some significant issues attached to working with respondents' stories and voices.

While to the researcher, this is a project (and a passion), to those being researched, this is their lives under scrutiny. There are implications here for how stories are written in doing justice to stories shared, by presenting them in all their complexity, thick with context, and in respecting respondent anonymity. These two interests clash regularly. It was important to protect the anonymity of respondents as had been promised; they are too easy to recognize in a small community. Some respondents have been written-up as two people, specifically to separate sensitive material from their other more recognizable stories. It is difficult to change minor details of a story without significantly altering its shape. Even a change of occupation mangles some of the best quotes.

How dare I/can I/will I write this thing? The main dilemma has been about privileges of access, and doing justice to the stories and lives shared:

> The feeling I get after conducting that interview, the phone one, is, a real hollowness. It's like I've, I have touched a sore spot and I've allowed her to pour out everything that's painful, and, I have nothing to offer her. She – she was very generous, they're generous with their pain, the people who talk, and generous with, with their lives, and I have only ears to offer them. I don't know what comfort that is, um, I don't know whether she gets anything out of it or whether she's just a – a truly generous being (Sigh). I'm thankful but I feel like I've been in a space where I shouldn't have been. (Researcher diary, 1999).

Respondents' trust and generosity means a responsibility for writing their stories well. More often than not in the first three years, this was paralysing. Regularly breaking through this paralysis relied on drawings, stories, poems, my journal tapes even have songs on them. In many instances to write anything in a linear form, or to make diagrams felt dangerously like making caricatures of people and issues that are, in reality, so much more complex. Audio tapes have been valuable, constantly bringing the respondents' voices back into the writing.

Another issue was the integrity of stories. When people are hearing about this project for the first time, 'returning to the same young people over years... making a life...' they often say: 'Like a miniature 7-Up?'. However, something different happens to respondents' stories when they are presented thematically, which is not like the recently screened '49 Up'(Apted 2006) at all. Michael Apted's refusal to voice-over and draw conclusions about participants lives in the current iteration of the project has been widely recognized. On the other hand, in my own research, the writer's voice is loudest and the individuals' lives are fragmented into themes, and they cannot properly be traced. This touches on significant issues and debates about what researchers actually do with people's stories (see Fine 1992; Richardson 1992; Hood et al. 1999; Frank 2004). In their book about 'streetkids' voices, Peter Cullen and Carol Ann Marshall (1999) present this challenge:

> It wasn't our intention to impose any hierarchy or structure on interviews... All we've changed is the interviewee's name... We've been sensitive to the danger involved in putting the book forward as yet another academic study by researchers who seem to know best about everyone else's life, especially disadvantaged people's life. (viii–ix)

Here, researchers really enter a world of clashing ideals. How we analyse is important and even to analyse *at all* is contentious.

The form of research will depend upon the purpose for which it is conducted (Yates 1996). I analyse in the way I do because I want to understand and put a language around some all-too-familiar social processes. Respondents rarely, if ever, talk explicitly about the spheres of learning, social participation or wellbeing, yet it is in these areas where their detailed stories can yield some powerful insights. I want the things that kids say to inform policy and practice with young people. To this end perhaps there is something about aesthetics, comfort levels and researcher impunity that needs to give way at times. To reflect on what people tell us, it is sometimes important to look critically and explicitly at social structure and process, and in this case, to the new things that young people's stories can show us about them. A critical look at structure and process may sometimes involve going to places where few people will follow. Does that necessarily mean we should not go there? I think not.

My breaking-up of respondents' stories into themes is about this, and it also respects respondents' privacy. In an attempt to keep the integrity of the stories, extended quotes and abundant information about context has been included. In a small town, people are too easy to trace, and fragmented narratives is ironically one of the better protections that I can offer.

Alongside the issue of working with respondents' stories and voices sits the issue of *working with their silences.*

Practices of storying are intertwined with rapport, habit, culture. Within the research (like within young people's lives), these things form loops which are self-perpetuating. If a respondent is used to doing some self-contained storying (as compared to more collective storying), our rapport is generally stronger... so more rewarding storying exchanges follow. The converse is also true. Some interviews are long, fluent and generously worded. and there is plenty of text there to analyse. But some are very truncated, containing many 'I don't know's'. There is no less going on here. I suspect that often the young people with least to say have the most to teach us.

It is hard to analyze silence, and to do it ethically and respectfully. How dare I put words into her mouth? I cannot. But I can write, albeit very carefully. I can talk about patterns of practice that I see. I can talk about contextual factors that may have contributed to this silence (more on the politics of this later). Research is always a little inconclusive. I can write my hunches about why, as long as they are framed as such, but I cannot know. Does she even know? If knowing is about coherent stories, probably not.

I have found some good insights from observing the silences, and analyzing muted conversations. Hunches frame good future questions, if our verbal dialogue ever gets that far. Occasionally it does. With Elizabeth, and also with Beth, I had a chance to go back two years later and ask each what had been happening for them at the time of their first interviews. Each explained the crisis that she had been experiencing, but there was no way that she could have verbalized that at the earlier interview. For them, as they explained later, a lack of language about what was happening was a significant part of the problem that they were experiencing.

If we are prepared to sit with them over time, and observe the silences, *the ways in which young people do not talk to us can be as informative as the ways in which they do.*

Another result of getting close to important issues in people's lives was their *anger*. I learned not to flee from others' outbursts; as long as they wanted to keep talking (even heatedly) the channels of communication were open. The emotions were rarely directed at me but at the situation: 'What is it you want? Why do you keep ringing us? Why do you want to talk to him about choices? Look, he *had* no choice!' (Jenny).

Later that same hour, Jenny said: 'Sorry about that, I'm a bit under pressure at the moment', regarding just getting-by. Her son Richard, who had bellowed, 'I've got nothing to say to you!', translates his own words two years later: 'Right then I didn't know what I was going to do.'

Where emotional outbursts had happened and communication had stayed open (where trust had been tested), I found greater permissions to go into secret places. Respondents' generosity with their stories demonstrates trust, but this trust presents new challenges:

> I still feel really hollow. (Sigh) hollow like I (sigh) um offer them nothing but the chance to speak and that the speaking hurts them (silence). (Small voice) Still they choose to do it – what do these people get out of being interviewed? (Researcher journal, 1999)

Sometimes, researcher discomfort clashes with convictions that this is worth doing. There is a fine line between providing forums for others' voices and being a voyeur – especially with those who are being and/or feeling oppressed. I observed the need to keep at bay a kind of journalistic 'vulture' instinct. I learned to recognize and celebrate when individuals claim their *power to not speak* but also when they *claim their power to speak*.

Out of these things comes a recognition that power is not static but complex and multi-dimensional, and that the agency of the researched should not be overlooked (see Long and Long 1992). Much as the researcher position is a powerful one (in relation to 'voice' and publishing), there are different ebbs and flows of power here, and different currents operating at once. The young respondents have definitely been exercising their agency in this research process. Within their choices to be involved or not, when to be involved, to tell or not, how to tell the story, and how far they let me in, they are exercising considerable power. The wholeness of the story I tell is dependent upon being able to hear their stories. But the wholeness of this story also depends upon their ability or willingness to speak.

Sitting with respondents' stories for 12 years has meant slowly and cumulatively finding a language that made sense of the data. My most significant finding (and biggest nightmare at the time) was *how much data young people's stories actually carried about cultural and social pro-*

cesses. Every statement says something about available resources and relationships. The volume of data was overwhelming, everything was relevant, and it took literally years to sort it out under appropriate themes. The clear message here, though, is never to read young people's stories superficially. They have far more to teach us than we may expect.

Method and sociological insight

As well as telling us about their own agency and subjectivities, young people's stories can speak directly into our understandings of social structure and social process. If we listen well, we will find our own thin stories becoming thicker descriptions. Within the pages of this book, what I have been striving to do is to create a space of respectful dialogue between individuals' lives and sociological theory. I have discovered that creating safe spaces for that dialogue is important. It also needs to be done carefully, and there are some caveats that come from this work that I will explore below.

Listeners to young people's stories can expect to find many layers of meaning. Beyond things explicitly spoken, like passions or aspirations, are things implicitly spoken or unspoken. These take different forms: things communicated as bi-lines to other stories (list of resources, sources, common processes of resource flows) the unspoken but practised ('do things' or 'sorting it'); and finally the unspoken and equally significant (observing the silences with *retreating* young women). These more subliminal levels become particularly important for understanding social difference, social structure, and social process. We are the poorer if we do not attend to them.

Within the process of this dialogue, both respondents and researcher have had to wrestle with some *big questions*.

Good research is based upon trust relationships and it needs to be meaningful for respondents. If research ever becomes a violation, respondents close down. Violations potentially happen when a respondent is betrayed, is not well heard, is made very uncomfortable or is made wrong. Making research meaningful is easy with some, as is creating basic trust. These are the respondents: who are used to having others ask for, and listen to, their stories; those for whom 'past, future and me' are already clearly storied; and for whom what we are doing is already core business.

Other respondents, face, and present, more challenges. How to frame questions for (especially male *settling*) concrete thinkers? What are the best ways to ground conversations so that concrete thinkers can engage with the subject matter, and, at the same time, not limit the scope of their stories? How to organize the interview so that it is not limited to certain pre-conceived practical subjects?

Sometimes there is a fine line between bringing normally unspoken things to consciousness, and making respondents either wrong ('I've never thought about that') or very uncomfortable. Do questions need to be changed so that respondents are not wrong? What then does this say about consciousness-raising and about the ethics of consciousness-raising and the assumptions behind it? (Is it a kind of middle-class cultural imperialism?). For *settling* respondents, the research process is interesting if culturally unusual and amusing/bemusing. It may well be useful for them to think about options out loud before circumstances change around them (for example, jobs disappear).

Meanwhile, the questions linger. How to talk futures with young people with whom futures are bleak? How to do research with those who are already violated and closed down? Is it possible? Is it ethical to try? It seems that for some to speculate about the future is not at all rewarding, and to talk about the past is like ripping the scab off a wound.

During interviews I found a meeting place with some of the walking wounded, and their insights are some of the most profound for this research. An example is the lived experience of being within and/or emerging from crisis. Some say explicitly that the research process was useful in terms of their own storying (more on this later). Together, these things *present enough impetus to keep wrestling with these big questions.*

There are other hard issues with which to wrestle. Something distasteful happens if individuals' stories become simply examples of social and cultural theories. Young people are not just repositories of social process and group cultures. As one respondent proclaims in her grade seven essay: 'I'm an *indivigual*' (her own choice of spelling, Phoebe). As well as recognizing how individuals share qualities with others, it is important to also show some respect for each one's particular and unique story (see also Massey 1994; Frank 2004).

There is something ugly about taking another's story and working it to the point where they may not recognize it any more (Watts 1993). To do this represents a kind of symbolic violence (Bourdieu and Passeron 1977). This presents a dilemma, because concepts like 'class', 'gender', 'globalization', and 'rural decline' clearly have a significant role to play in the analysis of these young people's stories. Respondents actually know all too well the limitations that are imposed on their own lives and the lives of loved ones. Examples from their stories include: how other families (not theirs) 'run' the town; not being able to get a local mechanic's job as a girl; Dad's job disappearing; and not having enough people to be able to make up a local football team any more. They say things in fresh ways and in terms of lived experience, usually framed as troubles for private individuals, and not as major issues of populations (see Mills 1959:7).

Using ideal-types or models is one of the more controversial features of this research. Many of my research colleagues have resisted the use of such models, and for good reason. Insightful questioning about the use of models in respectful methods reaches well beyond youth research. Canadian narrative theorist, Arthur Frank (2001) highlights that to type people according to extra-local categories can intensify suffering for those being researched (in his case, those experiencing illness), and feed into existing power relations. Method also ultimately depends on the purpose of the piece of research. I write to create possibilities for more effective practice. The simplicity of this recurring two-by-two model evokes recognition from the sector, and links groups to different possibilities for action. This, for now, means sitting with any discomfort associated with the use of this model, including my own.

There are more researcher dilemmas. It is a harsh judgement call to talk about inconsistent narratives, or to highlight goals without the means to achieve them (see Chapter 4). It may be politically incorrect, and it certainly feels disrespectful. Other colleagues have opted for a different approach, explaining they prefer to provide optimistic, generous readings even where young people's stories of the future seem unrealistic. A large part of me simply wants to support the young people in their stories and hope they make it. However, I suspect ultimately the practitioner in me is the one that is driving as I write this book. I have seen too many young people for whom dreams do not work. There is now evidence that mental health problems and suicide rates increase, not with harsh conditions, but where there is a widening gap between the real conditions of people's lives and their desires (Eckersley 2005). Even where a sense of respect leaves me in two minds, to dig into the dynamic of what is happening for these young people, I believe that this analysis needs to go there.

These are real researcher dilemmas, and there are no easy answers. The real injustice would come from not representing respondents' narratives well, and not being open to learn from the stories that they bring. For instance, to simply use individuals' stories as exemplars of some theory we already knew, would be abhorrent. In every chapter

I have tried to establish a dialogue between respondents and researcher, between their stories (as I hear them) and broader theories.

Not surprisingly, these methodological/political issues seem not to bother respondents. Some are, however, interested in how the things that they (personally) said are being used, and so, in later interviews, we re-checked the themes that arose from their input. This accords with a grounded theory approach. First-order constructs met their approval (or not) and were shaped accordingly. At earlier stages, my writing was not at a point where I could show them their quotes enmeshed in my text. Later, it was, and in places this book has documented their responses and dialogue with the text. This did not happen with all respondents; there are researcher ideals, and then there are real-world constraints.

If I am honest, I am actually writing some things that I would not wish some respondents to understand, as the social-systemic picture regarding life-chances and opportunities can be really nasty. As we bur-rowed deeper into text and abstraction and layers of analysis, some would be excluded from engaging even more than before. And to insist that they did would be culturally violent.

Methodologies of hope

In the story related last chapter, Kylie says 'Tell me how I've changed.' I say 'That's your job.' She playfully grabs me around the neck: 'I need this Ani!' Especially where young people are devalued in their relation-ships, simply listening well to their stories may be the most powerful contradiction, affirmation and validation that can be offered.

Being acknowledged and reflected by another person creates a new experience of the 'looking glass self' (see Cooley 1922). Richly re-telling what I had just heard, I found myself cast in a collaborative 'co-storying' role. Michael White (1995) explains the role of audiences as *co-authors* in the narrative process, assisting people to create and consolidate alterna-tive storylines. I discovered that this is a bigger process which does not respect the neat, rigid distinctions of youthwork practitioner/researcher. Ironically, although this research began for me as a way of bailing out of youthwork for a while, it was probably the most effective piece of youth-work I have ever done (Wierenga 2002).

Concluding remarks

For me, the biggest surprises in the whole project have involved how often the research process came to be an embodiment of the issues

being studied. Themes of power and efficacy in negotiations, engagement and meaning, storying and making sense, different resources,
resource flows, trust and mistrust were all graphically lived-out in the
relationships between researcher and respondents. This research process
has clearly embodied some empowering social processes but at other
times has embodied the opposite, leaving unresolved some issues for
further thought.

Feminist and action researchers have drawn attention to the fact that
all too often, social research processes replicate other oppressive social
patterns (see Bowes 1996). They and other researchers (for example, see
Hood et al. 1999; Mayall 1999) are seeking to conduct research in ways
that challenge patterns of oppression.

As noted by other researchers, young people can often share richly of
themselves in research for very little direct return (Ram 1995; White et
al. 1996). In this study, when respondents were able to engage, it seems
the research process is one that directly resourced them:

> Kylie: Can you come back again in two years and interview me
> again?
> AW: But I will have finished in two years.
> Kylie: That doesn't matter! Come back and interview me anyway!

Initially, I was surprised at how some young people warmed to being
interviewed, and at *them* being the first to say: 'Thankyou!' afterwards.
Some say it was a chance to think out loud:

> AW: It makes me realize how little you might get to talk about
> what you're thinking.
> Alex: Yeah, this is a good chance to get stuff off our chest.

and a forum where their voices could be heard:

> Really good that you're doing all this 'cos I think it's good that you
> ask what we think. We get to say what we think. (Joel 3:19)

Interviews were claimed as a surprisingly rare, safe and available space
for storying, even amongst young people who had very good home
relationships. Ironically, some respondents explained that they welcomed talking to an outsider who was external to what they saw as
small-town-gossip, even though they knew I would publish what they
said. Perhaps to be an outsider also meant being naïve, and this created

a freedom to re-construct themselves in the encounter, to test sub-jectivities and voices outside the collective or all-too-familiar stories.

Sadly (and with some very notable exceptions), it was usually the young people who already came to this research process more equipped, who seemed in turn to be best resourced by the process. Rebekah is fully engaged: 'I've made a list…' and using the interviews as a forum for self-development. She already has the habits and symbolic tools in place to do that.

When individuals are not able to engage with a particular other (individual, group or institution), these social encounters become a hassle (see Chapter 6). This applies to research and to sympathetic researchers as much as it does to school and sympathetic teachers. This may have been what led to the four withdrawals from this study. With every respondent though, it became a challenge to frame interviews to be both as meaningful and as accessible as they could be.

However, questions like: 'What are you doing and why?'; 'What do you really want to do next?'; 'How did you get here?'; and 'What would you like to see when you are 60 and look back on your life?' are *big questions*.

What do big questions do to the way we think? For a time, if we allow them, they can jar us out of what Schuetz (1944) calls 'thinking as usual' where things taken-for-granted remain unquestioned. Indi-viduals can shift into a state where assumptions and normal things are examined differently. Then the big questions get bracketed as the world of everyday life takes over again. But as chapter 8 teaches us, once the questions have been asked (exposure) and thought about (engaged with), they are *there* for the re-visiting.

Engaging with the big questions is potentially very useful. On the other hand, what we did was actually a 'tough ask' for *all* respondents. As Pete (one of the most articulate respondents) glibly said:

> Umm, not really. I haven't thought much about the future, it's like… I think about what I'm going to do tomorrow, pretty much.

As explained in Chapter 7, to answer questions like: 'What's changed?' and 'What surprises you?' in re-interviews actually compounds cultural differences further, making a fascinating picture of the different cultural resources and practices that respondents bring. However, it also becomes a tougher assignment for some than for others. Before we had spent some time on their new stories, first responses ranged from: 'This is what I've learned…'; to 'I haven't thought about it'; 'I don't know'; and 'I was stupid'. This leaves plenty of challenges and food for further thought. There is a fine line between researching different cultural practices and running conversational experiments on people, between awakening consciousness and, on the other hand, making young people who are already being disempowered wrong yet again.

Then there are other issues involving the research 'gaze' and surveillance. Often, being an outsider who is interested in someone's life is welcomed. I remember finding a young man's home and, in our first conversation, his mum, stressed-out with said son, says: 'Are you a social worker?' I hurriedly replied that I was not, expecting to see the outside of the door if I was. 'Too bad,' she said 'I could use some help right now.' Her son was not home yet and we had a 'cuppa' anyway. Some people welcome the chance to talk over their live issues with an outsider (even a fully confessed researcher!) to story it, and, in so doing, to make sense of it for themselves.

Some thrive or grow within the experience of being researched, being reflected and reflexive: 'Oh we [the class of '97] will have to have a reunion and ring you up and invite you!' (Sonia); 'Gosh how could one person write so much about me!' (Suzy); 'Play the tape again, can y' play the tape again...' (Simon, after interview three). I was reminded of the power of being socially acknowledged/heard/reflected (as in Cooley's 'looking-glass-self' 1922) and how simply listening to young people powerfully does this, contradicting other dominant social patterns:

> AW: You all talked out?
> Kylie: No I could talk all day if you wanted me to.
> AW: You also say that you get sick of talking...
> Kylie: Yes, but you're listening so I could talk forever.

Everything in this book highlights the importance of a trusted audience for every story that is authored, the role of conversation in reflection, and the value of providing a safe space for young people to story their lives. But while during this research some respondents found this to be a very creative process, others did not want to go there. Where it was embraced by some, it was resisted by others. 'Not that I really wanted to be reminded...' (Fieldnotes, 1999). Worse still, at least once, I become part of the siege dynamics:

> I um, when I first saw Lisa down at the shop yesterday I said: 'Lisa, I wanted to ring you!', and she says: 'What about?' and so on, and

> she said: 'What for, interview me what for?', with a sense of Oh
> God, aggravation or something, um and I said, don't worry it's only
> for my research, I'm not a secret agent for anybody or whatever, and
> she laughed but she laughed in a way that says *these people get asked*
> *too many questions by too many people who have too much power over*
> *them, all the time.* (Taped researcher journal, 1999)

As a researcher, when I am not trusted I become part of that surveillance, add to it, accentuate it. I need to be aware of that.

> When I got there, I had to walk around the place a couple of times
> before I realized that she was actually there – recognized the car – so
> I'd been staking out the house effectively – I knocked on both doors,
> and on my second circumnavigation around the house I was looking
> down The Valley, turned around and suddenly saw her stand back
> from the window – and said: 'Lisa!' just as I saw this white t-shirt dis-
> appear from my peripheral vision, no sound. [I remember feeling the
> hair on the back of my neck stand up – realizing the awfulness of the
> situation – here she is, noiselessly watching me watching her.] So
> I very obviously walked down the middle of the driveway and down
> the road – where she could see me – I'm not here any more, I'm not
> bugging you any more. (Taped researcher journal, 1999)

As explained earlier, four out of 32 respondents said or demonstrated
that they would no longer be involved in the research. It seems that
even though they had each done interviews in the past, a one-on-one
encounter was too big an 'ask'. With clear hindsight, I could have differently approached conversations with the four young women who
withdrew from the study. In 1997 they could have been presented with
an option to be interviewed with somebody else. Although they would
produce qualitatively different kinds of results, joint interviews may
have given a voice to those who might otherwise be silent. They would
have changed power dynamics and provided a less fearsome interview
space for cultures of people who story in more collective ways. In their
previous interviews (1995), three out of these four chose to be interviewed with a friend present. Earlier chapters have revealed how for
some, collective practice is a far more familiar and safe way of engaging
with the world and with new things. What could their collective voices
have explained?

When already socially voiceless people also become voiceless in this
research, what does this mean about the efficacy of the research? About

the ethics? About the politics? Refusal is valuable data about social process and about difference, but it is also reinforcing existing social patterns. It becomes a powerful exemplar of social processes (like trust and resource flows, meaning and engagement) but also a ghastly perpetuation of familiar dynamics.

To become privy to these young people's stories (if possible) may mean working longer and harder on trust relationships. To what end? To write about them and leave?

When respondents opt out of research, hassling them is not an option and working around them is also a poor solution. Ignoring that they were there in the first place is even worse – as if to obliterate their presence or their impact on this study. Using external sources of information (for example, saying most of these are young women from violent homes) means talking *about* them. Using a spokesperson is a possibility. For example, Beth found her way out of a violent home and crisis and was able to name what had been happening for her, and then stayed involved in the study. To merge her stories with some of the others is to make some assumptions, but it is the best information we have. Every preceding chapter shows these tensions: giving space to the young women who negotiated without words, observing, keeping and respecting their silence. I have hoped at the very least to amplify the silence to the point where it cannot be ignored.

I have no doubts that this research was, is, and will continue to be valuable, and my research goals have been met. Fourteen years after the project started, these young people are still teaching me as I write. However the process has also raised some questions, above, that have not been satisfactorily answered. Still the most privileged (plus several notable others) are also the ones who say most clearly that they benefited from this process. Is this realistically the best that I could hope for? The challenge stands: how to better construct research so that it embodies less of the unhealthy social processes being studied. Rather, how can a researcher engage in work that more consistently confronts and challenges these patterns? Clearly, there is room for more work.

References

Abbott-Chapman, J. (1999). The work, study and unemployment mosaic for youth: the search for adult status, *Social policy for the 21st century: justice and responsibility*. Sydney: University of New South Wales.

Abbott-Chapman, J., Hughes, P., & Wyld, C. (1992). Changes and challenges in senior secondary education in Tasmania 1982 to 1991. Hobart: Youth Education Studies Centre, University of Tasmania.

ABC (1999a). Lateline: Now we are 42: Australian Broadcasting Corporation.

—— (1999b). The Trouble with George, *Australian Story*. Australia: Australian Broadcasting Corporation.

—— (2004). Positive Approach Regenerates Timber Town, *Landline*. Australia: Australian Broadcasting Corporation.

ABS (1994). 1991 Census of population and housing basic community profile, Tasmania, urban centre/locality: 06200. Canberra: Australian Bureau of Statistics.

—— (1996). 1996 Census of population and housing Tasmania: statistical local areas, ranked by median personal income. *ABS Website:* http://www.abs. gov.au/websitedbs/D3110124.NSF/4a3fed835c77efdd4a2564d4001de2e5/ce4b 1543349b5ef74a2564d4001e1cc3!OpenDocument 1 June 2001.

—— (1997). Youth Australia: a social report. Canberra: Australian Bureau of Statistics.

—— (1997a). 1996 Census of population and housing: basic community profile. Canberra: Australian Bureau of Statistics.

—— (1997b). 1996 Census of population and housing: selected social and housing characteristics, Australia. Canberra: Australian Bureau of Statistics.

—— (1997c). Mental health and wellbeing: profile of adults, Australia 1997. Canberra: Australian Bureau of Statistics.

—— (1999). Health and socio-economic disadvantage of area. Australian social trends. Canberra: Australian Bureau of Statistics.

—— (2000a). ABS finds suicide highest in 25–44 age group. Canberra: Australian Bureau of Statistics.

—— (2000b). Special article – suicide (year book Australia, 2000). Canberra: Australian Bureau of Statistics.

—— (2001a). Labour force figures for May 2001. Canberra: Australian Bureau of Statistics.

—— (2001b). Regional population growth. Canberra: Australian Bureau of Statistics.

—— (2003). 2035.0 – Census of Population and Housing: Population Growth and Distribution, Australia, 2001: Australian Bureau of statistics.

AIHW (2002). Australia's Health 2002. Canberra: Australian Institute of Health and Welfare.

—— (2005). Australia's Welfare 2005 AIHW Cat. No. AUS 65. Canberra: Australian Institute of Health and Welfare.

—— (2006). Australia's Health 2006 AIHW Cat. No. AUS 73. Canberra: Australian Institute of Health and Welfare.

Apple, M. W. (2002). Interrupting the Right: On Doing Critical Educational Work in Conservative Times. *symploke*, 10.1–2, 133–152.

Apted, M. (2006). 49 Up. UK: BBC Television.

Banks, M., Bates, I., Breakwell, G., Bynner, J., Emler, N., Jamieson, L., & Roberts, K. (1992). *Careers and identities*. Buckingham: Open University Press.

Barker, L., & Milligan, K. (1990). Improving services for rural young people: strategies for change, *National Youth Affairs Research Scheme*. Hobart: National Clearinghouse for Youth Studies.

Beck, U. (1992). *Risk society: towards a new modernity*. London: Sage.

Beck, U., & Beck-Gernsheim, E. (2002). *Individualization*. London: Sage.

Beck, U., Giddens, A., & Lash, S. (1994). *Reflexive modernization: politics, tradition and aesthetics in the modern social order*. Cambridge: Polity Press.

Becker, H. S. (1963). *Outsiders: studies in the sociology of deviance*. Glencoe: Free Press.

Bell, C., & Newby, H. (1971). *Community studies*. New York: George Allen and Unwin.

Berger, P. L., & Berger, B. (1975). *Sociology: a biographical approach*. New York: Basic Books.

Berger, P. L., & Luckmann, T. (1967). *The social construction of reality: a treatise in the sociology of knowledge*. London: Penguin.

Bernstein, B. B. (1977). *Class, Codes and Control*. London: Routledge and Kegan Paul.

Bessant, J. (1996). An early survey of the Howard Government's policies of young people, *Revisiting: pathways, personal issues and public participation* (pp. 37–49). Melbourne: Youth Research Centre.

Bourdieu, P. (1973). Cultural reproduction and social reproduction. In R. Brown (ed.), *Knowledge, education and cultural change* (pp. 71–112). London: Travistock.

—— (1977). *Outline of a theory of practice*. New York: Cambridge University Press.

—— (1984). *Distinction: a social critique of the judgement of taste*. London: Routledge and Kegan Paul.

Bourdieu, P., & Passeron, J.-C. (1977). *Reproduction in education, society and culture*. London: Sage.

Bourke, L. (1997). Outlook of rural secondary students. *Youth Studies Australia*, 16, 11–16.

—— (2003). Toward understanding youth suicide in an Australian rural community. *Social Science & Medicine*, 57, 2355.

Bourke, L., & Geldens, P. M. (2007). Subjective Wellbeing and its Meaning for Young People in a Rural Australian Center. *Social Indicators Research*, 82, 165–187.

Bowes, A. (1996). Evaluating an empowering research strategy: reflections on action-research with South Asian women. Scotland: Department of Applied Social Science, University of Stirling.

Brady, M. (1991). The health of young Aborigines: a report on the health of Aborigines aged 12 to 25 years. Canberra: National Clearinghouse for Youth Studies.

Bruner, J. (1987). Life as narrative. *Social Research*, 54, 11–32.

Burgess, J., & Campbell, I. (1998). The nature and dimensions of precarious employment in Australia. *Labour and Industry*, 8, 5–21.

Cahill, H., Shaw, G., Wyn, J., & Smith, G. (2004). Translating Caring into Action. Melbourne: Australian Youth Research Centre.

Cartmel, F. (2004). Book Review: Young people in Rural Areas of Europe. *Journal of Social Policy*, 33, 687–689.

Centrelink (2001). Payment statistics by local government area. Hobart: Centrelink, Tasmania.

Charmaz, K. (2000). Grounded theory: objectivist and constructivist methods. In N. K. Denzin & Y. S. Lincoln (eds), *Handbook of qualitative research* (pp. 509–535). Thousand Oaks, California: Sage.

Coleman, J. (1971). *The adolescent society – the social life of the teenager and its impact on education*. New York: The Free Press.

Commonwealth of Australia (1994). Working nation: policies and programs. Canberra: Australian Government Printing Service.

Commonwealth of Australia (2007). Northern Territory National Emergency Response Act 2007, available at http://www.comlaw.gov.au/ComLaw/Legislation/ActCompilation1.nsf/0/68914A40CCE87B0FCA2573F0000ADD3?OpenDocument

Connell, R. (2006). Northern Theory: the political geography of general social theory. *Theory and Society*, 35, 237–264.

Connell, R. W., Ashenden, D. J., Kessler, S., & Dowsett, G. W. (1982). *Making the difference: schools, families and social division*. Sydney: Allen and Unwin.

Cooley, C. H. (1922). *Human nature and the social order*. New York: Transaction Publishers.

Corbett, M. (2006). We're practical people: schooling and identity in a Canadian coastal community. In P. L. Jeffrey (ed.), *Australian Association for Research in Education (AARE)*. Parramatta NSW: Australian Association for Research in Education.

Corrigan, P. (1982). Doing nothing. In S. Hall & T. Jefferson (eds), *Resistance through rituals* (pp. 103–105). London: Hutchinson & Co.

Côté, J. E. (2000). *Arrested Adulthood: The Changing Nature of Maturity and Identity. What Does it Mean to Grow Up?* New York: NYU Press.

Côté, J. E., & Allahar, A. L. (1994). *Generation on hold: coming of age in the late twentieth century*. Toronto: Stoddart.

Cox, E. (1995). *A truly civil society*. Sydney: ABC Books.

Cullen, P., & Marshall, C. A. (1999). *Voices of the streets*. Hawthorn, Vic: John Garratt Publishing.

Cunningham, R., Choate, J., Abbott-Chapman, J., & Hughes, P. (1992). Rural disadvantage and post compulsory participation. Hobart: Youth Education Studies Centre, University of Tasmania.

Currie, G., Gammie, F., Waingold, C., Paterson, D., & Vandersar, D. (2005). Rural and regional young people and transport. Canberra: A report to the National Youth Affairs Research Scheme, FACSIA.

Dempsey, K. (1990). *Smalltown: a study of social inequality, cohesion and belonging*. Melbourne: Oxford University Press.

Denzin, N. K. (1989). *Interpretive interactionism*. Newbury Park: Sage.

Department of Health and Family Services (1997). Youth suicide in Australia: a background monograph. Canberra: Mental Health Branch, Commonwealth Department of Health and Family Services.

Dewey, J. (1933). *How We Think. A restatement of the relation of reflective thinking to the educative process*. Boston: D. C. Heath.

Dick, R. (1995). *You want to do an action research thesis?* Brisbane: Interchange.

Du Bois-Reymond, M. (1998). 'I don't want to commit myself yet': Young people's life-concepts. *Journal of Youth Studies*, 1, 63–79.

Dudley, M. J., Kelk, N. J., Florio, T. M., Howard, J. P., & Waters, B. B. H. (1998). Suicide among young Australians 1964–1993. *Medical Journal of Australia*, 169, 77–80.

Dussledorp Skills Forum (1998). Australia's youth: reality and risk. Sydney: Dussledorp Skills Forum.

Dwyer, P. (1996). *Opting out: early school leavers and the degeneration of youth policy*. Hobart: National Clearinghouse of Youth Studies.

Dwyer, P., Harwood, A., & Tyler, D. (1998). Life-patterns, choices, careers: 1991–1998 (p. 59). Melbourne: Youth Research Centre.

—— (1999). Seeking the balance: risk, choices and life priorities in the Life-patterns Project 1998–1999 (p. 45). Melbourne: Youth Research Centre.

Dwyer, P., Smith, G., Tyler, D., & Wyn, J. (2005). Immigrants in Time: Life-Patterns 2004. Melbourne: Australian Youth Research Centre.

Dwyer, P., & Wyn, J. (2001). *Youth, Education and Risk*. London and New York: Routledge/Falmer.

Eckersley, R. (1992). Youth and the challenge to change, *Apocalypse? No! essay series no 1*: Australian Commission for the Future.

—— (2005). *Well & Good: Morality, Meaning and Happiness (2nd edition)*. Melbourne: Text Publishing.

Eckersley, R., Cahill, H., Wierenga, A., & Wyn, J. (2007). Generations in dialogue about the future: the hopes and fears of young Australians (Available online at: http://www.australia21.org.au/whats_new.htm). Melbourne: Australian Youth Research Centre, University of Melbourne.

Eckersley, R., Wierenga, A., & Wyn, J. (2006a). Flashpoints and Signposts: Pathways to success and wellbeing for Australia's young people. Melbourne: Australia 21 Ltd, the Australian Youth Research Centre and Victorian Health Promotion Foundation.

—— (2006b). Success & wellbeing. *Youth Studies Australia*, 25, 10–18.

Economou, N. (2001). The regions in ferment? The politics of regional and rural disenchantment. *Alternative Law Journal*, 26, 69–73.

Elder, G. H. J., King, V., & Conger, R. D. (1996). Attachment to place and migration prospects: a developmental perspective. *Journal of Research on Adolescence*, 6, 397–423.

Epps, R., & Sorensen, T. (1996). The nature of leadership in rural Australia: A case study of four central western Queensland towns. In G. Lawrence, K. Lyons & S. Momtaz (eds), *Social Change in Rural Australia* (pp. 154–166). Rockhampton: Rural Social and Economic Research Centre, Central Queensland University.

Epston, D., & White, M. (1992). *Experience, contradiction, narrative and imagination: selected papers of David Epston and Michael White*. Adelaide: Dulwich Centre Publications.

Escobar, A. (2001). Culture sits in places: reflections on globalism and subaltern strategies of localization. *Political Geography*, 20, 139–174.

Etzioni, A. (1993). *The spirit of community: rights, responsibilities and the communitarian agenda*. New York: Crown Publishers.

Evans, K. (2002). Taking control of their lives? Agency in young adult transitions in England and the New Germany. *Journal of Youth Studies*, 5, 245–269.

Everett, J. (2001). We're not lost, *Message Stick*: ABC Television.

Fagan, G. (2001). Building Sustainable Communities: Capacity, Understanding and Action: CADISPA.

Fine, M. (1992). *Disruptive voices: the possibilities of feminist research*. Ann Arbor: University of Michigan Press.

Finn, B., & Australian Education Council Review Committee (1991). *Young people's participation in post-compulsory education and training*. Canberra: Australian Government Printing Service.

Forestry Tasmania (2001). Forest products: hardwood pulpwood, *Forestry Tasmania, growing our future* (http://www.forestrytas.com.au/). Hobart: Forestry Tasmania.

Foucault, M. (1980). *Power/knowledge: selected interviews and other writings*. New York: Panthenon Books.

Frank, A. W. (2001). Can we Research Suffering? *Qualitative Health Research*, 11, 353–362.

Frank, A. W. (2004). After the Methods, the Story: From Incongruity to Truth in Qualitative Research. *Qualitative Health Research*, 14, 430–440.

Freeman, M. (1998). Heywire. Newcastle, Upper Hunter-Muswellbrook: ABC Online, http://www.abc.net.au/heywire/heywire2000/true/nsw.htm.

Freire, P. (1973). *Education for critical consciousness*. New York: Seabury Press.

Friend, R. (1992). *We who are not here: Aboriginal people of the Huon and Channel today*. Huonville, Tasmania: Huon Municipal Association.

Fukuyama, F. (1995). *Trust: the social virtues and the creation of prosperity*. London: Penguin Books.

Furlong, A. (2000). Introduction: youth in a changing world. *International Social Science Journal*, 52, 129–134.

Furlong, A., & Cartmel, F. (1997). *Young people and social change: individualisation and risk in late modernity*. St Leonards, NSW: Allen and Unwin.

Garfinkel, H. (1967). *Studies in ethnomethodology*. New Jersey: Prentice-Hall.

Geertz, C. (1975). *The interpretation of cultures: selected essays*. London: Hutchinson.

Geldens, P. (2005). Wanted: 'Place' to fill vacancy in roomy, well appointed 'space' within youth sociology, Available immediately. *TASA Conference*. University of Tasmania, Australia.

Gergen, K. J., & Gergen, M. M. (1988). Narrative and the self as relationship. *Advances in experimental social psychology*, 21, 17–56.

Giddens, A. (1979). *Central problems in social theory: action, structure, and contradiction in social analysis*. Berkeley: University of California Press.

—— (1991). *Modernity and self-identity: self and society in the late modern age*. Oxford: Polity.

—— (1994a). Living in a post-traditional society. In U. Beck, A. Giddens & S. Lash (eds), *Reflexive modernization: politics, tradition and aesthetics in the modern social order* (pp. 56–109). Cambridge: Polity Press.

—— (1994b). Replies and critiques: risk, trust, reflexivity. In U. Beck, A. Giddens & S. Lash (eds), *Reflexive modernization: politics, tradition and aesthetics in the modern social order* (pp. 184–197). Oxford: Blackwell.

Glaser, B. (1992). *Basics of grounded theory analysis: emergence vs. forcing*. Mill Valley, California: Sociology Press.

Glaser, B., & Strauss, A. (1967). *The discovery of grounded theory: strategies for qualitative research*. Chicago: Aldine.

Glendinning, A., Nuttall, M., Hendry, L., Kloep, M., & Wood, S. (2003). Rural communities and wellbeing: A good place to grow up? *Sociological Review*, 51, 129–156.

Goffman, E. (1961). *Asylums*. Harmondsworth: Penguin Books.

—— (1969). *The presentation of self in everyday life*. London: Allen Lane.

Granovetter, M. (1982). The strength of weak ties: a network theory revisited. In P. V. Marsden & N. Lin (eds), *Social Structure and Network Analysis* (pp. 105–130). Newbury Park, Beverly Hills: Sage.

Gray, I. (1991). *Politics in place: social power relations in an Australian country town*. Oakleigh: Cambridge University Press.

Gray, I., & Phillips, E. (1996). Sustainability and the restructuring of tradition: a comparative analysis of three rural localities. In G. Lawrence, K. Lyons & S. Momtaz (eds), *Social Change in Rural Australia* (pp. 276–289). Rockhampton: Rural Social and Economic Research Centre, Central Queensland University.

Green, E. (1996). Rural youth suicide: the issue of male homosexuality. In G. Lawrence, K. Lyons & S. Momtaz (eds), *Social Change in Rural Australia* (pp. 85–94). Rockhampton: Rural Social and Economic Research Centre, Central Queensland University.

Green, R., & McDonald, J. (1996). Transport for young people in rural areas: patterns, problems and prospects. *Youth Studies Australia*, 15, 38–42.

Greens, T. (2001). Jobs versus forests logged, *The future is Green*: Tasmanian Greens.

Haberkorn, G., Kelson, S., Tottenham, R., & Magpantay, C. (2004). Country Matters – Social Atlas of rural and regional Australia: Australian Government, Bureau of Regional Sciences.

Hall, T., Coffey, A., & Williamson, H. (1999). Self, Space and Place: youth identities and citizenship. *British Journal of Sociology of Education*, 20, 501–513.

Harris, A. (2002). Young Australian Women: Circumstances and Aspirations. *Youth Studies Australia*, 21, 32–37.

Hawken, P. (2007). *Blessed unrest: how the largest movement in the world came into being, and why no one saw it coming*. New York: Viking.

Heidegger, M. (1962). *Being and time*. New York: Harper & Row.

Helve, H., & Holm, G. (2005). Contemporary Youth Research: Local Expressions and Global Connections. England and USA: Ashgate.

Higgins, J., & Nairn, K. (2006). 'In transition': choice and the children of New Zealand's economic reforms. *British Journal of Sociology of Education*, 27, 207–220.

Hillier, L., Warr, D., & Haste, B. (1996). The rural mural: sexuality and diversity in rural youth. Carlton South: Centre for the Study of Sexually Transmissible Diseases, La Trobe University.

Holden, E. (1992). Getting a life: pathways and early school leavers. Melbourne: Youth Research Centre.

Holdsworth, R. (2004). Real learning real futures. Sydney: Dussledorp Skills Forum.

Hood, S., Mayall, B., & Oliver, S. (1999). Critical issues in social research: power and prejudice. Philadelphia: Open University Press.

HREOC (1999). Bush talks. Sydney: Human Rights and Equal Opportunity Commission.

—— (2000). Education access: national inquiry into rural and remote education. Sydney: Commonwealth of Australia: Human Rights and Equal Opportunity Commission.

—— (2006). A statistical overview of Aboriginal and Torres Strait Islander peoples in Australia. Canberra: Human Rights and Equal Opportunity commission.

Irvine, S. (1999). 'You can take the boy out of Bundy, but you can't take Bundy out of the boy": Regional youth and community. *Social Alternatives*, 18, 22–24.

James, R., Wyn, J., Baldwin, G., Hepworth, G., McInnis, C., & Stephanou, A. (1999). Rural and isolated students and their higher education choices. Canberra: National Board of Employment, Education and Training, Higher Education Council.

Jones, G. (1999). 'The Same People in the Same Places'? Socio-Spatial Identities and Migration in Youth. *Sociology*, 33, 1–22.

—— (2002). *The Youth Divide: Diverging paths to adulthood*. York: Joseph Rowntree Foundation/York Publishing Services.

Jones, G., & Wallace, C. (1992). *Youth, family and citizenship*. Buckingham: Open University Press.

Just Tasmania Coalition (1999). Life on a low income: a consultation with the people of the Huon Valley, July 1999. Hobart: Social Action and Research Centre, Anglicare Tasmania, The Poverty Coalition and TasCOSS.

Kelly, P. (2003). Growing Up as Risky Business? Risks, Surveillance and the Institutionalized Mistrust of Youth. *Journal of Youth Studies*, 6, 165–180.

Kenway, J., Collins, C., & McLeod, J. (2000). Factors influencing the educational performance of males and females and their initial destinations after leaving school. Canberra: Department of Education, Training and Youth Affairs.

Lahelma, E., & Gordon, T. (2008). Resources and (in(ter))dependence: Young people's reflections on parents. *Young*, 16, 209–226.

Lamb, S., Dwyer, P., & Wyn, J. (2000). Non-completion of school in Australia: the changing patterns of participation and outcomes. Camberwell, Vic: Australian Council for Educational Research.

Lash, S. (1994). Reflexivity and its doubles: structure, asesthetics, community. In U. Beck, A. Giddens & S. Lash (eds), *Reflexive modernization: politics, tradition and aesthetics in the modern social order* (pp. 281–308). Cambridge: Polity Press.

Lawrence, G. (1996). Rural Australia: insights and issues from contemporary political economy. In G. Lawrence, K. Lyons & S. Momtaz (eds), *Social change in rural Australia* (pp. 332–349). Rockhampton: Rural Social and Economic Research Centre, Central Queensland University.

Lenehan, C. (2000). *Visiting Tasmania: images of the margin*. PhD thesis, School of Sociology and Social Work, University of Tasmania.

Long, N., & Long, A. (1992). Battlefields of knowledge: the interlocking of theory and practice in social research and development. London: Routledge.

Looker, D., & Dwyer, P. (1997). Education and negotiated reality: complexities facing rural youth in the 1990s. *Journal of Youth Studies*, 1, 5–22.

MacDonald, R., & Marsh, J. (2001). Disconnected Youth? *Journal of Youth Studies*, 4, 373–391.

MacDonald, R., Shildrick, T., Webster, C., & Simpson, D. (2005). Growing Up in Poor Neighbourhoods: The Significance of Class and Place in the Extended Transitions of 'Socially Excluded' Young Adults. *Sociology*, 39, 873–891.

Marsden Jacob Associates (2001). Forestry and national competition policy. Camberwell, Victoria: Australian Conservation Foundation.

Massey, D. (1994). Human identity and change: the educational challenge, *Identities, ethnicities, nationalities: Asian and Pacific contexts*. Melbourne: La Trobe University.

Mayall, B. (1999). Children and childhood. In S. Hood, B. Mayall & S. Oliver (eds), *Critical issues in social research: power and prejudice* (pp. 10–24). Philadelphia: Open University Press.

McDonald, K. (1999). *Struggles for subjectivity: identity, action and youth experience.* Cambridge: Cambridge University Press.

McLeod, J. (2000). Metaphors of the self: searching for young people's identity through interviews. In J. McLeod & K. Malone (eds), *Researching youth.* Hobart: Australian Clearinghouse for Youth Studies.

McPherson, D. (2006). Is Australia doing all it can to encourage young people to stay on the land? Melbourne: Australian Broadcasting Corporation.

Mead, G. H. (1955). *Mind, self and society: from the standpoint of a social behaviourist.* Chicago: University of Chicago Press.

Measor, L. (1985). Interviewing: a strategy in qualitative research. In R. G. Burgess (ed.), *Strategies of educational research: qualitative methods* (pp. 55–77). London and Philadelphia: The Falmer Press.

Mills, C. W. (1959). *The sociological imagination.* New York: Penguin.

Minichiello, V., Aroni, R., Timewell, E., & Alexander, L. (1995). *In-depth interviewing: principles, techniques, analysis.* Melbourne: Longman.

Morris, C. (1974). In pursuit of the travelling man: a study of Tasmanian tourism to 1905, *Honours thesis,* Hobart: History Department, University of Tasmania.

Moyle, S. (2006). Dirt, dust and heartache. Melbourne: Australian Broadcasting Corporation.

Myrtle Vale Youth Outreach (1993). *Myrtle Vale youth, gateway to our future: a study of the issues surrounding our young people.* Myrtle Vale: 'Explosive Light', and Lightwood Valley Youth Service.

Nairn, K., & Higgins, J. (2007). New Zealand's neoliberal generation: tracing discourses of economic (ir)rationality. *International Journal of Qualitative Studies in Education,* 20, 261–281.

Neimeyer, R. (2000). *Lessons of loss: a guide to coping.* Clayton South: Centre for Grief Education.

Nilan, P., & Feixa, C. (2006). Global Youth? Hybrid identities, plural worlds. London and New York: Routledge.

O'Connor, P. (2005). Local embeddedness in a global world: Young people's accounts. *Young,* 13, 9–26.

OECD, & Canadian Policy Research Networks (2005). From Education to Work: A Difficult Transition for Young Adults with Low Levels of Education: OECD Publishing.

Polk, K., & White, R. (1999). Economic adversity and criminal behaviour: rethinking youth unemployment and crime. *The Australian and New Zealand Journal of Criminology,* 32, 284–302.

Poulos, C. N. (2006). The Ties That Bind Us, the Shadows That Separate Us: Life and Death, Shadow and (Dream)Story. *Qualitative Inquiry,* 12, 96–117.

Presdee, M. (1990). Creating poverty and creating crime: Australian youth policy in the eighties. In C. Wallace & M. Cross (eds), *Youth in Transition: The*

Sociology of Youth and Youth Policy (pp. 146–189). Basingstoke: The Falmer Press.

Pusey, M. (2007). The changing relationship between the generations ...It could even be good news? *Youth Studies Australia, 26*, 9–16.

Putnam, R. (1995). Bowling alone: America's declining social capital. *Journal of Democracy, 6*.

Quixley, S. (1992). Living, learning and working: the experiences of young people in rural and remote communities in Australia. Canberra: National Youth Coalition for Housing.

Ram, M. (1995). The politics of research: local consultation in a city challenge context. *Sociology, 29*, 275–292.

Richardson, L. (1992). Consequences of poetic representation: writing the other, rewriting the self. In C. Ellis & M. Flaherty (eds), *Investigating subjectivity: research as lived experience*. California: Sage.

Rimmer, G. (1989). Hobart: a moment of glory. In P. Statham (ed.), *The origins of Australia's capital cities*. Cambridge: Cambridge University Press.

Schuetz, A. (1944). The stranger: an essay in social psychology. *The American Journal of Sociology, 49*, 499–507.

Schwab, R. G. (1999). Why only one in three? the complex reasons for low indigenous school retention. Canberra: Centre for Aboriginal Economic Policy Research.

Seligman, M. (1975). *Helplessness: On depression, development, and death*. San Francisco: W. H. Freeman.

Semmens, B. (2000). Summary of the interim report of the ministerial review of post compulsory education and training pathways in Victoria. *Youth Research News, 9*, 7.

Sercombe, H. (2006). Going bush: youth work in rural settings. *Youth Studies Australia, 25*, 9–16.

Sercombe, H., Omaji, P., Drew, N., Cooper, T., & Love, T. (2002). Youth and the Future: Effective youth services for the year 2015. Report to the National Youth Affairs Research Scheme. Hobart: Australian Clearinghouse for Youth Studies.

Shields, R. (1991). *Places on the margin: alternative geographies of modernity*. London and New York: Routledge.

Sidoti, C. (2001). Time is now to address bush education. *Campus Review, 11*, 11.

Silverman, D. (2000). Analyzing talk and text. In N. K. Denzin & Y. S. Lincoln (eds), *Handbook of qualitative research* (pp. 821–833). Thousand Oaks, California: Sage.

Simmel, G. (1950). The stranger in K. Wolff (ed. and translator) The sociology of Georg Simmel, pp. 402–408. New York: Free Press.

Smith, M. (2003). From youth work to youth development: the new government framework for English youth services. *Youth and Policy, 79*, Available in the informal education archives: http://www.infed.org/archives/jeffs_and smith/smith_youth_work_to_youth_development.htm.

Stokes, H., Stafford, J., & Holdsworth, R. (1999). Final report, rural and remote school education: a survey for the Human Rights and Equal Opportunity Commission. Melbourne: Youth Research Centre, University of Melbourne.

Stokes, H., Wierenga, A., & Wyn, J. (2003). Preparing for the future and living now: young people's perceptions of VET, part-time work, career education and enterprise education. Melbourne: Australian Youth Research Centre, for the Enterprise Career Education Foundation (ECEF).

Strauss, A. (1987). *Qualitative analysis for social scientists*. New York: Cambridge University Press.

Strauss, A., & Corbin, J. (1990). *Basics of qualitative research: grounded theory procedures and techniques*. Newbury Park, California: Sage Publications.

Strauss, A. L. (1977). *Mirrors and masks: the search for identity*. London: M Robertson.

Taylor, C. (1989). *Sources of the self: the making of the modern identity*. Cambridge, Massachusetts: Cambridge University Press.

Thomson, R., Bell, R., Holland, J., Henderson, S., McGrellis, S., & Sharpe, S. (2002). Critical Moments: Choice, Chance and Opportunity in Young People's Narratives of Transition. *Sociology*, 36, 335–354.

Thomson, R., & Holland, J. (2003). Hindsight, foresight and insight: the challenges of longitudinal qualitative research. *International Journal of Social Research Methodology*, 6, 233–244.

Thomson, R., Holland, J., McGrellis, S., Bell, R., Henderson, S., & Sharpe, S. (2004). Inventing adulthoods: a biographical approach to understanding youth citizenship. *The Sociological Review*, 52, 218–239.

Turner, R. H. (1976). The real self: from institution to impulse. *Psychological Review*, 55, 189–208.

Ukeje, C. (2006). Remarks on the Status of Youth Research in Africa, and the Future, *International Sociological Association at the 16th World Congress of Sociology, Sociology of Youth*. Durban, South Africa.

Voth, D. E. (1979). Social action research in community development. In E. J. Blakely (ed.), *Community development research: concepts, issues, and strategies* (pp. 69–81). New York: Human Sciences Press.

Voyce, M. (1996). Ideas of rural property in Australia. In G. Lawrence, K. Lyons & S. Momtaz (eds), *Social Change in Rural Australia* (pp. 95–105). Rockhampton: Rural Social and Economic Research Centre, Central Queensland University.

Wadsworth, Y. (2006). The Mirror, the Magnifying Glass, the Compass and the Map: Facilitating Participatory Action Research. In P. Reason & Bradbury, H. (eds), *Handbook of Action Research*. London: Sage.

Watts, R. (1993). Doing ethnography with young people: How and why? In R. White (ed.), *Youth Subcultures* (pp. 54–60). Hobart: National Clearinghouse for Youth Studies.

Wax, R. H. (1971). *Doing fieldwork: warnings and advice*. Chicago: University of Chicago Press.

Weber, M. (1969). Subjective meaning in the social situation I. In L. A. Coser & B. Rosenberg (eds), *Sociological theory: a book of readings* (pp. 248–259). New York: Macmillan.

White, M. (1995). *Re-authoring lives: interviews and essays by Michael White*. Adelaide: Dulwich Centre.

—— (2000). *Reflections on narrative practice: essays and interviews*. Adelaide: Dulwich Centre Publications.

White, M., & Epston, D. (1990). *Narrative means to therapeutic ends*. New York: Norton.

White, R. (1997). Young men, violence, and social health. *Youth Studies Australia*, 16, 31–37.

—— (1999). Rural youth and remote communities, *Hanging out: negotiating young people's use of public space* (pp. 140–154). Canberra: National Crime Prevention, Attorney General's Department.

—— (2001). Restorative community justice: community building approaches in juvenile justice, *Paper presented at 4th National Outlook Symposium on Crime in Australia*. Canberra: Australian Institute of Criminology.

White, R., McDonnell, L., & Harris, A. (1996). Researching youth, a practical guide. *Youth Studies Australia*, 15, 18–25.

White, R., & Wyn, J. (1998). Youth agency and social context. *Journal of Sociology*, 34, 314–327.

—— (2008). *Youth and Society: exploring the social dynamics of youth experience*. South Melbourne: Oxford University Press.

Wierenga, A. M. (1995). *Growing up in Myrtle Vale: social reproduction, life choices and cognitive mapping in a rural Tasmanian community*, Honours thesis, School of Sociology, University of Tasmania.

—— (1999). Imagined trajectories: local culture and social identity. In R. White (ed.), *Australian youth subcultures: on the margins and in the mainstream* (pp. 189–199). Hobart: Australian Clearinghouse for Youth Studies.

—— (2001). *Making a life*, PhD thesis School of Sociology and Social Work, University of Tasmania.

—— (2002). Losing and Finding the plot: storying and the value of listening to young people. *Scottish Journal of Youth Issues*, 9–30.

—— (2006). Thick and thin stories of citizenship, *Three Deans conference*. University of Madison Wisconsin, USA.

Wierenga, A., Wyn, J., Glover, S., & Mead, M. (2003). Application of enabling state principles in the delivery of youth services: a report for Social Policy Branch, Department of Premier and Cabinet. Melbourne: Youth Research Centre and the Centre for Adolescent Health, University of Melbourne.

Wild, R. A. (1978). *Bradstow: a study of status, class and power in a small Australian town*. Melbourne: Angus and Robertson.

Williams, C. (1981a). *Open cut: the working class in an Australian mining town*. Sydney: George Allen & Unwin.

Williams, R. (1981b). *Culture*. London: Fontana.

Williamson, H. (1997). Status Zero Youth and the 'Underclass': Some Considerations. In R. MacDonald (ed.), *Youth, the 'Underclass' and Social Exclusion* (pp. 83–95). London: Routledge.

Willis, P. (1979). *Learning to labour: how working class kids get working class jobs*. Westmead: Saxon House.

Wiseman, J. (2006). Local Heroes? Learning from Recent Community Strengthening Initiatives in Victoria. *Australian Journal of Public Administration*, 65, 95–107.

Wyn, J. (2000). The postmodern girl: education, 'success' and the construction of girls' identities. In J. McLeod & K. Malone (eds), *Researching Youth* (pp. 59–70). Hobart: Australian Clearinghouse for Youth Studies.

—— (2007). Learning to 'become somebody well': challenges for educational policy. *Australian Educational Researcher*, 34, 35–52.

—— (2008). *Youth Health and Welfare: The Cultural Politics of Education and Wellbeing*. Melbourne: Oxford University Press.

Wyn, J., & Stokes, H. (1998). Community strategies: address the challenges for young people living in rural Australia, *Learning Communities, Regional Sustainability and the Learning Society – International Symposium Conference Proceedings*. Launceston: Centre for Research and Learning in Rural Australia.

Wyn, J., Stokes, H., & Stafford, J. (1998). Young people living in rural Australia in the 1990s. Melbourne: Youth Research Centre.

Wyn, J., & White, R. (1997). *Rethinking youth*. St Leonards: Allen and Unwin.

—— (2000). Negotiating social change: the paradox of youth. *Youth and society*, 32, 165–183.

Yates, L. (1996). How do we generate useful knowledge about young people?, *Pathways, personal issues and public participation* (pp. 9–16). Melbourne: Youth Research Centre.

Yndigegn, C. (2003). Life Planning in the Periphery: Life Chances and Life Perspectives for Young People in the Danish-German Border Region. *Young*, 11, 235–251.

Index